M000196046

Published by Sightline Institute
1402 Third Ave. Suite 500
Seattle, Washington 98101

For ordering information, go to: *BecomingADemocracy.org*

Print ISBN: 978-0-9894740-2-3
EBook ISBN: 978-0-9894740-3-0

First Edition

BECOMING

—— A ——

DEMOCRACY

HOW WE CAN FIX THE ELECTORAL COLLEGE, GERRYMANDERING, AND OUR ELECTIONS

BY KRISTIN EBERHARD

Table of Contents

Introduction

If you've picked up this book, welcome! I'm Kristin Eberhard. I am a researcher and the director for the democracy and climate programs at Sightline Institute, a think tank. I've put in years of reading and writing, and have earned a law degree and a master's degree, to hone the expertise that informs this book. I am also a mom; a resident of Portland, Oregon; a fantasy fiction aficionada; the only member of my family of origin who is not a public school teacher; and an aspiring contender for best family Halloween costume coordinator, the fruits of which grace our holiday card to friends and family every year. (In fact, here we are in 2019 as Bellatrix Lestrange, Severus Snape, Harry Potter, and the Golden Snitch, in celebration of my older son's completion of the first four books of the series.)

All this is to say, I'm human!

And I know you may be wondering if you can trust me as your guide as you dive into this book.

Since you've picked up a book about U.S. democracy, you may feel strongly affiliated with either the Democratic or the Republican Party and wonder where I fall. I lean left politically, but I am not a member of the Democratic Party. I'm a proud member of the Independent Party of Oregon. While I do care about many of the policy priorities of Democrats, what I care about most is that our democracy works for everybody.

This isn't just an empty platitude — I want my children to live in a democracy. I'd also like them to live in a stable climate. The world is facing a climate crisis that will likely make my children's lives harder than mine has been, and the United States has been unable to act on this issue in part because of deep flaws in our democracy. Those flaws have escalated into fractures and are on their way to chasms that, if left unchecked, could so delegitimize our democracy that people give up on it entirely.

Who is this book for?

If you care about democracy in the United States, this book is for you.

If you lean left, many of the solutions will resonate with you right away, especially the ideas of helping more people vote and of making the U.S. Senate and the Electoral College more responsive to all voters, not to the minority of voters they now serve. But this is not simply a playbook for the Democratic Party. It's a playbook for a resilient democracy. For example, in my home state of Oregon, Democrats control the legislature, and the legislature controls the redistricting process, giving Democrats an opportunity to gerrymander. This book is adamantly against gerrymandering and presents a solution that would likely give more seats in Oregon's legislature to Republicans and Libertarians, but that would make our government more representative of all my fellow Oregonians, and thereby stronger. If you lean right, this book is also for you! One of the biggest risks to democracy is a decline of the center-right party, leaving a vacuum in which extremists gain power. Center-right Americans may be the most critical players in helping the United States to weather the brewing storms and come out the other end as a strong and fair democracy. While the current incarnation of the Republican Party has chosen to appeal to a smaller number of mostly white voters and grab power without winning the most votes, many conservative-leaning Americans do believe that our country is stronger when everyone has a fair shot at participating in its affairs. You might believe, as I do, that not only American democracy but the American conservative movement itself would be stronger if the Republican Party had to compete on a level playing field rather than on the tilted one we have now.

This book is probably not for you if you

- believe "your" party should win at any cost,
- are willing to sacrifice democracy to get a policy or political result you want,
- support corporations and their lobbyists having more influence than everyday people on decisions about our health-care costs, our drinking-water safety, our school funding, and other priorities, or
- believe that some Americans' views should be excluded or discounted.

If that's you, I hope you might still give the book a try, but unfortunately we are not starting from the same values.

Everything seems to be about red and blue these days. If you browse the politics section of any bookstore, you'll see lots of red and blue covers and elephants and donkeys. Not so with this book. But I know we humans love a good "us versus them" story line, so I'd like to invite you to start thinking of a *different* "us" and "them": not red versus blue, but pro- versus anti-democracy. If you believe in the solutions in this book, welcome. You are officially part of the pro-democracy *us*.

We are committed to delivering on the promise that all Americans are created equal and deserve the right to vote, the right to a voice in elections, the right to fair representation in our halls of government, and maybe even a chance to take part in writing the laws, either by running for office (see chapter 5) or by participating in a citizens' assembly (see chapter 10).

Think of it like building a bridge. Anti-democracy forces might say, for instance, that only redheaded people should have a say in when, where, and how to build a bridge. Or maybe only right-handed people. Or only landowners. The possibilities for exclusion are endless. Truly, only bridge engineers should be allowed to design the trusses. But we in the pro-democracy club would say that everyone should have a chance to give their input about whether, where, and how big to build a bridge. If some people were systematically excluded from the planning, the community could end up with a bridge to nowhere that destroyed a thriving neighborhood to boot.

Policy-making can work the same way, and in a country of more than 300 million people, there are many sources of knowledge to gather. Elections are our primary tool for making sure that all the relevant knowledge is brought to bear anytime our councilors, mayors, legislators, governors, or president are making important decisions. Making sure that elections are free and fair so that every voice is heard can lead to healthier, more balanced decision-making.

How to use this book

You could read this book straight through for an overview of the ways in which American democracy was designed to *not* work well in the modern era, as well as ten solutions.

Or you could take a look at the table of contents and go directly to the section that interests you the most. The section overview will provide you with context, and each chapter in the section will present a proven solution. For instance, if you are most concerned about voting rights, read the section I overview for context and chapters 1 through 4 for solutions.

Or you could just turn to the chapter you are most interested in to find out how that solution works and how you can help make it happen. Maybe the Electoral College bothers you — go straight to chapter 7!

Organization and elements

Each section of this book focuses on an overarching problem, and each chapter presents a policy solution to address that problem. All the solutions in this book are road-tested, meaning that at least some cities or states have already implemented them. The book moves roughly from the lowest-hanging fruit (very proven and easy-to-implement solutions, often those that many states have already put in place) to fruit that is harder to reach but just as sweet (solutions that have less of a track record at the state or federal level, or that have bigger political hurdles to overcome). In broad terms:

- Section I is about honoring the **right to vote** by making it easy to register and stay registered, convenient to cast a ballot, and impossible to permanently lose your right to vote;

- Section II is about how to counterbalance **moneyed special interests'** overwhelming influence on our elections; and

- Section III is about how to **make every vote matter** no matter what state or district the voter lives in or what party they affiliate with; key terms here include gerrymandering and the Electoral College.

These three sections lay out nine proven ways to make voting and elections work better. Then there's a bonus tenth chapter, because I think one important twenty-first-century solution to the problems of representative democracy is to move beyond elections and get us *ordinary people directly involved* in the lawmaking process.

Many of the section overviews also contain historical information about how our systems came to be the way they are. If you appreciate learning the "why" behind the "what," you'll get starter background here, and you can check the endnotes for further reading if you want more.

Each chapter kicks off with a story about an individual whose voting experience could have been improved by the solution presented in the chapter. These stories have been drawn from true accounts in news articles about real people's experiences and combined into a single story of a fictional person.

Key terms are boldfaced and defined in the text, but they are also compiled in the glossary at the end of the book for easy reference.

Read, then act!

My dearest hope is that this book will spur you to action. That could mean helping these solutions catch on by bringing the book to your book club, happy hour or church group, or League of Women Voters unit for a meaty discussion. To aid that effort, each chapter ends with discussion questions to get the conversation started. Which problems are most pressing for your community? Which solutions seem most promising? Where do you have relationships to leverage for change? What skills do you have to lend to the cause, and what solutions inspire your passion?

I hope you'll take the next step and become active in making these solutions a reality. The final pages of each chapter will point you to groups that are working on that solution, and you can learn more about each group in the appendix. If you read only chapter 7, for example, I hope you'll become involved in getting your state signed on to the National Popular Vote Interstate Compact. Or, if you read the whole book and become fascinated with the idea of citizens' assemblies, I hope you'll work to create one in your city or town. The book aims to give you background and context, especially in the section overviews, but mostly to give you concrete actions and groups to connect with to turn your interest into real change in the world.

This book is *your* book. Please use it to help make this your democracy, too.

A hard look at history, a hopeful view of the future

The Declaration of Independence, penned in 1776, expressed some ideals that our country, at its best, is still trying to truly realize. But there has always been a thread of thought running counter to the ideals that we are all created equal with a right to life, liberty, and the pursuit of happiness. For much of our country's early years, some white Americans enslaved Black Americans and the Constitution counted them as three-fifths of a person. Fewer than 10 percent of all Americans were allowed to vote. It took a bloody Civil War for the United States to grudgingly extend rights to Black men, and almost a century more for it to come around to allowing women to vote.

To this day, many Americans are still, in practice, excluded or undervalued. As I write this book, we are gearing up for a momentous presidential election in which many will not be able to vote, whether because they were previously convicted of a felony, because they don't have the right kind of ID, or because they can't take hours off work on a Tuesday to wait in line at a polling place. The people facing more barriers to voting aren't a random sample of Americans — they are more likely to be Black, Latino, or Native American. Several U.S. Senate races are being very closely fought, yet no matter how many people turn out to vote, the Senate will continue to grossly underrepresent the majority of Americans (because more than half of Americans live in just nine states) and to overrepresent white Americans (because the Senate overrepresents small states, which are whiter than the rest of the country). In the presidential election, some people's votes won't really matter because only a handful of swing states determine who wins the presidency, and the Electoral College system ignores the votes of most Black Americans living in the South.

This book is mostly about solutions. But along the way it reveals some of the history that got us to a place where, in 2020, most Americans don't bother to vote in most elections, politicians can draw the lines that determine election outcomes, and just 18 of 100 U.S. senators represent half of all Americans. If we want to truly become a democracy, we have to understand both where we came from and where we can go from here.

And to those who may read that and respond, "We're not a democracy, we're a republic": nice try, but don't drop the mic yet. If you want to get technical, the United States is a democratic republic. A democracy is a country where the people, not a king, have the power, and a republic has a constitution and the rule of law to protect the rights of minorities even if a majority of voters tries to exploit them. We are both. But on both these definitions, we are falling far short. Understanding how many of our systems were designed to subvert these principles can help us see how to make the changes necessary to truly empower the people and protect all Americans from exploitation.

I believe we *can* live up to our founding principles. My ambition, my optimism, my earnestness that we can do this are all well founded — based on the research I have done and the examples I have found of jurisdictions already using the following chapters' measures to great success, yes, but even more so on the legacy of the many Americans who have come before me — before us, with their own bold dreams and stories, their own fight, as part of the pro-democracy *us*. Let us honor their hope by adding our own. To that end, I invite you to turn the page.

I. FREE VOTERS TO VOTE

MAKE IT EASIER, CHEAPER, AND MORE SECURE FOR ALL AMERICANS TO VOTE.

We'll start our journey toward a better democracy in an obvious place: voting. When most people think of a healthy representative government, they think of that most concrete and fundamental right allotted to every one of a country's citizens. Voting should be an easy, efficient, inclusive, secure process that makes everyday people feel that their voices matter and makes them want to vote.

Unfortunately, this is not the case in the United States, as the following four chapters will discuss:

- It can be hard to get and stay registered to vote, from registering in the first place (chapter 1) to dodging the suppressive tactics of voter roll purges and Voter ID laws (chapter 2).

- It can be a hassle to vote, with distant polling places, long lines, and expensive, questionably secure voting machines (chapter 3).

- Some states have stripped the right to vote from millions of people on the basis of felony convictions, the definition of which varies greatly from state to state. This is frequently the case even after those people have served their sentences (chapter 4).

These conditions are no accident. Some are the result of policy and legal decisions that have systematically disenfranchised certain groups of people for decades or even centuries, and some are more recent incarnations motivated by partisan politics. Others have resulted from a failure to modernize, despite opportunities to do so and proof that new programs would better serve the public. Below, we'll briefly discuss three major components of this suppression.

States control who votes and how, with widely varying effects on voting rights

Most Americans would consider the right to vote to be fundamental. But at its founding, fewer than 10 percent of people living in the United States were allowed to vote. The Constitution was silent about who could vote, so states decided for themselves. Mostly, they decided that only white, Protestant, property-owning men could exercise that right. Over time, Americans amended the Constitution to allow men of color to vote (the **15th Amendment,** in 1870), and eventually to allow women to vote (the 19th Amendment, in 1920), and finally to allow people who can't afford to pay to vote (the **24th Amendment,** in 1964). Today, most Americans assume everyone has the right to vote.

Not so. Though **poll taxes** and **literacy tests** are technically no longer part of our elections process, some states have found ways to institute policies with much the same effect, and the Supreme Court has let them. These states make it difficult for voters to register or to stay registered, forcing them to jump through hoops only to later purge them from voter rolls anyway. Or they require voters to show identification they don't have or might have difficulty obtaining. Or they make it hard to vote, holding elections on a workday and limiting polling places so that long lines at the polls force some Americans to choose between casting their votes and keeping their jobs. Or they take away voting rights from people with felony convictions and never give them back, even when those people have served their time. None of these practices encourages citizens to exercise their democratic right. Rather, these suppressive practices are part of the reason the United States has some of the lowest rates of voter participation among wealthy nations.

Disenfranchisement by design: A closer look at racism embedded in voting rights laws

The **14th Amendment**, ratified in 1868 after the Civil War, gave formerly enslaved people born or naturalized in the United States the right of citizenship. But the amendment also created a gaping constitutional loophole: section 2 allowed states to deny people the right to vote for "participation in rebellion or other crime." This clause gave states a reliable and expansive qualification by which to strip former enslaved people and their descendants of voting rights.

The architects of state criminal disenfranchisement laws were not vague about their purpose, either. They intended to stop Black Americans from voting. Florida, for instance, which established its state constitution after the Civil War, passed a raft of "Black Codes" that made it easier to convict Black men of felonies and then permanently disenfranchised all felons.[1]

Not far away in Virginia, a delegate to that state's 1902 Constitutional Convention addressed reporters: "I told the people of my county before they sent me here that I intended, as far as in me lay, to disenfranchise every negro that I could disenfranchise under the Constitution of the United States, and as few white people as possible."[2] In a supposed justification for this, he reminded the convention's attendees that in the South, 6 whites out of 10,000 were in prison compared to 29 Blacks out of 10,000 — a result, he doubtless intended to infer, of moral inferiority rather than racist laws. (The United States now imprisons many more people, and the racial disparity has only gotten worse: as of 2014, 46 of every 10,000 whites and 272 of every 10,000 Blacks were in prison.[3] Most are serving time for drug offenses.[4])

The Virginia Constitution that delegates helped ratify included a clause that disenfranchised any Virginian who committed any of a broad swath of crimes, including "treason or any felony, bribery, petit larceny, obtaining money or property under false pretenses, embezzlement, forgery, or perjury."[5] The legacy of that sweeping law? Today, Virginia is one of three states[6] whose constitution permanently takes away people's right to vote if they are convicted of a felony.

The Constitution does not guarantee the right to vote, and the Supreme Court does not reliably protect voting as a "fundamental right"

The first ten amendments to the Constitution are known as the Bill of Rights, and they protect freedom of speech, freedom of the press, freedom to gather in an assembly, and other rights. But an important right is missing: the right to vote. Several subsequent amendments have given piecemeal voting protections for people of color, women, and people who can't pay poll taxes,[7] but none goes so far as to state that all Americans have a right to vote.

But that's okay; the Supreme Court justices can read those amendments, all of which reference the "right to vote," and conclude that Americans have the right to vote, correct? Maybe.

While the Bill of Rights states broadly that its rights "shall not be infringed" for any reason, the amendments related to voting all name *specific* ways that voting rights cannot legally be denied (such as on the basis of race, skin color, or sex), leaving open to interpretation whether states may find other, more creative ways to limit voting rights.

Here is another angle: the Court has found some rights merely implied in the Constitution to be **fundamental rights,** deserving of the same respect and protection as those explicitly laid out in the Bill of Rights. These include the right to marry, to engage in interstate travel, and, yes, to vote. But unfortunately, the Court has been inconsistent on this last item, sometimes declaring boldly that the right to vote is indeed fundamental, but other times treating it as a privilege rather than a right.[8]

It is important that the Court recognize voting as a fundamental right, because then it will almost certainly strike down any law that infringes on that right or is "burdensome" to those wishing to exercise it. In some cases where the Court has declared voting to be a fundamental right, it has applied a **strict scrutiny test** to the burdensome law in question. This means the entity supporting that law — say, a certain state legislature or the U.S. Congress — must prove that the law passes three tests. The law must be

1. justified by a compelling governmental interest,
2. narrowly tailored to achieve that compelling interest, and
3. the least restrictive means of achieving the compelling interest.

In other words, the defenders of the burdensome law must basically say, "We *know* this law is infringing on an important right, but it *has* to, and there's no other way!" The Court then asks, "Okay, if you have an *incredibly important purpose*, you *might* need to infringe on basic rights, but is there *any other way* for you to accomplish your purpose in a *less burdensome* manner?" Often the answer is yes, and the law is therefore struck down. The strict scrutiny test has worked to strike down a poll tax[9] and limits on who is eligible to vote.[10] But again, the Court applies it only in cases where it recognizes voting to be a fundamental right.

In cases where the Court has not recognized voting as a fundamental right, it generally has given great deference to governmental entities, applying the more lenient **rational basis test**. The rational basis test says that as long as a law is rationally related to a legitimate government interest, the Court will uphold it. The state whose law is in question can usually claim some interest in preventing fraud or ensuring election integrity, and the Court then upholds that state's law. This test has worked to uphold a slew of voter-suppressive measures over time, including a literacy test for would-be voters,[11] a requirement to enroll in a political party before being allowed to vote,[12] a prohibition on voting for write-in candidates,[13] and a strict Voter ID law.[14]

The Voting Rights Act is under attack

Congress did try to protect Americans by passing the **Voting Rights Act of 1965**, and for a while that federal law made important strides in defending the votes of **people of color**. But in recent years, a number of Supreme Court decisions have eroded that law's core protections.

Section 4 of the Voting Rights Act required states or counties with a history of racial discrimination in their elections to preclear with the federal government any changes to their election rules, creating a safeguard against racist restrictions on Americans' right to vote.[15] But in the 2013 decision ***Shelby County v. Holder***,[16] the Court effectively disabled section 4 by ruling that the coverage formula for determining which jurisdictions required preclearance was out of date.[17] In essence, the Court said, "Those places may have been racist in the past, but it's 2013 now, and we can't be sure they still are. Congress needs to come up with a new way to identify racist places. Until it does, we will not require preclearance by these jurisdictions."

So until Congress can agree on a new coverage formula — and seven years later, it still hasn't[18] — states with a history of racial discrimination are free to restrict voting. And they have. Within 24 hours of the ruling, Texas announced it would implement a strict photo ID law. Two other states, Mississippi and Alabama, began to enforce photo ID laws that had previously been barred because of the federal preclearance requirement.[19] Jurisdictions no longer subject to preclearance also began purging more voters from their rolls when *Shelby* freed them to do so. The Brennan Center for Justice estimates that lifting preclearance enabled states to purge an additional 2 million people from American voter rolls between 2012 and 2016.[20]

What's more, the 2018 Supreme Court decision *Husted v. Randolph*[21] eviscerated another Voting Rights Act protection that had prevented states from removing eligible voters from their rolls just because they hadn't voted in a recent election. Purges based on missing a vote force voters to "needlessly reregister" (as Justice Sotomayor pointed out in her dissent) and disproportionately affect people of color as well as low-income, disabled, and veteran voters[22] (more on that in chapter 2).

In short, Americans can't count on state laws or the Supreme Court to reliably protect our right to vote — sad but true. Also true, though, is that there's plenty that regular citizens, and our representatives at the state and national levels, can do about it.

Honor the right to vote

Right now, at this very moment, Americans and their representatives have ready-to-launch solutions that could enfranchise millions more voters and make it easier to participate in that foundational act of democracy: voting. In other words, we can treat Americans as if they have the right to vote, without changing the Constitution or relying on the Supreme Court:

- **Automatically register voters.** States or Congress can show they want citizens to vote by automatically registering eligible voters through modern and secure registration systems, as Oregon already does (chapter 1).

- **Use modern, standardized technology to clean voter rolls.** States can keep their voter rolls clean and updated by joining the 30 states plus DC that already use the Electronic Registration Information Center (chapter 2).

- **Let voters vote conveniently.** States or Congress can do away with long lines, confusing or burdensome Voter ID requirements, and the costly and hacker-vulnerable infrastructure of dispersed voting sites by implementing Vote At Home (chapter 3).

- **Preserve or restore voting rights.** States can show people with felony convictions that they still matter as citizens and that their crime does not define them, either by allowing them to vote while still in prison, as do Maine, Vermont, and DC, or by automatically restoring that right once they have served their time (chapter 4).

There are, of course, many more ways that states and Congress can ease burdens on voters. But these four are solutions that many states are already implementing and that many voters are benefiting from. So it's not a question of reinventing the wheel, but just one of pushing it around to more places. Let's get rolling . . .

Chapter 1:
Make Voter Registration
Easy and Secure

Enact robust Automatic Voter Registration in all states.

Daniel's story

Daniel Jones had voted his whole adult life. When the 34-year-old school-teacher moved from Utica, New York, to Syracuse, New York, for a new teaching position in fall 2016, he went to the Department of Motor Vehicles to update his driver's license and voter registration. In November, he went to his polling place with his five-year-old daughter in tow, proud to show her the importance of voting. But he and his daughter got a different lesson that day. The poll workers informed Jones that he was not on the voter rolls. Surprised, he explained that he had registered recently and asked if he could cast a provisional ballot while they sorted out the paperwork. A few weeks later, he received a notice in the mail: his provisional ballot had not been counted. The next day, he received his voter registration card with his new Syracuse address, too late.

"I've been voting since I was 18," Jones said. "I'm a U.S. citizen, and that's an important right that I take seriously. To be told my vote didn't count, to have to tell my daughter that I tried to vote but wasn't allowed to, and I can't even explain to her why . . . it's just not right. My voice wasn't heard, and it should have been."[23]

Barrier 1: Americans must proactively register to vote (and reregister when they move)

In every American state except North Dakota, eligible voters can't vote unless they register to do so, in a process separate from and in addition to the other types of registration that most of us engage in, like applying for a driver's license. The result: one in five eligible American voters is not registered to vote.[24] And even when they've taken the trouble to register, outdated and error-prone voter registration systems have blocked millions of eligible voters from voting.[25]

In other countries, including Canada, France, and Germany,[26] the state takes responsibility for registering eligible voters and keeping its list of voters up to date. Eligible voters can just vote. American voters in most states, though, must first opt into the system. This means they need to register to vote when they become eligible and also reregister every time they move. This sort-of system works to the disadvantage of first-time voters, like young people and immigrants, as well as people who move frequently, like renters, people with lower incomes, and (again) young people.

Barrier 2: Some states punish registration errors

In 2019, Tennessee passed a law to impose fines and penalties on voter registration groups that submit incomplete forms to the state.[27] Laws like this have an obvious chilling effect on largely volunteer-powered organizations such as Rock the Vote, which are trying to make up for their states' failure to automatically enroll eligible voters, even when these eligible voters have already proven their citizenship and eligibility to a qualified state agency.

Meanwhile, in Texas, legislators are considering a law that would punish people for errors on their voter registration forms or for voting if they are ineligible.[28] While some may feel the latter action merits punishment, cases of ineligible people intentionally voting are nearly nonexistent. The real targets of this law are perfectly eligible voters registering for the first time (who are more likely to be young) or updating their registration (more likely to be low-income voters, because they tend to move more and so need to update their addresses more often). If this law passes, members of both these groups could be punished for making any errors. Those Americans might wonder if their one vote is really worth possible punishment for an inadvertent error on a form and forgo registering to vote at all.

The reform: Automatic Voter Registration

What if instead of an opt-in registration system, we had an opt-out one? That's the promise of **Automatic Voter Registration (AVR)**, and it's already well at work across the United States. As of May 2020, fully 19 jurisdictions had adopted this more modern and secure policy.[29] Another four states (Connecticut,[30] Kentucky, New Mexico, and Utah[31]) use a somewhat weaker version in which voters applying for licenses or updating their addresses at the DMV cannot complete their transactions without either accepting or declining voter registration.[32]

Under AVR, eligible citizens are automatically registered, or if they were already registered their information is electronically updated, when they present proper documentation at a single state agency such as the Department of Motor Vehicles (where people get not only driver's licenses but other ID cards too), the health benefit exchange, or departments of social services. People may opt to stay unregistered if they like.

If Daniel lived in a state with AVR, when he moved and updated his driver's license, the DMV would have electronically transferred his updated information to the voter rolls so he could vote. Or if he got married and registered a name change, his voter registration would automatically stay up to date.

	In just four years, 22 states and DC have started automatically registering voters.	
	Approved	**Passed by**
ALASKA	2016	Ballot
CALIFORNIA	2015	Bill
COLORADO	2017	Administrative
CONNECTICUT	2016	Agency agreement
DC	2016	Bill
GEORGIA	2016	Executive order
ILLINOIS	2017	Bill
KENTUCKY	2019	Administrative
MAINE	2019	Bill
MARYLAND	2018	Bill
MASSACHUSETTS	2018	Bill
MICHIGAN	2018	Ballot
NEVADA	2018	Ballot
NEW JERSEY	2018	Bill
NEW MEXICO	2019	Bill
NEW YORK	2020	Bill
OREGON	2015	Bill
RHODE ISLAND	2017	Bill
UTAH	2018	Bill
VERMONT	2016	Bill
VIRGINIA	2020	Bill
WASHINGTON	2018	Bill
WEST VIRGINIA	2016	Bill

Source: National Conference of State Legislatures; Brennan Center for Justice

Table 1.1: *Jurisdictions that use Automatic Voter Registration.*

 # Case study: Oregon

Oregon, for one, is committed to honoring its residents' right to vote. The Beaver State was the very first to pass and implement Automatic Voter Registration in 2015 under what was called the New Motor Voter Law, because it automatically registered people to vote when they used the DMV, thereby implementing the opt-out system.[33] The results were stunning. In less than three years, Oregon registered nearly half a million people. As shown in figure 1.1 below, through 2018 (the most recent year for which data on the **voting-eligible population** is available), Oregon's percentage of unregistered eligible voters decreased from nearly 30 percent to under 10 percent.

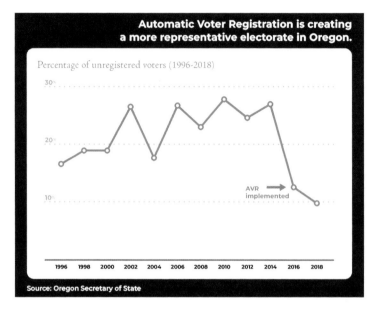

Automatic Voter Registration is creating a more representative electorate in Oregon.

Percentage of unregistered voters (1996-2018)

AVR implemented

1996 1998 2000 2002 2004 2006 2008 2010 2012 2014 2016 2018

Source: Oregon Secretary of State

Figure 1.1: *Eligible but unregistered voters in Oregon.*

What's more, most of these newly registered voters were young people, a notoriously difficult-to-engage demographic. In 2015, before AVR was implemented, voters over 60 were overrepresented among registered voters, making up more than one-third of the state's voters but only about one-quarter of the general population. Young people ages 18 to 24, on the other hand, were slightly underrepresented among registered voters, accounting for 10 percent of voters but 13 percent of the general population.

Now, though, Oregon's New Motor Voter Law is getting more young people onto the voter rolls. Since its implementation, more than half of newly registered voters have been young people ages 18 to 34, while 14 percent have been over age 60, a near flip of the previous registration statistics for the two groups. Oregon doesn't maintain information on each voter's race, ethnicity, or income, but a 2017 analysis showed that the areas where the new voters lived tended to be more suburban, low- and middle-income, and Hispanic, while already-registered voters tended to come from areas that were more urban, high-income, and white.[34]

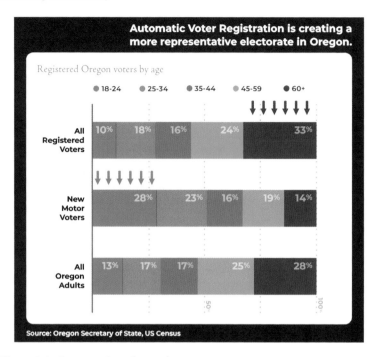

Figure 1.2: *Oregon registered voters by age.*

Swing states usually see the highest rates of voter turnout, but Oregon, a reliably blue jurisdiction, consistently makes the top ten, showing that voter-friendly policies like Automatic Voter Registration pay off handsomely in voter participation levels. Indeed, Oregon's system helped push its voter turnout even higher in the 2018 midterms. That year, the United States as a whole was proud to hit a 50-year high for midterm turnout at 49 percent.[35] Oregon, meanwhile, blew that number out of the water: 63 percent of eligible Oregonian voters turned in a ballot, the highest midterm turnout Oregon had seen in at least a quarter century.

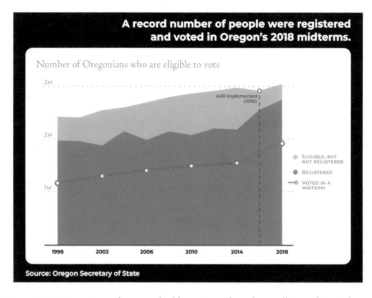

Figure 1.3: *Oregonians who were eligible, registered, and actually voted in midterms.*

 ## Case study: Georgia

Kitty-corner across the country in Georgia, the state Attorney General's Office and the Secretary of State's Office implemented their own Automatic Voter Registration policy in fall 2016.[36] Since implementation at the beginning of 2017, the Peach State's new system has led to a whopping 93 percent increase in voter registration rates there, with the Department of Driver Services adding more than 12,000 new voters to the rolls each week. Analysis by the Brennan Center for Justice indicates that without Automatic Voter Registration, Georgia would have registered only half that.[37] In its first three years of operation, Georgia's Automatic Voter Registration system added about 1 million voters to the rolls, bringing the state to an unprecedented 7.4 million registered voters.[38]

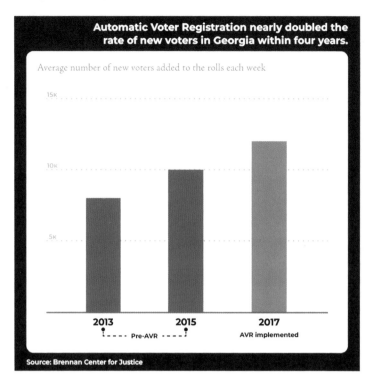

Figure 1.4: *Voter registrations in Georgia.*

As in Oregon, Georgia's Automatic Voter Registration system is registering more young first-time voters. Only 14 percent of all Georgia voters are age 30 or younger, but they make up about 45 percent of new voters.[39] New voters are also somewhat more likely to be people of color. While 40 percent of all Georgia voters are people of color, they make up 47 percent of new voters.[40]

Record registration rates went hand in hand with record voter turnout: a resounding 74 percent.[41] Georgia also saw additional benefits from Automatic Voter Registration, including voter applications being processed more quickly, fewer election-day complaints about voters having to go vote where they were formerly registered, fewer provisional ballots, and overall cost savings.[42]

That's not to say all is well in Georgia. Voter purges, which the next chapter discusses in greater detail, removed 1.5 million names from Georgia voter rolls between 2012 and 2016 — twice as many as were removed between 2008 and 2012[43] — and in December 2019 the state removed nearly 300,000 more, about 4 percent of all registered voters in Georgia.[44]

Still, Automatic Voter Registration has been a success, and one with bipartisan support. Though in many states it's Democrats who are championing voting rights, Georgia's Republican Secretary of State, Brad Raffensperger, touts voter registration and accessibility improvements as "Republican initiatives with bipartisan support."[45]

The payoffs: Ease, accuracy, cost savings, and voter turnout

Automatic Voter Registration is undoubtedly easier for voters. They can go about their lives, getting a driver's license or other ID as they normally do, and their voter registration stays accurate. But it's also easier for the states. They can maintain clean and accurate voter rolls with the paperwork that state agencies are already processing for other purposes. What's more, they can avoid confusion and delays at election time, due to fewer mistakes and outdated voter records.

> **Automatic Voter Registration helps maintain clean and accurate voter rolls with less paperwork.**

Oregon pioneered Automatic Voter Registration in 2015, and 21 other states plus the District of Columbia have so far followed suit, as shown in table 1.1 above. Most states use records from the Department of Motor Vehicles, but some collaborate with other agencies that may require proof of citizenship, such as health benefit exchanges and social services departments. Together, these jurisdictions have honored the right to vote for nearly 90 million eligible voters by making it far easier to keep their registration records up to date.

Make it happen: By legislature, governor, or ballot measure

If you live in one of the 28 states that have not yet adopted Automatic Voter Registration or one of the four that could strengthen its process, you can check this endnote to see whether your state lawmakers have introduced Automatic Voter Registration bills in recent years and their status.[46] Then you could join with others in your state to

- urge your lawmakers to pass a law, as Oregon and 14 other states plus DC have done;

- push your governor to sign an executive order, as Colorado, Georgia, and Kentucky have done;

- ask the state elections agency to sign an agreement with the DMV, as Connecticut did; or

- if your state allows citizens' initiatives, run a ballot measure asking voters to approve it, as voters did in Alaska, Michigan, and Nevada.

No matter where you live, you could encourage your Congress members to pass H.R. 1, which would require all states to implement AVR. The House passed the bill in 2019, but the Senate blocked it.

Organizations that can connect you with like-minded advocates and campaigns include Let America Vote, Indivisible, Common Cause, RepresentUs, I Vote for America, and the League of Women Voters.

If the first step to voting is being registered to vote, and if we as Americans value every citizen's right to vote, then we have to make it easier to register, plain and simple. If every state followed Oregon's example, the United States as a whole could achieve close to 100 percent voter registration within just a few years.

Once more citizens are registered to vote, the record suggests that more of them will vote.[47] Indeed, the ten states with the highest voter participation rates in the 2018 midterms all use Automatic Voter Registration,[48] having increased their registration rates on average four times faster than states that did not adopt Automatic Voter Registration. In short, more voters on the rolls meant more voters at the polls.

Discussion questions

☐ Do you remember when you first registered to vote? How did you do it? Did you find it easy or cumbersome?

☐ Do you know a young person who recently registered for the first time or who is about to register? How have they found the registration process?

☐ Can you think of reasons *not* to register people or keep their registration up to date once they have submitted verifying paperwork to a state agency?

☐ If your state does not have Automatic Voter Registration, how might it adopt it? Through administrative action, like Georgia? Through legislation, like Oregon? Or through a ballot measure, like Michigan?

Summary: Make Voter Registration Easy and Secure

- The United States has historically used an opt-in voter registration system, meaning voters are responsible for registering and keeping their voting registration up to date; if they don't, they can't vote.

- Many American states are shifting to an opt-out system known as Automatic Voter Registration (AVR), meaning eligible citizens are automatically registered when they present proper documentation at a state agency, unless they ask not to be registered.

- Under AVR, the state keeps voters' addresses up to date on the voting rolls if they move within the state and update their new address with a state agency.

- Twenty-two states, plus the District of Columbia, have adopted Automatic Voter Registration, helping more than 90 million eligible voters in those jurisdictions get and stay registered.

- Automatic Voter Registration helps more people vote: the ten states with the highest voter participation rates in the 2018 midterms all use it.

Chapter 2:
Protect Voter
Registration Records

Use the Electronic Registration Information Center rather than purges to keep voter lists clean and secure, and to reduce the need for Voter ID laws.

Joe's story

Joe Harmon is a U.S. Army veteran who was deployed abroad for years and didn't vote while he was away. After returning from tours in Iraq and Afghanistan, he proudly went to his polling place in Dayton, Ohio, but was turned away because he was no longer registered.

"I started crying," Joe said. "To come home after defending that fundamental right and to be told that I couldn't exercise it—that was heartbreaking."[49]

Ada's story

Ada was born in 1925 in Joplin, Missouri. Her name then was Ada Davis, but her mom remarried when she was ten and changed her name to Ada Williams. That's the name she has gone by for more than 80 years, and she has voted in every presidential election since 1948. In 2011, though, she lost her right to vote when Wisconsin, where she had lived for the past 20 years, passed a strict Voter ID law that requires all voters to present specific forms of ID before being allowed to vote at their polling places on Election Day.

Ada was determined to get the required ID so that she could continue to vote. She can no longer drive, so her daughter took her to the DMV, where she presented to the clerk her 1925 birth certificate, an old photo ID from Missouri, an expired Wisconsin ID, and proof of residence in Wisconsin. These weren't enough; the clerk needed to see the name-change certificate her mother had filled out in 1935. Ada explained that that certificate had been lost long ago, but that she had gone by Ada Williams for over 80 years without issue. The clerk had to insist: without the certificate, Wisconsin wouldn't let her vote.

Ada then sought out a lawyer who agreed to help her free of charge. The lawyer assessed the new law as it applied to Ada's situation and found that she indeed would need a name-change certificate. The only way to obtain one, though, was to go to court and pay $300.[50] Ada didn't have the money, so in 2016, for the first time in nearly a century, she didn't vote.

"I'm so mad, I could spit," Ada said. "Why are they trying to stop good, honest Americans from voting? I feel like I am not wanted here. After all these years, I don't matter."

Barrier 1: Voter ID laws bar eligible voters from the polls

In the last chapter, we looked at barriers to registering to vote. In this one, we learn that even after a would-be voter surmounts those hurdles, in some states she still must work each year to ensure she stays registered and that she indeed can vote when she arrives at the polls. Sound repetitive? Burdensome? Confusing? Well, it is.

All states keep lists of voter names and addresses. Some states treat voting as a right: they try to keep their lists as accurate as possible to make it easy and smooth for people to cast their votes. Other states treat voting as a privilege: they focus on blocking any potentially ineligible people[51] from voting, which may block *eligible* voters from casting their fully legitimate votes, too.

Unfortunately, these attitudes are often animated by which party is in charge and what they perceive will help them stay in control. In general, Democrats believe that more people voting is better for their electoral chances, while Republicans believe that a smaller pool of voters is better for them. Recently, the Democratic Party has attracted more people of color, young people, lower-income people, and single women. All of these groups are more likely to change their place of residence and to lack certain types of ID. Because of this, the Republican Party often sees policies that require voters to jump through hoops every time they move, or to show a particular type of ID that these (more likely Democratic) voters might not have,[52] as opportunities to keep opposition voters out of the voting booth, boosting Republican candidates' chances of winning.[53]

One way these "voting is a privilege, not a right" states prevent certain people from voting is with strict **Voter ID laws**, which require voters to present specific forms of ID at their polling places in order to obtain their ballots and cast their votes. The justification for such laws is that they are supposed to prevent in-person **voter fraud**, which would go something like this: Al Alive happens to know that his neighbor Dan Dead, who died last year, is still on the voter rolls. Al casts a legitimate vote for himself in the morning, but later that day, when the poll workers have changed shifts, he returns to the polls and claims he is Dan. Al fraudulently casts a second vote, as Dan. One man, two votes: not fair. Some states argue the best way to prevent this type of cheating is to make Al show ID to prove his identity before they hand him a ballot.

But this is a solution without a problem, because in-person voter fraud like Al's is *exceptionally* rare.[54] As in, more people get struck by lightning than commit voter fraud.[55] As in, more people escape from maximum-security prisons than commit voter fraud.[56] Because . . . *why would you?* For just one extra vote, out of however many thousands or millions of votes people cast in an election, Al risks five years in prison, a $10,000 fine, and other penalties.[57] In short, it's not worth it. Very few races turn on the one vote Al can get by fraudulently voting as his dead neighbor.

Okay, you might think, but is it really so burdensome to ask people to show photo ID? For some: yes, it is. Many eligible voters don't have the particular kind of ID that Voter ID states require, be that a driver's license, a passport, or a concealed-carry handgun license.[58] Why? Well, sometimes the type of ID deemed acceptable seems tailor-made to allow certain kinds of people to vote and to stop others. For example, Texas accepts a handgun license but not a student photo ID issued by a Texas state university.[59] That might sound arbitrary unless you know (a) that the lawmakers who passed the bill are Republican, (b) that gun owners are more likely to vote for Republicans, and (c) that university students are more likely to vote for Democrats. Similarly, until its Voter ID law was struck down by a federal court, North Carolina prohibited public assistance IDs and state employee ID cards, which are disproportionately held by Black voters.[60]

And sometimes the right ID is expensive or difficult to get. Yes, voting is free, thanks to the 24th Amendment, but getting a photo ID is not.[61] Courts have required states with restrictive Voter ID laws to provide qualifying IDs for free, but there are still plenty of costs involved in getting that ID in the first place that the courts can't erase: would-be voters must get to the issuing government office within business hours, perhaps navigating limited transportation options, long or conflicting work hours, and lack of childcare.[62] Not coincidentally, more restrictive states often have limited locations where, and hours when, people can get the appropriate ID. For example, some Texas residents must travel 170 miles to get to the closest office.[63] Or would-be voters may not have, be able to obtain, or be able to pay the price of obtaining copies of the required supporting documentation.[64] Or, especially in the case of Native Americans living on reservations, the state may not acknowledge a person's address as valid when she tries to obtain an ID to be able to vote.[65]

The result? More than one in ten voting-age citizens do not have a current, government-issued photo ID.[66] Put another way, some 23 million American citizens who are eligible to vote cannot exercise that right in states with strict Voter ID laws.[67]

 More than one in ten voting-age citizens do not have current, government-issued photo ID.

Put another way, some 23 million American citizens who are eligible to vote cannot exercise that right in states with strict Voter ID laws.

What's more, Voter ID laws are costly to implement — ironic, given the often fiscally conservative politics of their advocates. Even though the problem that Voter ID laws supposedly protect us from is almost nonexistent (that is, in-person voter fraud is almost unheard of), the state often spends three to five dollars per registered voter to enforce Voter ID laws.[68] This can cost state taxpayers millions of dollars.[69]

Notably, the harm of Voter ID laws falls disproportionately on people of color.[70] For example, one study in Michigan showed that people of color were between two and a half and six times more likely than white voters to lack a photo ID.[71] And while one Al voting as his dead neighbor is not going to swing an election, a law that systematically prevents millions of Americans from voting could very much do so. For some proponents, that's the real point. In 2012, for example, a legislative leader in Pennsylvania said that the state's Voter ID law[72] was "gonna allow [Republican presidential candidate] Governor Romney to win the state of Pennsylvania."[73] In Alabama, a state senator publicly said he championed a strict Voter ID law because it would undermine the state's Black leaders.[74]

 # Barrier 2: States have barred less active voters from the polls

Imagine that you own a home. One day while you're at work, someone knocks on your door to see if anyone's there. When no one answers, they mark your home vacant and for sale. You return that evening to discover you're no longer a homeowner.

That's pretty absurd, right? But that's effectively what's happened to many voter registration records in states using what we'll call "postcard purges." The National Voter Registration Act requires states to "make a reasonable effort" to remove voters from their rolls when they move, and some states treat this as a license to purge. States do remove some voters who are genuinely no longer eligible, but purge rates have noticeably jumped since the Supreme Court's 2013 decision in *Shelby v. Holder* (see the section overview), suggesting that states are removing plenty of eligible voters from their rolls. Between 2016 and 2018 alone, at least 17 million voters — that's more than 10 percent of all registered voters — were purged nationwide.[75]

Compared to pro–voting rights states, which take a careful and diligent approach to keeping their voter rolls clean so all eligible voters can have a smooth and easy voting experience, these "voting is a privilege" states presume that voters have moved and disenroll them if they haven't voted in an election in a while. State election officials send a postcard to voters' homes to ask whether they still live there. If they ignore the postcard, miss it, misplace it, or are off fighting for their country for months or years on end — like our combat veteran Joe Harmon above — they may return to find they are no longer registered to vote.

Here are a few of the types of scenarios that states are protecting against when they remove someone who has in fact moved: Marvin Mover registers to vote in County Hometown, then moves to County Newtown and registers to vote there, too. He votes in County Newtown and then drives back to County Hometown to vote again. Or, unbeknownst to Marvin, his old neighbor Stan Staid knows that Marvin moved away but is still on the rolls, so Stan votes as himself in County Hometown, then goes back to the polls pretending to be Marvin and votes again. In both these scenarios, one person has two votes: not fair.

But both these scenarios are vanishingly rare. Because again: *Why would you bother?* Why would Marvin drive across the state, and why would he or Stan risk fines and jail time, for the chance at one additional vote?

New scenario: Stan Staid is still at the same old address, but he was feeling disenchanted with the available candidates and decided not to vote in a couple of elections. The state sent him a postcard asking if he still lived there, but it looked like junk mail and he threw it away. This year he is fired up and wants to vote. He shows up at his usual polling place but is turned away because he isn't on the list. One person, no vote: not fair.

The state should keep its voter lists clean and accurate and remove Marvin from the rolls in County Hometown. But how to know when Marvin has in fact moved? It could use the U.S. Postal Service's change-of-address records to see that Marvin moved, or it could search the rolls for duplicates and see that Marvin is registered in two counties. Or it could . . . purge Stan if he skips an election and doesn't respond to a postcard.

Wait, what? Fewer than half of registered voters actually vote in most federal elections, so using skipped elections and a postcard to trigger a purge could eliminate many eligible voters from the rolls. Stan hasn't moved; he just skipped a few elections and missed a postcard. But now he tries to vote and finds he can't. Some states are willing to deny Stan his right to vote rather than use a more reliable method for identifying that Marvin has actually moved.

Case study: Ohio

Is a not-returned postcard plus sitting out a couple of elections enough to prove someone has moved and should be stricken from the voter rolls? That's what some states are claiming.[76] In Ohio, for instance, if a registered voter does not vote in a federal election, the state suspects he may have moved and sends him a "last chance" postcard asking him to verify that he still lives in the Buckeye State. If he doesn't return the postcard and doesn't vote in the next two federal elections (two being the figure required by the **National Voter Registration Act of 1993**[77]), the state presumes he has moved and purges him from the voter rolls.

In this way, voter inactivity, plus inattention to what we might safely assume not to be the flashiest item in one's mailbox, can get a person disenrolled. Put more plainly, doing nothing can mean disenfranchisement. In the 2018 Supreme Court case *Husted v. Randolph*[78] that examined this "postcard purge" practice and upheld it as legal, Justice Stephen Breyer dissented:

> *Very few registered voters move outside of their county of registration. But many registered voters fail to vote. Most registered voters who fail to vote also fail to respond to the State's "last chance" notice. And the number of registered voters who both fail to vote and fail to respond to the "last chance" notice exceeds the number of registered voters who move outside of their county each year. . . .*
>
> *[I]n 2012 Ohio identified about 1.5 million registered voters — nearly 20% of its 8 million registered voters — as likely ineligible to remain on the federal voter roll because they changed their residences. Ohio then sent those 1.5 million registered voters "last chance" confirmation notices. In response to those 1.5 million notices, Ohio only received back about 60,000 return cards (or 4%) which said, in effect, "You are right, Ohio. I have, in fact, moved." In addition, Ohio received back about 235,000 return cards which said, in effect, "You are wrong, Ohio, I have not moved." In the end, however, there were more than 1,000,000 notices — the vast majority of notices sent — to which Ohio received back no return card at all. What about those registered voters — more than 1 million strong — who did not send back their return cards? Is there any reason at all (other than their failure to vote) to think they moved? The answer to this question must be no. There is no reason at all.*

Despite Justice Breyer's earnest reasoning on behalf of voters' rights, the majority of the Supreme Court upheld Ohio's voter-purging scheme in a ruling that, unfortunately, is emboldening other states to undertake similar measures.

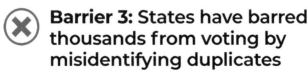

✖ Barrier 3: States have barred thousands from voting by misidentifying duplicates

Another tactic some states employ that makes it hard for voters to stay registered is purging large numbers of voters for supposedly being registered more than once, but using a defective method of identifying duplicates. The most egregious example of this practice was a program the state of Kansas developed in 2005 called the Interstate Voter Registration Crosscheck Program, or just Crosscheck. **Crosscheck** was a software system designed to identify and disenroll duplicate voter registrations within and between states. By 2017, 30 states with more than 100 million voter records — that's nearly half of all American voters — were participating.

To say Crosscheck was problematic would be an understatement. For every record it identified as a likely legitimate duplicate, Crosscheck flagged 300 non-duplicate records.[79] This means that states participating in Crosscheck could delete 300 eligible voters from their rolls for every one real duplicate, in some cases without those voters ever receiving notice until they showed up to vote on Election Day and learned they couldn't do so.

According to a 2015 report, Crosscheck's program disproportionately affected Black, **Hispanic**, and Asian American voters.[80] Why? In large part because many members of these communities are more likely to share the same last name, such as Washington, Gonzales, Lee, Patel, or Kim.[81] This built-in racial bias may have been an innocent flaw of the Crosscheck system, or it could have been a feature for some states. Because Blacks, Hispanics, and Asian Americans are all more likely to vote for Democrats, Republican state officials may have seen political benefits in a system that disproportionately removed those voters from the rolls.

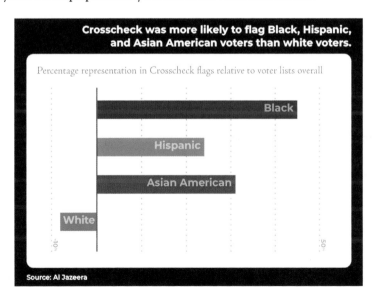

Figure 2.1: *Crosscheck flags by race.*

If its sloppy and discriminatory voter identification practices weren't bad enough, Crosscheck also poorly secured voter information as it stored and transmitted it between users. Non-secure servers, hackable passwords, and emails including usernames and passwords[82] would all be poor practice just for personal documents, but for a database responsible for tens of millions of voter records . . . well, in the words of the chief technologist for the Center for Democracy and Technology, "It blows my mind — this is complete operational security incompetence."[83]

In December 2019, the American Civil Liberties Union (ACLU) of Kansas settled a lawsuit that effectively shut down Crosscheck.[84] By that time, many states had already dropped the program,[85] but sadly, Crosscheck may have already considerably damaged their voter rolls. Come 2020, we may still see voters showing up to vote only to learn for the first time that Crosscheck removed them and they can't.

 # The reform: The Electronic Registration Information Center (ERIC)

None of the above means that pro-voter states don't want clean voter rolls. They do! When people move from one place to another, of course they shouldn't be double registered. Nor should outdated voter rolls be allowed to gum up the polls on Election Day. Nor should the costs to fix this fall to taxpayers in election cycle after election cycle. States need to maintain clean voter rolls to enable smooth and efficient election administration.

Luckily, there is a system that is reliable, secure, and unbiased (unlike Crosscheck). The **Electronic Registration Information Center (ERIC)** is a modern, secure system that searches for actual duplicates and deceased individuals within and across state voter rolls. ERIC compares voter registration information not only between its member states but also — and this is key, going well beyond Crosscheck's methods — against data from several official sources typically quite current on a person's whereabouts, like the U.S. Postal Service, motor vehicle licensing agency data, and the Social Security Administration death index.[86] It also looks for more than a first and last name match to ensure it is identifying an actual duplicate and not two unrelated Barry Washingtons or Betty Kims. In other words, ERIC cross-references existing databases and uses multiple data points to clean and update voter rolls. Already, it has successfully cleaned millions of voter records.[87] Unlike Crosscheck, ERIC also shares information with member states in a secure manner.

Thirty states plus the District of Columbia are members of ERIC.[88] These states give a bipartisan vote of confidence to the necessity of clean and modern voter rolls. Together, ERIC states account for a little more than half of the **voting-age population** of the United States, whose records are now kept cleaner and more accurate because ERIC helps identify

- updated addresses of voters who move across state lines,
- updated addresses of voters who move within a state,
- duplicate registrations, and
- deceased people still on the voter rolls.

Over the years, ERIC has identified hundreds of thousands of deceased people for states to remove from their rolls, flagged millions of voters who moved across state lines so their former states of residence can remove them, and alerted states to updated address information for nearly 10 million voters.[89] ERIC has also identified more than 30 million eligible voters who were not yet registered,[90] giving member states the chance to reach out and get them registered. If all the eligible voters identified by ERIC registered, the ranks of the approximately 160 million registered voters in the United States would swell by about one-fifth.

Better together: ERIC + Automatic Voter Registration

Sixteen jurisdictions — Alaska, Colorado, Connecticut, DC, Georgia, Illinois, Maryland, Michigan, Nevada, New Mexico, Oregon, Rhode Island, Vermont, Virginia, Washington, and West Virginia — are members of ERIC and *also* use Automatic Voter Registration (chapter 1). These states are using the best available systems for keeping their voter rolls clean, modern, and up-to-date while making it easy for voters to get registered and stay registered. When a voter moves within these states and updates their address on their driver's license or other ID, they are automatically registered to vote at the new address. Meanwhile, ERIC has definitive confirmation that they have moved and that their registration at their prior address should be removed.

Fifteen states — Alabama, Arizona, Delaware, Florida, Iowa, Kentucky, Louisiana, Minnesota, Missouri, Ohio, Pennsylvania, South Carolina, Texas, Utah, and Wisconsin — are members of ERIC but do not yet use Automatic Voter Registration. ERIC is helping them take steps to maintain accurate voter lists but still has less information to work with when identifying voters who have moved.

Four states — California, Maine, Massachusetts, and New Jersey — have adopted Automatic Voter Registration but are not yet members of ERIC (as of this writing, Massachusetts is in the process of joining). These states are getting voters onto their rolls but could keep those rolls cleaner with ERIC.

Figure 2.2: *Jurisdictions using AVR, ERIC, or both.*

Both ERIC and AVR	ERIC	AVR	Neither ERIC nor AVR
ALASKA	ALABAMA	CALIFORNIA	ARKANSAS
COLORADO	ARIZONA	MAINE	HAWAII
CONNECTICUT	DELAWARE	MASSACHUSETTS	IDAHO
DC	FLORIDA	NEW JERSEY	INDIANA
GEORGIA	IOWA	WISCONSIN	KANSAS
ILLINOIS	LOUISIANA		MISSISSIPPI
KENTUCKY	MINNESOTA		MONTANA
MARYLAND	MISSOURI		NEBRASKA
MICHIGAN	OHIO		NEW HAMPSHIRE
NEW MEXICO	PENNSYLVANIA		NEW YORK
NEVADA	SOUTH CAROLINA		NORTH CAROLINA
OREGON	TEXAS		NORTH DAKOTA
RHODE ISLAND	UTAH		OKLAHOMA
VERMONT			SOUTH DAKOTA
VIRGINIA			TENNESSEE
WASHINGTON			WYOMING
WEST VIRGINIA			

Table 2.1: *Jurisdictions using AVR, ERIC, both, or neither.*

The payoff: Efficient, accurate, secure voter rolls

Clean voter rolls allow election administrators to make voting a smooth experience. Americans receive the correct ballot or polling place assignment in the mail, and polling places are appropriately staffed to meet the needs of each precinct. Clean rolls also nearly eliminate the (say it with me now: *already all but nonexistent*) likelihood of in-person voter fraud.

The reality is that most voting glitches arise not from people trying to defraud election officials but rather from errors in the voting rolls.[91] Clerks typing in information from handwritten paper registration forms sometimes make mistakes, voters sometimes don't complete the forms, and people stay on the voter rolls after they die — simple, honest errors or oversights. Throwing sand in the gears of the democratic process with expensive Voter ID requirements doesn't solve these problems. Utilizing technology to maintain clean and accurate voter rolls does.

Ditching Crosscheck is a no-brainer for states still subscribed to it, especially because such a better, proven tool exists for them to switch to in ERIC. Pair ERIC with Automatic Voter Registration, and the results would be a real win for voters and voting rights.

And the more states that join ERIC, the more effective it gets. If every state joined, ERIC could compare records across all states to ensure they were properly updated when someone moved, no matter where in the United States they moved. All citizens who had proved their citizenship to a relevant agency in any state would automatically be ready to vote at their home address, and ERIC would notify election administrators in their prior jurisdiction to remove them from the rolls there. In this way, Americans' voter registration would follow them when they moved or else expire when they died, without their needing to jump through Voter ID or postcard hoops. Whenever an election rolled around, voters could simply vote.

Make it happen: Join ERIC (plus adopt AVR)!

If you live in one of the 20 states that has not yet joined ERIC (see ericstates. org for an updated list), you could urge your secretary of state to join. Helpful organizations in that effort would be Common Cause,[92] the Brennan Center for Justice, and the League of Women Voters. If you live in one of the 25 states that is still a member of Crosscheck, pressure your state to get out. The organization

Indivisible has a great tool kit to help and might have a local chapter in your area already working on this issue.[93]

No matter where you live, you could encourage your Congress members to pass H.R. 1, which would require all states to use ERIC, or ERIC-level quality standards, before removing anyone from the voter lists. The House passed the bill in 2019, but the Senate blocked it.

 ## Discussion questions

☐ Do you believe voting should be a right or a privilege? Why?

☐ What do you think would happen if we acted as though all citizens have a right to vote? What do you think would happen if we acted as though voting is a privilege that only the most dedicated citizens are allowed to participate in?

☐ What ID does your state require to vote?

☐ Do you know anyone who is a citizen but doesn't have a driver's license or other form of ID required to vote in their state?

☐ Under what circumstances can you imagine someone risking five years in jail to get one extra vote?

☐ What would you do if you showed up to vote and found out you were no longer on the voter rolls? Do you know someone this has happened to?

☐ What do you think are the most important things a state can do to protect against voter fraud?

☐ Have you heard anyone complain that dead people are voting in elections? Did you wonder why your state doesn't remove deceased people from the voter rolls? What would you say to them now if you heard someone complain about dead people voting?

☐ If you heard someone say that we have to purge voters to avoid voter fraud, what would you say to them?

Summary: Protect Voter Registration Records

- Voter ID laws are supposed to protect against in-person voter fraud, something that can only happen if voter rolls are inaccurate. But in-person voter fraud almost never happens. Americans are more likely to get hit by lightning.

- Some 23 million American citizens, or about 10 percent of the voting-eligible population, don't have the type of ID that strict Voter ID laws require.

- Rather than carefully curating accurate lists, some states purge eligible voters from their rolls without sufficient information. Between 2016 and 2018 alone, at least 17 million voters were removed nationwide.

- In some cases, the motivation behind Voter ID laws and voter purges is that the Republican Party is trying to boost its chances of winning elections by preventing likely Democratic voters from casting a ballot.

- Nonetheless, both parties can strive for clean voter rolls. Fully 31 jurisdictions (including both Democratic-leaning and Republican-leaning states) already use a better system for maintaining clean and accurate lists of voters: the Electronic Registration Information Center (ERIC), which compares voter data securely across several databases to help states maintain accurate voter rolls. The other 20 states could join them and ensure that deceased people don't stay on American voter rolls.

Chapter 3:
Make Voting Convenient

Enact Vote At Home to let people vote on their own time.

Nia's story

Nia Taylor arrived at her polling place in Snellville, Georgia, at 6:45 a.m. to find 100 people already in line ahead of her, all eager to vote in the 2018 midterms. The line wasn't moving, though, because the machines that scan ballots had broken down. Nia, a 35-year-old African American social worker, waited in line for an hour before she had to leave to get to her job. Once there, she explained the situation to her boss, who gave her permission to leave work a little early. She was able to arrange for her mother to babysit her children, and she was back in line by 5:00 p.m.

Talking with her neighbors there, she learned that some people had been waiting in line for hours and many had simply given up and left. Nia waited for two more hours and was tired, hungry, and frustrated when her mother called: Nia's children were wondering if she'd be home to put them to bed. Finally, Nia gave up and went home to her two children.

"What does a person have to do to vote around here?" Nia asked, exasperated. "I got up early. I stayed late. I arranged for childcare and to get out of work early so I could vote. My voice still wasn't heard. I'm an American! Why is it so hard to vote?"[94]

Barrier 1: Voting is inconvenient or difficult for voters

In many American jurisdictions, the only way to vote is by showing up at a single designated polling place during certain hours on a specific Tuesday. That usually means a voter must take time from work or home duties, travel to the polling place by personal vehicle or by transit, wait in line, bring the right ID, vote, and travel back to work or home. Every one of these steps is a barrier for many would-be voters. In 2016, nearly four of every ten registered voters who didn't vote said it was because they had trouble getting to their polling place during open hours.[95]

Barrier 2: States can't afford enough secure, modern voting infrastructure

In recent years, cash-strapped cities and counties — the government entities responsible for organizing and operating elections — have cut back on the number of polling places they offer their voters, the number of people staffing those stations, and the hours those remaining stations are open.[96] The result? Those iconic photos from our last several elections of voters across the United States, in places large and small, waiting in lines for up to five hours just to cast their votes.[97] Or tales of long trips to unfamiliar neighborhoods, perhaps inaccessible by transit, for voters to exercise their democratic rights.

What's more, voting machines are expensive, and many jurisdictions have not been able to upgrade their equipment in nearly two decades. This can mean widespread malfunctions or failures on Election Day, as at Nia's polling place above, as well as a higher risk of election hacking.

Cities' and counties' failure to support their polling infrastructure has especially hurt American voters of color. In recent years, many of the neighborhoods that lost a polling place or didn't have enough machines were ones where more people of color live. For example, voters in the heavily **Latino** Spruce Street neighborhood of Manchester, Connecticut, faced a journey of many more miles, to a polling location without bus access, when their local polling place closed in 2012.[98] In Atlanta, Georgia, a polling location serving a mostly Black neighborhood had only three voting machines, forcing would-be voters to wait in line for hours.[99] A recent study showed that voters in predominantly Black neighborhoods wait 29 percent longer to vote than those in white neighborhoods.[100]

The reform: Vote at Home

Now imagine this instead: several weeks in advance of an election, Nia received a text letting her know her ballot was on its way to her, and two days later, it arrived in the mail. She filled it out at her convenience, working away at it over the course of a few evenings while doing a little extra research on some unfamiliar candidates or measures and talking to her kids about the importance of voting. Once finished, she dropped it at a secure collection box on her way to work one day. The next afternoon, she got a text saying her ballot was received, and the following day another text told her that her vote was counted.

Doesn't that sound a lot easier than the polling place rigmarole? Well, many states think so, and they have implemented just that system, making it easier for their residents to vote. Instead of going to a designated polling place on Election Day, every registered voter automatically receives a ballot in their home mailbox a few weeks beforehand. They may take advantage of this extra time to talk with family and friends about candidates and policy proposals, or host a voting party, or do some extra research on their own. Then, on their way to work or to pick up the kids from school or when simply walking past a U.S. Postal Service mailbox or secure ballot drop box, they submit their vote. Poof! They've voted.

Every state gives at least some voters the convenience of voting at home. But in most states, the default is that voters need to show up at a polling place on Election Day, and voting at home in fuzzy slippers is the exception only for those who request it. Fifteen states make it particularly hard to get a mailed ballot, requiring voters to have an "excuse" such as being ill or disabled, to request an absentee ballot.[101] Most states allow any voter to request that a ballot be mailed to them.[102] A dozen of those mail ballots to *all* voters in certain elections (such as special elections)[103] or in certain jurisdictions (some counties or small precincts may find it more practical to mail out ballots than to run polling places).[104] Six make it easy for voters to always vote at home by allowing them to sign up to permanently continue receiving their ballots by mail.[105]

A note on terminology:

- An **absentee ballot** is one that a voter must request.

- Full **Vote At Home** means a state or jurisdiction automatically mails ballots to all registered voters.

- **Mailed-out ballots** and **Vote By Mail** can refer to any ballots that get mailed to voters, whether automatically or by request.

Five states have enacted full Vote At Home, meaning they automatically mail a ballot to each registered voter for all elections.[106] In these states, the default is to Vote At Home, and the exception is to show up at a polling place if you need special assistance.

Vote At Home: A resilient voting system during a pandemic

In 2020, as the global COVID-19 pandemic raged, many states had a hard time staffing their polling places. Many poll workers are older people, a class that is at particular risk if infected with COVID-19. And many voters preferred to vote from the safety of their homes rather than risk infection at crowded polling places, so they applied to vote absentee. This added up, for most states, to a crash course in how to help more voters Vote At Home.

During the primary, thirteen states waived or loosened their "excuse" requirements.

As of this writing, the primary results are in, and states are preparing for the November 2020 general election. In the primary, many states successfully counted orders of magnitude more absentee votes than in previous elections, and some states experienced problems. Notably, thousands of voters in Georgia, Wisconsin, and New York requested absentee ballots that did not arrive in time. But Idaho and Montana mailed ballots to all voters, with rave results: Idaho saw the highest voter participation in 30 years, while Montana saw the highest in more than 40 years. Michigan voters presciently passed a ballot measure in 2018 allowing any voter to request an absentee ballot. Michigan shattered its voter turnout record, and two-thirds of those voters opted to vote absentee.

During the general, nine states again loosened the "excuse" requirement.[107] And ten states plus DC mailed ballots to all registered voters (the five that had already implemented full Vote At Home, plus five more and DC).[108]

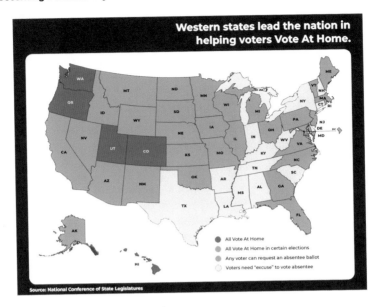

Figure 3.1: *Vote At Home across the states.*

All Vote At Home	All Vote At Home in certain elections	Any voter can request an absentee ballot	Voters need "excuse" to vote absentee
Colorado	Alaska	Georgia	Alabama*
Hawaii	Arizona	Illinois	Arkansas*
Oregon	California**	Iowa	Connecticut*
Utah	DC**	Maine	Delaware*
Washington	Florida	Massachusetts	Indiana
	Idaho	Michigan	Kentucky*
	Kansas	North Carolina	Louisiana
	Maryland	Ohio	Mississippi
	Minnesota	Oklahoma	New Hampshire*
	Missouri	Pennsylvania	New York*
	Montana**	Rhode Island	South Carolina
	Nebraska	South Dakota	Tennessee
	Nevada**	Virginia	Texas
	New Jersey**	Wisconsin	West Virginia*
	New Mexico		
	North Dakota		
	Vermont**		* "Excuse" temporarily waived for Covid-19
	Wyoming		** All ballots mailed in November 2020

Table 3.1: *Vote At Home across the states.*

The payoffs: Ease, accessibility, engagement, cost savings, and security

Vote At Home isn't just easier for voters. It has also proved to be highly secure, to increase turnout, and to significantly lower the cost to local governments of managing an election — which should be great news to all those cash-strapped cities and counties struggling to keep up the old-fashioned way.

Vote At Home empowers voters, letting them decide when, how, and where they vote. They don't have to take time off work, travel to a polling place, or stand in long lines, and the flexibility ensures that all eligible voters can actually vote. Seniors and voters with disabilities who might have trouble getting to the polls; rural voters a long way from a voting site; single parents working three jobs; people with inflexible work schedules, sick kids, or a business trip: all have equal access to the ballot. And equal access means higher rates of voter participation.

Vote At Home gives voters the chance to more thoughtfully peruse the entire ballot as they vote, looking up information about candidates and initiatives as they go and discussing the options with family and friends.[109] This can introduce minors to a more communal and engaged sense of civic participation, engendering good voting habits early on. (It certainly beats trying to get your kid to stand in line with you for hours and telling them this is an example of great democracy.)

An abundance of studies bear this out, finding that across different states, Vote At Home increases turnout. This is even true in low-turnout elections such as local elections; among typically less engaged voters, like younger people; and for people with disabilities, for whom Vote At Home is a game changer.[110] For example, in the 2014 midterm elections, voter participation in Vote At Home states across the nation was on average 23 percent higher than in other states.[111] In Anchorage, Alaska, which held its first Vote At Home election in the 2018 midterms, voter turnout positively shattered prior records.[112] When Garden County, Nebraska, tried Vote At Home that same year for a state primary, it more than doubled voter participation compared to other Nebraska counties.[113] St. George, Utah, used Vote At Home in 2019 and saw double the usual turnout.[114] Tucson, Arizona, conducted a Vote At Home election in 2019 and was delighted to see turnout above 37 percent (high for a city election).[115] Similarly in Kansas, a county clerk estimated that Vote At Home increased voter participation by 20 percent in a 2018 local election on a sales tax.[116] In Las Cruces, New Mexico, voter turnout in local elections skyrocketed from its abysmal historical levels of just 5 to 10 percent, to 25 percent.[117] In California, Vote At Home increased voter turnout by 7.6 percent in local special elections.[118] In 2016, Vote At Home counties in Utah saw 4 to 9 percent more voters than their neighboring counties still using polling sites, as well as a 10 percent increase in turnout among 25- to 34-year-olds.[119] And statewide in Washington, Vote At Home boosted voter participation by 2 to 4 percent.[120] Michigan voters are also embracing their newly implemented "no excuse" model, which allows anyone to request a Vote At Home ballot without having to give a reason (such as being abroad during the election), with large turnout increases.[121]

Vote at Home increases voter participation

In addition to boosting turnout, Vote At Home is also considerably less expensive. Colorado cut costs by about 40 percent when it implemented Vote At Home in 2014,[122] and in San Diego, which is considering adopting Vote At Home, the registrar estimates the city could cut its election costs by about one-third.[123] Colorado shed the expense of thousands of poll workers; of equipment needed at each polling site, as well as repairs and updates to that equipment; and of printing so many provisional ballots.[124]

What's more, Vote At Home means more secure elections. First, Vote At Home systems use hand-marked paper ballots, the gold standard for election security because voters can personally verify that their selections are correct. This means there's a paper trail that officials can audit should the need arise, and they don't rely on hackable electronic voting machines.[125] Second, jurisdictions process Vote At Home ballots at fewer locations and with fewer machines. This means fewer opportunities for hackers or other bad actors to intervene. Fewer machines also mean that officials can better afford the maintenance and software to ensure that they are updated and reliable.

Perhaps intuitive, but most important of all, *voters love Vote At Home.* Would you rather have Nia's experience of voting from the beginning of the chapter, or the flexible and comfortable experience described above? Considering how many Americans have grown accustomed to home delivery of everything from diapers to produce, who wouldn't appreciate the same convenience and control with their ballot? Indeed, a poll of voters in Oregon found that fully 87 percent of them support Vote At Home.[126]

Vote At Home makes so much sense that it is spreading across the country. In 2016, one-quarter of all American voters used a ballot that had been mailed to them.[127] In the 2018 midterms, 27 percent of all votes cast nationally and 69 percent of votes cast in the West were from mailed-out ballots.[128]

Case study: Colorado

In 2008, a handful of Colorado counties began using Vote At Home as a pilot for the state. Five years later, with the support of a broad coalition of civic and nonprofit groups,[129] the Colorado legislature took Vote At Home statewide with the Voter Access and Modernized Elections Act. Key to passing the bill was that election administrators themselves had helped to craft it and so were glad to support it as it moved through the legislature. Notably, the Colorado County Clerks Association, which is 65 percent Republican, also voted to support it,[130] likely in part due to the considerable cost savings they foresaw from Vote At Home.

Thus, since 2014, all registered voters in Colorado have received their ballots in the mail. The county clerks weren't wrong in their prediction, either: implementing Vote At Home in Colorado reduced election costs by 40 percent, saving more than six dollars per voter per election.[131] What's more, Coloradoans voted in higher numbers in 2014 than in any prior election, including typically low-turnout groups of voters like young people.[132]

Case study: Montana

Montana was well positioned to move to full Vote At Home in response to the risks of COVID-19. In Big Sky Country, voters are allowed to sign up to permanently vote by mail, and three-quarters of voters already do. In spring 2020, Governor Steve Bullock (a Democrat), with full support of House Speaker Greg Hertz (a Republican), announced that counties could choose to mail ballots to all their voters. Every single county opted in.

Local election administrators were well prepared for a full Vote At Home election, not just because most Montana voters already vote from home, but because state law puts in place many of the safeguards and best practices to ensure it works well. For example, clerks compare signatures against a signature on file to verify voters' identity, and clerks are allowed to start processing mailed ballots as soon as they receive them. This spreads out the work over a longer time period so that clerks don't have to rush their work directly after Election Night. Voters have an easier time of things, too, since they can register to vote and request replacement ballots online. Montana's preparations paid off: the state's full Vote At Home primary yielded the highest voter turnout of any primary since 1972.

Better together: Vote At Home + ERIC

When mailing ballots to all voters, it's important to have the most up-to-date addresses for those voters. By joining ERIC (see chapter 2), states can keep their voter lists clean and updated, removing voters who have passed away or moved out of the state, and updating addresses for voters who have moved within the state.

Clean voter rolls mean mailed-out ballots will get to the right voters. According to a U.S. Government Accountability Office report, "King County, Washington, which conducts elections entirely by mail, saw a 38 percent drop in undeliverable ballots in just one year! County election officials attributed this improvement to Washington's participation in ERIC."[133]

Make it happen: Vote At Home at state or local levels

States usually take two important steps before adopting a full Vote At Home system. First, they *let any voter request an absentee ballot.* If you live in one of the 15 states that requires voters to provide an "excuse" to vote absentee, you first need to convince your legislators to remove that barrier. The groups listed below can help you contact your state representatives. A warning: you might have a particularly uphill battle in Arkansas, Mississippi, and Texas, which didn't even let voters request an absentee ballot to avoid poll-based exposure during the COVID-19 pandemic.

The second step is letting voters *sign up to permanently vote absentee.* This is a cost saver for election administrators because they don't have to continue mailing and processing applications to vote absentee. If a voter knows they want to keep filling out their ballots in the convenience of their home, they sign up for the permanent list, and their election administrator mails them a ballot for every election. Once states start this list, voters flock to it. In California, Arizona, and Montana, most voters permanently vote absentee. You could contact your state lawmakers or your secretary of state and ask to be allowed to sign up to permanently vote absentee.

If you live in one of the six jurisdictions that already lets voters sign up for permanent absentee voting — Arizona, California, DC, Montana, Nevada, and New Jersey — your area is ripe to go all the way to mailing out all ballots. Indeed, all these except Arizona already mailed ballots to all voters in 2020, so they have at least one full Vote At Home election under their belts. Idaho and Vermont also mailed ballots to all voters in 2020, so they might be ready to think about full Vote At Home as well. If you live in any of those places, get in touch with the organizations listed in the section on taking action, below, to find out the best way to help push your lawmakers to take the next step.

How to do it right

Those are the big steps to get to full Vote At Home, but there are lots of other implementation details to get right. States that have been mailing out ballots for decades have figured out a lot of ways to make the process smooth and secure. Here are a few of the best practices they employ.

Keep the process secure from fraud without sacrificing votes by using signature verification and a "cure" process. To ensure that every ballot is filled out by a different eligible voter, most states use the voter's signature to verify the ballot. Trained workers compare the signature on the ballot to one or more signatures on file for each voter, from their voter registration, driver's license, or other government file. If it matches, their vote is counted. If it doesn't match, they notify the voter and give her a chance to cure the problem, that is, to prove she is who she says she is so her vote can be counted. Thirty-two states don't require that voters be given this chance.[134] To avoid inadvertently disenfranchising voters just because they wobbled on their signature, these states would need to implement a cure process.

Increase confidence with comprehensive ballot tracking. So that election officials and voters know where their ballots are at all times, some states use a comprehensive tracking system that uses the postal service's unique election bar-coding system to track ballots. It gives voters greater confidence that their vote is properly counted and can help election administrators head off potential problems if they see that ballot deliveries are delayed. Some states use more limited ballot tracking that lets voters check online to see if their ballot was received, but the comprehensive systems give more transparency, accountability, and security.

Start checking early. Checking signatures takes time. To make sure they can release election results quickly, Vote At Home states start checking signatures early, so they can start counting on Election Day. Unfortunately, 15 states don't allow local officials to start processing absentee ballots early enough.[135]

Good design makes it easy for voters. Since there are no poll workers at home to help voters figure out their hanging chads, Vote At Home materials need to be well designed so that voters know exactly what to do. Poorly designed ballots and envelopes can confuse voters and even lead to their voice not being heard if they, for example, forget to sign their envelope or sign in the wrong place. Luckily, design experts and election experts have worked together to create a tool kit showing election officials how to make it easy on voters.[136]

Make returns a breeze with prepaid postage and secure drop boxes. In the Vote At Home states of Colorado, Oregon, and Washington, about half of voters return their ballots in person to an official location such as a secure drop box or election center, while the other half mail them in.[137] Locating a stamp can be a barrier for some voters,[138] so 17 states provide postage-prepaid return envelopes so voters don't have to worry about locating a stamp; they can just drop their ballot in the mail.[139] Many states also provide secure drop boxes in convenient locations so voters can simply drop their ballot in one, no postage needed. Delivering to an official drop box or election office offers voters the additional benefit of not needing to worry about how fast the mail will be delivered.

Account for voters with nonstandard addresses. Native American voters living on tribal lands often have mailing addresses that don't adhere to U.S. Postal Service standards, making it difficult for them to register to vote and receive ballots in the mail. People experiencing homelessness may also have problems requesting a ballot. To ensure that all residents can vote, states can allow Native Americans to designate a building on their nation's land to receive their ballot[140] and can allow community members experiencing homelessness to receive their ballots at a shelter, park, motor home, or other identifiable location.[141]

Take action

A good place to start is sightline.org/votebymail2020, where you can find the in-depth report for your state. It will tell you which policies your state has already enacted to help voters vote from home and which policies your state lawmakers or election administrators still need to implement. Organizations that can help connect you with like-minded advocates include the National Vote at Home Institute, RepresentUs, Indivisible, the League of Women Voters, Let America Vote, the Campaign Legal Center, Unite America, and Rock the Vote.

If your state officials aren't ready to make changes, you can still contact your local officials. They have the authority to take some steps and build expertise while giving their voters a chance to experience Vote At Home. Utah started out piloting Vote At Home at the county level before taking it statewide. Dozens of counties in Nebraska and North Dakota are using Vote At Home, as is the city of Anchorage, Alaska.

If you live in Colorado, Hawaii, Oregon, Utah, or Washington, which have all implemented full Vote At Home,[142] you can tell your friends and family members in other states how easy it is for you to vote. Make them envious, and then spur them to take action to bring Vote At Home to their own state!

 ## Discussion questions

- ☐ Have you ever voted at a polling place? What was your experience?
- ☐ Do you know anyone who has had trouble voting at a polling place due to travel difficulties or long lines?
- ☐ Do you think your Black and Latino friends have had more trouble voting than your white friends?
- ☐ Have you ever voted at home? What was your experience?
- ☐ If you have never voted at home, do you know someone who has? What do they say about it?
- ☐ During the COVID-19 pandemic in 2020, did you vote in person or at home? How did you feel about your voting options? Where did people you know vote?
- ☐ Do you have any concerns about Vote At Home?
- ☐ If your state does not already use Vote At Home, what could you do to encourage it to adopt the system?

Summary: Make Voting Convenient

- Due to restricted funding and polling place closures, many Americans have to travel long distances and wait in long lines on a workday to vote. Some people can't do this, and so they can't vote.

- Vote At Home means that states mail ballots to all registered voters before the election so voters can fill them out at their convenience and return them either by mail or in person at a secure location.

- All states allow some or all voters to request that an absentee ballot be mailed to them so they can complete it at their convenience. At the time of publication, 33 states allow voters to request a Vote At Home ballot without requiring a justification ("no-excuse absentee voting"), while 5 of those states use full Vote At Home — they automatically mail ballots to all registered voters. Because of the COVID-19 pandemic, an additional 6 states mailed ballots to all active voters for the election in November 2020.

- In counties and states that use Vote At Home, voter turnout is higher.

- Vote At Home saves counties and states money because they don't have to run polling stations or buy polling station equipment, and they can consolidate vote counting.

- People love Vote At Home! It gives them time to research their options and vote on their own time, rather than missing work or other duties to wait in line at a polling place on a Tuesday.

Chapter 4: Restore Voting Rights

Give back the right to vote to those who have served their time; or, better yet, never take away their vote in the first place.

Darnell's story

Darnell Brown got involved with gangs as a young man. At 19, he was sentenced for drug trafficking charges and served 11 years in prison, plus an additional 6 years of probation. After serving his term, he was determined to live within the law. He now works full-time at an organization in Tallahassee, Florida, that helps people transitioning from prison back into society, much like a program that had helped him adjust to life outside after his own release. In 2018, when Florida voters overwhelmingly approved a referendum to allow people with a past felony conviction to vote, Brown was thrilled.

"I hadn't voted in almost 20 years," he explained. "To get to vote again, to feel like a real American — oh man, I can't even tell you what it was like."

But his joy was short-lived. Just months after Brown had cast that thrilling vote, Florida governor Ron DeSantis signed a bill requiring people with a past felony conviction to pay all outstanding court costs, fees, fines, or restitution before they could vote. Brown, now 41, discovered that he owed $1,800 due to court orders he hadn't known about. The fees had been sent to collection agencies that had never contacted him. Brown is now making small payments, trying to chip away at the debt, but interest keeps accruing.

"It seems like every time I pay them a dollar, they add a dollar in interest. At this rate, I'll be dead before I can vote again." He wonders why he is being doubly punished, first with a prison sentence and now by withholding his voting rights.

"I did my punishment; I served my time. But they've gotta take away my right to vote, too. Now I'm giving back, I'm working, and I'm paying taxes. I'm a citizen of this country, but I'm not treated like one."[143]

 ## The problem: Rampant disenfranchisement with racist roots

As of 2016, 6.1 million Americans were prohibited from voting due to laws that disenfranchise citizens convicted of felony offenses.[144] That's nearly 3 percent of voting-age Americans.[145] Of those, more than half have been released from prison but are still denied the right to vote.[146]

As table 4.1 below shows, two states, Maine and Vermont, protect citizens' right to vote while incarcerated. Eighteen states and DC automatically restore voting rights after a citizen has served a prison sentence and returned to the community. In 20 states, those convicted of a felony may need to wait to vote again not just through the duration of their prison sentences but also through their parole and probation.[147] But in 11 states, serving time in prison, parole, and/or probation is not enough to win back voting rights — people must take extra steps such as paying fees, waiting for an additional period, or requesting a pardon from the governor. If they don't, they might never be allowed to vote again.

Felonies differ by state but may include everything from murder and rape to burglary, robbery, damage to property, camping on state property, or multiple DUIs.

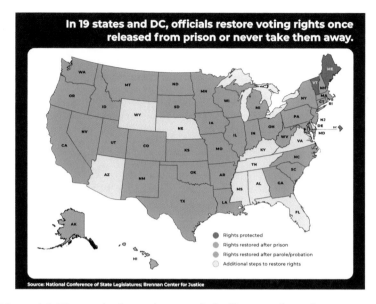

Figure 4.1: *Voting rights for people convicted of a felony in each jurisdiction.*

Rights protected	Rights restored after prison	Rights restored after parole/probation	Additional steps to restore rights
DC	COLORADO	ALASKA	ALABAMA
MAINE	HAWAII	ARKANSAS	ARIZONA
VERMONT	ILLINOIS	CALIFORNIA	DELAWARE
	INDIANA	CONNECTICUT	FLORIDA
	MARYLAND**	GEORGIA	KENTUCKY
	MASSACHUSETTS	IDAHO	MISSISSIPPI
	MICHIGAN	IOWA	NEBRASKA
	MONTANA	KANSAS	TENNESSEE
	NEVADA	LOUISIANA	VIRGINIA*
	NEW HAMPSHIRE	MINNESOTA	WYOMING
	NEW JERSEY	MISSOURI	
	NEW YORK*	NEW MEXICO	
	NORTH DAKOTA	NORTH CAROLINA	
	OHIO**	OKLAHOMA	
	OREGON	SOUTH CAROLINA	
	PENNSYLVANIA	SOUTH DAKOTA	
	RHODE ISLAND	TEXAS	
	UTAH	WASHINGTON	
		WEST VIRGINIA	
		WISCONSIN	

*THE GOVERNOR ISSUES RESTORATIONS.
**ELECTION FRAUD LEADS TO PERMANENT LOSS OF VOTING RIGHTS.

Table 4.1: *Voting rights for people convicted of a felony in each jurisdiction.*

Criminal disenfranchisement disproportionately affects Black Americans. As of 2016, 1 in every 13 Black adults could not vote as the result of a felony conviction, making Black citizens four times more likely than the general population to be barred from voting.[148] In four states — Florida, Kentucky, Tennessee, and Virginia — this figure rises to more than one in five.[149] While those are shameful numbers, they are no accident. As discussed in the section overview, states originally passed felon disenfranchisement laws with the express purpose of disenfranchising freed slaves and their descendants. The 15th Amendment prevented states from disenfranchising Black people and former slaves, but the 14th Amendment gave the states a loophole: they could constitutionally remove voting rights from people convicted of crimes. Because states did, and continue to this day, to convict Black people of crimes at much higher rates than white people, this loophole becomes a shorthand for disenfranchising Black voters.

> **As of 2016, one in every 13 Black adults could not vote as the result of a felony conviction.**

The reform: Continual or restored enfranchisement for people with felony convictions

States should want to protect the democratic rights of and inspire civic pride in all their citizens, and one way to do this is by upholding their voting rights. States could either never take away people's right to vote in the first place, regardless of carceral status, or they could at least restore their right to vote after incarceration.

Maine, Vermont, and DC are the gold standard in this arena. The two states have always protected full and **continual enfranchisement** for their citizens throughout and after their prison terms. DC recently extended the right to vote to residents incarcerated for a felony conviction.[150] But other states can make progress toward this ideal, merely by looking to their many neighbors who at least **re-enfranchise** their citizens after imprisonment. Returning to the table above, moving states even just one or two columns to the left would be a step forward for millions of Americans. For example, the most restrictive 11 states (those in the right-most column) could shift to restore voting rights once a person has served their time in prison, parole, and probation. Or the next most restrictive 20 states (those that wait until parole and possibly probation to re-enfranchise) could join the states that automatically restore people's voting rights as soon they are freed from prison.

This shift is happening, if slowly. Since 1997, two dozen states have reconsidered their archaic disenfranchisement policies and enacted reforms.[151] In 1997, Texas repealed a post-incarceration waiting period to restore voting rights.[152] In 2018, Florida, New York, and Louisiana all improved voting rights for people with convictions.[153] In 2019, Colorado, Kentucky, Nevada, and New Jersey all accomplished reforms.[154] In 2020, Iowa finally stopped permanently disenfranchising its citizens.[155] And in California, Connecticut, Minnesota,[156] Washington,[157] and other states, advocates are working to automatically restore voting rights to residents upon their release from prison.[158] If society intends for these individuals to reintegrate into their communities, then society must treat them as valued citizens.

Case study: Flip-flopping re-enfranchisement in Virginia and Kentucky

Virginia, the state profiled in the section overview as having helped codify racism into U.S. voting laws, has more recently worked to change tack, including by restoring voting rights to people previously convicted of a felony.[159] In 2013, then governor Bob McDonnell restored rights for those who had completed their sentences and paid all fines.[160] The following year, Governor Terry McAuliffe changed the restoration-of-rights process to automatically restore voting rights to people convicted of nonviolent crimes who had completed their prison term, probation, and parole, as well as paid all fees, and who had no pending felony charges. In 2016, he went further and signed an order restoring voting rights for more than 200,000 Virginians who had completed their prison time, probation, and parole.

But the Virginia Supreme Court overturned the governor's order, saying he could not make a blanket restoration. Instead, he had to consider each person on a case-by-case basis. The governor acquiesced and started issuing restorations on an individual basis. Within a year, McAuliffe had restored rights to more than 156,000 people with past felony convictions.[161] Unfortunately, because the restoration depends on executive order rather than law,[162] progress in Virginia is tenuous. McAuliffe's successor could choose not to continue the practice of restoring voting rights.

Indeed, that very thing happened in Kentucky. Toward the end of his term in 2015, then governor Steve Beshear signed an executive order[163] restoring voting rights to people convicted of nonviolent felonies who had completed their prison sentence, probation, and parole.[164] But that December, a new governor, Matt Bevin, took office and promptly reversed the order.[165] Four years later, in 2019, in a twist that would be Hollywood-worthy if not so consequential for tens of thousands of people, Steve Beshear's son Andy was elected governor of Kentucky — and he promptly signed an executive order nearly identical to his father's.[166] The back-and-forth in both Virginia and Kentucky has been trying for those states' voters with felony records.

Case study: Florida's re-enfranchisement and fees debacle

Florida voters are often closely divided. Many Americans will remember the 2000 presidential election "hanging by a chad," and the margin for the 2018 gubernatorial race in the Sunshine State was so razor-thin that the state had to do a recount. But when it came to restoring voting rights to disenfranchised citizens, voters were overwhelmingly supportive of the idea. A hefty 65 percent voted in favor of Amendment 4,[167] which on January 8, 2019,[168] restored voting rights to some 1.4 million people. That's 6.5 percent of Florida's total population, or 10 percent of its registered voters.[169] One in ten more Floridians suddenly could vote, a stunning achievement after 150 years of its state constitution's legally codified racism and the unfairness of a system that forever took away a citizen's right to vote with almost no recourse.[170] The amendment particularly benefited Black people, who make up 15 percent of adults in Florida but nearly 30 percent of those whose voting rights were restored.[171]

Sadly, though, that's not the end of the story. Florida legislators swiftly passed a bill preventing individuals with past felony convictions from regaining the right to vote if they still owed any fees — including court costs, fees, fines, or restitution. These legislators knew well that many of these individuals owe such fees because, since the mid-1990s, they have mandated more than 20 new categories of fees,[172] using convicted people's money to pay for court clerks and state agencies.[173] Further, these debts accrue penalty fees if people cannot pay them.

In total, Floridians convicted of crimes owe more than a billion dollars in fees,[174] and for many, paying them off is next to impossible. Since people with a criminal record have a harder time getting hired into jobs and thereby earning any money to start to pay off these charges, they often fall into an unbreakable cycle of debt, which means they are forever barred from voting, like Darnell Brown, whose story begins this chapter. Of course, the United States more broadly has a long history of excluding Black and poor people from voting via mechanisms like poll taxes.[175] Our country finally outlawed poll taxes in federal elections in 1964, when the states ratified the 24th Amendment.[176] Two years later, the Supreme Court extended the principle to state and local elections.

But if eligible voters must pay off court fees before voting, doesn't that constitute a poll tax? That's one of the arguments that advocates made in an attempt to overturn the Florida law.[177] In February 2019, a unanimous three-judge panel of the 11th Circuit Court of Appeals forbade Florida from prohibiting the registration of people with past convictions who couldn't pay fees and fines. The court concluded that "once a state provides an avenue for ending the punishment of disenfranchisement," it can't use lack of wealth as a reason to withhold access to the ballot box.[178] But in February 2020, in a 6-4 ruling, the Court upheld the Florida law, preventing 800,000 people from voting in the 2020 presidential election.[179] The ACLU, the Brennan Center for Justice, and the NAACP plan to appeal to the Supreme Court.

Better together: Continual or re-enfranchisement + ERIC + Vote At Home

Protecting voting rights for people with convictions could be even more powerful if combined with reforms discussed in prior chapters. Specifically, consider the potential of piling on the Electronic Registration Information Center (ERIC), from chapter 2, and Vote At Home, from chapter 3.

In the case of continual enfranchisement, ERIC could coordinate information between criminal justice agencies and elections agencies to ensure that Vote At Home ballots reach voters who are currently incarcerated. In states at least re-enfranchising their citizens after their prison terms, ERIC could mark people as inactive upon imprisonment and active again upon release, with Vote At Home making certain that each person receives their ballot at their new address on the outside. Together, these measures make for a system that is more accurate, efficient, and just.

DC will be piloting this combination of best practices. It is a member of ERIC, it will mail absentee ballots to all registered voters in November 2020, and it has restored voting rights for incarcerated individuals.

The payoff: A more robust, inclusive voting public

If every state guaranteed the right to vote during a person's incarceration, 6 million more Americans could participate in democracy. That's 1 in 25 more of all voting-age Americans — *4 percent*. Or, if every state at least automatically restored voting rights once convicted people had served their sentences, over 3 million more Americans could vote. Americans like Darnell, who have already served their sentences and then some, could authentically reengage in civic life as part of their full reintegration into life outside prison.

> ## If every state guaranteed the right to vote during a person's incarceration, 6 million more Americans could participate in democracy
>
> ### That's 1 in 25 more of all voting-age Americans — 4 percent.

And because a disproportionate share of people in prison or who were formerly incarcerated are Black or poor, continual or re-enfranchisement measures would help address systemic racism and classism. For example, 34 percent of people behind bars are Black,[180] compared with just 13 percent of the total U.S. population.[181] Incarcerated people in all gender, race, and ethnicity groups earned substantially less income prior to their incarceration than their non-incarcerated peers.[182] So we can anticipate that many of the newly enfranchised voters would also be Black or poor.[183] That is, people whom systemic discrimination already disempowers could have much to gain from voting rights restoration, starting with a real voice in their community.

 # Make it happen: Honor everyone's right to vote

If you live in one of the 48 states that take away citizens' right to vote based on carceral status or history, or especially in one of the 30 states that prevent people from voting even after they have re-entered the community, you could join a campaign to (a) urge your lawmakers to pass a law, (b) push your governor to sign an executive order, or (c) run a ballot measure directly with voters — all options with an end goal of restoring voting rights sooner or never taking them away in the first place. Some organizations to help connect you with campaigns to restore voting rights include the Sentencing Project, Prison Policy Initiative, NAACP, Forward Justice, the Brennan Center for Justice,[184] Demos, Let America Vote, Common Cause,[185] Indivisible, RepresentUs, the League of Women Voters, and the ACLU.

 ## Discussion questions

☐ Do you think taking away someone's right to vote is an appropriate punishment for some crimes? Why?

☐ Do you believe voting is a fundamental right all citizens should have?

☐ Do you think felony disenfranchisement has a racist impact? A classist impact?

☐ Do you know anyone with a felony conviction? (Felonies differ by state but may include everything from murder and rape to burglary, robbery, damage to property, camping on state property, or multiple DUIs.) Do you think they should be able to vote?

☐ Where is your state in table 4.1 above? What could you do to encourage your state representatives to expand voting rights?

Summary: Restore Voting Rights

- Millions of American citizens, many of whom have already served their prison sentences, can't vote due to a felony conviction.

- This especially affects citizens of color and poor citizens.

- Some states are moving to restore voting rights for people with a felony conviction in their past, but other governors and legislators are pushing back against voting rights.

- Each state could expand voting rights by restoring them more quickly or never taking them away in the first place.

II. DROWN OUT BIG DOLLARS

BECAUSE WE CAN'T STOP SPECIAL INTERESTS' BIG-MONEY FLOOD, LET'S WIDEN ORDINARY CITIZENS' SMALL-MONEY STREAMS.

The second major issue we'll address with this book concerns one of the most common complaints about American elections: there's simply too much money involved in campaigns. And it's true. The United States stands well above peer democracies in terms of how much it costs for an individual who wishes to serve her community to run for office. To have a fighting chance in a competitive campaign, candidates must raise huge sums of money: a billion dollars to run for president, tens of millions to run for the Senate, and millions to run for the House of Representatives. Compare this with other wealthy nations like Canada and Germany, where national campaigns cost in the tens or hundreds of thousands of dollars. That's two to four orders of magnitude less than in the United States.[186] Even local races in big cities can cost over $100 million, and midsized cities' campaigns can cost over $1 million.[187]

The high cost of running for office has several cascading negative effects:

- Candidates are generally from wealthier backgrounds and narrower, less representative social and demographic groups.

- Candidates, including elected officials seeking reelection, must spend lots of time raising money rather than talking about issues or doing the work of legislating.

- Donors who can make large gifts, whether they are individuals or corporations, get more attention from fundraisers — as do the issues they care about, which may well differ from the priority issues of the general public.

- Voters grow annoyed with the constant requests for money and begin tuning out candidates altogether, even when they do discuss the issues.

- Voters grow cynical about a system that seems to privilege the wealthy few over the middle-class many, and they further disengage.

We'll dig into these problems in this section's chapter, but to understand how we got here in the first place, let's take a brief look at a few recent U.S. Supreme Court decisions.

Citizens United flooded elections with untracked money

Few Supreme Court decisions have lodged in the public consciousness like *Citizens United v. Federal Election Commission* (FEC). It has entered the ranks of rulings that many Americans can name unprompted, like *Brown v. Board of Education* or *Roe v. Wade*. In combination with a number of other lesser-known cases, this ruling undammed a tidal wave of spending in U.S. elections.

63

Citizens United, a Supreme Court case decided in 2010, split the Court in a 5–4 decision. Five justices asserted that corporations are people, striking down a provision of the 2002 McCain-Feingold Act that banned corporations and unions from broadcasting "electioneering communications" in the 30 days before a presidential primary and in the 60 days before the general elections.

While lawmakers can still limit the amount of money that corporations and unions can contribute directly to a campaign, *Citizens United* gives corporations and unions free rein to spend unlimited sums, anonymously, on **independent expenditure campaigns** — that is, money coming from outside the candidate's election organization that is not coordinated with the campaign. This includes donations to **political action committees (PACs)** (committees that may accept contributions of up to $5,000 per year from any individual) and **super PACs** (committees that may accept unlimited contributions from any non-foreign source) that pool donations and spend substantial sums, sometimes more than the campaigns themselves, in support of candidates. In other words, Big Corp. might be limited in how big of a check it can write to Candidate Needsmoney, but it can write an infinitely large check to the Support Corporate Hacks super PAC, which runs ads supporting Candidate Needsmoney or attacking his opponent. In short, it's a shell game.

The dissent, penned by Justice Stevens and joined by Justices Ginsburg, Breyer, and Sotomayor, railed against the majority conclusion that corporations are people, saying the majority never explained "why corporate identity demands the same treatment as individual identity." Because corporations "are not natural persons, much less members of our political community, and the governmental interests are of the highest order," the dissent argues that regulating corporate money is justified. The dissent also presciently warned about the risks of the majority opinion. "The Court's ruling threatens to undermine the integrity of elected institutions across the Nation.... Take away Congress' authority to regulate the appearance of undue influence and the cynical assumption that large donors call the tune could jeopardize the willingness of voters to take part in democratic governance."[188]

Alas, the majority pushed on.

People of all political stripes loathe the *Citizens United* ruling[189]: three-quarters of Republicans and more than four in five independents and Democrats oppose it.[190] The unchecked funding frenzy and barrages of attack ads that *Citizens United* unleashed are repulsive to most voters, reinforcing their negative impression that their government is bought and paid for.

McCutcheon lifted contribution limits

Four years later, the Supreme Court's 2014 decision in *McCutcheon v. Federal Election Commission*[191] only made things worse. Another 5–4 decision[192] extended the "money is speech and speech is sacred" logic of *Citizens United* and also implied that only one kind of corruption is illegal: explicit *quid pro quo* ("this for that") corruption, in which a donor gives a politician money explicitly in return for some desired action by that politician.

Under this definition, quid pro quo dealings must be blatant and direct. For instance, a chemical manufacturer might donate money to a candidate's campaign in return for that politician working to turn back regulations on dangerous chemicals, or a farm-business owner might make a contribution with the understanding that the politician would ensure that he received a lucrative subsidy.

Section 441 of the Federal Election Campaign Act had previously capped the amount an individual could donate to political parties and PACs at around $100,000. *McCutcheon* eviscerated that section of the law, freeing the uber-wealthy to donate sums into the millions — two orders of magnitude more than the previous limits. Five members of the Court reasoned that if someone donates money to a political party, and then the party bundles it out to politicians, that is not a quid pro quo arrangement because the donor is not interacting directly with the politician. The chemical manufacturer or farm-business owner can give their money to a political party or a super PAC, which in turn can give money to candidates who then roll back regulations or grant subsidies. Congress can't limit the amount the donor gives to parties and PACs because the donor isn't giving directly to the candidate, so it can't be quid pro quo.

In his vehemently dissenting opinion, Justice Breyer (joined by Justices Ginsburg, Sotomayor, and Kagan) pulled back the curtain on this flimsy facade and showed how donors can now give millions to a single candidate, currying that politician's gratitude and indulgence. Breyer ran the numbers on how a donor (he called him "Rich Donor") could give millions to a single politician (hypothetically called "Candidate Smith")[193]:

> *Before today's decision, the total size of Rich Donor's check to the Joint Party Committee was capped at $74,600 — the aggregate limit for donations to political parties over a 2-year election cycle. After today's decision, . . . without an aggregate limit, the law will permit a wealthy individual to write a check, over a 2-year election cycle, for $3.6 million.*

65

Breyer went on to point out that "Candidate Smith will almost certainly come to learn from whom he has received this money" and will likely feel "particularly grateful to the large donor."

Past Supreme Court decisions had warned against not only corruption but "the appearance of corruption." These rulings recognized that if Americans feel the system is rigged, that alone can be damaging to democracy. When the people lose faith in the institutions of democracy, they may stop participating in elections, trusting their elected leaders, and believing in laws and norms. Things can quickly fall apart from there.

The rulings in *Citizens United* and *McCutcheon* together not only turned American campaign finance into a shell game but also added a lot more shells beneath the cups. The system now looks to most Americans like a scam game open only to an elite few with enough shells to ante into play.

How to beat the game

The long play: Try to limit big-shot players

Many advocates are working tirelessly to amend the U.S. Constitution to stem the tide of big money in politics. Their chief goal is to make clear that free speech protections don't apply to corporations.

"The history of campaign finance reform," writes law professor Lawrence Lessig in his influential book *Republic, Lost*,[194] "is water running down a hill. No matter how you reform, the water seems to find its way around the obstacle." No sooner do you restrict gifts directly to candidates than **soft money** (money donated to political parties rather than specific candidates) gushes around the corner into those same candidates' pockets. Stop that, and the money flows through PACs that run advertisements explicitly supporting a candidate but that are technically separate from the candidate's own campaign. Limit donations to PACs, and corporations and unions will fund super PACs (political action committees that can receive unlimited contributions and spend an unlimited amount supporting or opposing candidates).

For every obstacle reformers erect, political fundraisers circumvent them. Now we're in a game of whack-a-mole — only in this game, the moles are moneyed, well-connected corporations and individuals accustomed to getting their way. The odds are not in our favor.

The short play: Let regular people become donors

Fortunately, there is a shorter road to reform. Rather than trying to limit the flood of money from wealthy individuals (how many shells under which cups), reformers could instead focus on setting up alternative game tables that regular people can access. That is, they could provide a different source of political money, one that is easier for candidates to collect in quantity and that is divorced from political patronage.

And what would these alternative game tables look like? Here, everyday people would be offered their own shells to play, no ante required — so firstly, many more would be able to participate. Second, the cups would disappear, allowing for transparency and sunlight on what had been a shady exchange. Third, there would be no corporations (or representatives of corporations) at this table, because only living, breathing people would be able to play.

Okay, so it's not much of a game anymore ... but that's the point! Our elections and the support behind them shouldn't be a game in the first place. They should be accessible and engaging for anyone who wishes to get involved, not just those who can afford the ante to sit at the table. Even if each American had just one shell to play, together our shells would well outnumber those of even the Koch brothers and George Soros combined. And that would turn the heads of candidates and their professional fundraisers.

Shells for all

If this sounds too good to be true, it's not. Indeed, a system of just this design is successfully at work in elections in the city of Seattle, Washington, as we'll learn in chapter 5. It gives every eligible resident $100 in Democracy Vouchers to support their favorite local candidates.

And yes, this section on resolving the issue of money in politics has but one lonely chapter offering a solution — but it is by far the best one! While I could have mentioned other measures like New York's public matches, this book (as noted in its introduction) aims to feature the best-of-the-best, road-tested, highest-return-on-investment reforms for Americans to claim the democracy we deserve. Democracy Vouchers are that reform. So without further ado ...

Chapter 5:
Amplify Small Donors' Power

Implement an inclusive, transparent system of Democracy Vouchers.

Susan's story

Susan Lee is a 64-year-old Seattle resident raising three grandchildren. One day last year, she opened her mail and found $100 of Democracy Vouchers.

"It was like getting a surprise check for your birthday," she said.

Carrying her vouchers in her purse, she went to a town hall debate between candidates for Seattle City Council to learn more about how to use them and to hear the candidates discuss their priorities. One particular candidate stood out to Lee, and after the event finished, she offered him all four of her $25 vouchers, then asked for a photo. In it, she is grinning hugely, with one arm around the candidate and the other hand holding up the vouchers.

"I felt like a bigwig donor," she gushed. "Like Bill Gates! I had never been able to donate before, and being able to contribute like that . . . I felt like I'm part of the system, like I'm valued, like my voice matters. It was wonderful."[195]

 ## Problem 1: The current system privileges wealthy and extremist donors . . . and their policy priorities

The quest for money dominates American elections. To have a chance at competing for votes, candidates must first compete for dollars. Sky-high campaign costs require candidates to appeal to big-money donors — those with pockets deep enough to give the maximum allowed by law — and to extreme partisans who write smaller checks but are fired up enough to do so.

Most of us are aware of this at the national level, where presidential races cost billions of dollars and congressional races millions. But it is also true for state and city races, which can cost hundreds of thousands of dollars. For example, Portland, Oregon, is not remarkably large or wealthy, but it routinely costs nearly $1 million to run for mayor, and hundreds of thousands to run for city council.[196] One candidate for city council had to raise $400,000 in just four months, meaning she had to spend hours a day on the phone with mostly wealthy white men with business interests in city decisions.[197]

Taking a campaign donation does not obligate a candidate to do favors for that donor once elected. It's difficult to draw a straight line between a $5,000 donation and a yes-or-no vote on a bill.[198] But private interests clearly influence public decisions. Back to the national level: two of the 2020 presidential front-runners, from both sides of the aisle and both sides of the dance between those who have money and those who run for office, agree:

> "*I was a businessman. . . . When [candidates] call, I give. And do you know what? When I need something from them two years later, three years later, I call them, they are there for me. And that's a broken system.*"
> —**presidential candidate Donald Trump, in 2015**[199]

> "*[As a candidate] you have to go where the money is. Now where the money is, there's almost always implicitly some string attached. . . . It's awful hard to take a whole lot of money from a group you know has a particular position, then you conclude they're wrong [and] vote no.*" —**Vice President Joe Biden, in 2015**[200]

A recent painstaking analysis of the final language of the Affordable Care Act traced the paths of amendments and found that hosting a fundraiser increased your chances of getting your words into the bill.[201] Most individuals don't have the resources to host a fundraiser. They are excluded from the donor class of corporate lobbyists and wealthy individuals whose money, in our current system, shapes how candidates spend their time, with whom they are in close and regular contact, and what policies they ultimately pass.

Even with the rise of small-dollar contributions in recent years, figures like the Koch brothers on the right, and Tom Steyer and George Soros on the left, have outsized influence on our elections, and in turn on the people who run in them and the issues they prioritize once in office. The same goes for lobbying groups like political action committees (PACs) and super PACS, whose power has been amplified in the last decade especially. Since the candidates who can raise the most money are often the ones who win, the campaign process elevates politicians most attuned to the rich. Law professor Lawrence Lessig calls this the "donor election." First, donors decide who is acceptable and use their dollars to increase the visibility of those candidates to the broader public. Then voters choose from among these candidates, their options shaded, if not dictated, by who has the money to dominate the airwaves.

Problem 2: Candidates spend more time fundraising than legislating

One week after the 2012 election, the Democratic Party sent newly elected members of Congress an orientation packet. The packet for new House members contained a suggested schedule: nearly half of a representative's day was to be spent soliciting campaign funds, compared with just one to two hours for constituent visits and two hours for committee and floor time.[202] That is, on a representative's very first day in an office that she may have fought tooth and nail to win, she is already having to raise funds for her next race. The message is clear: money is the priority.

Representatives seeking reelection or simply supporting their respective parties, as well as future representative hopefuls, must spend hours every day, month after month, year after year, listening to the views of wealthy individuals, corporate lobbyists, and organized special interest groups. In other words, elected officials are spending most of their time interacting with only a tiny slice of their constituents, those wealthy enough to make a difference in their campaign coffers. It's no surprise that candidates develop a sixth sense for how this class will respond to legislative proposals, all the while trading time legislating for time soliciting gifts from this donor class by phone or in-person meeting.

The reform: Democracy Vouchers

As the section overview showed, two recent Supreme Court decisions have made it especially hard to limit Big Money's influence over campaigns. Advocating for a reversal of these decisions is a long game with poor odds, and we can't afford to wait.

So if we can't limit big money right now, what if we could leverage small money? That is, give average voters an equally powerful pool of funds to support candidates they believe in. Candidates spend their time raising money from wealthy donors and special interests because that's where the money is. But what if everyday people had just as much money to give?

Enter: Democracy Vouchers. Here's the idea: everyone can be a donor, even if they can't afford it. Everyone gets vouchers that they can give to candidates who opt to accept only small donations. Those candidates start chasing everyday people for their vouchers, instead of chasing wealthy people for their big checks. Everyday people, like Susan Lee, become important participants in campaigns. It's already working in Seattle.

Case study: Seattle

In 2015, a large coalition of community-based organizations and advocates in Seattle ran the Honest Elections Seattle campaign, or Initiative 122, to bring Democracy Vouchers and other good-government reforms to the Emerald City. Seattle voters overwhelmingly approved the measure, which tightened lobbying and contribution limits while implementing a first-in-the-nation Democracy Vouchers program.

How Democracy Vouchers work

Honest Elections Seattle gives every registered voter in the city (as well as other adult residents eligible to donate under federal law, if they apply) four $25 Democracy Vouchers to support candidates for city council and mayor. Every voter — barista or banker, janitor or judge — gets exactly the same $100 of vouchers, which they can contribute to any voucher candidates.

Meanwhile, voucher candidates must agree to play by the Honest Elections rules: no contributions from any one person or business of more than $250 for city council seats or $500 for mayor, limits on total campaign spending, strict rules maintaining distance between candidates and independent expenditure campaigns like those described in the section overview, and penalties for benefiting from spending by outside campaigns.

Where does the $100 per voter come from? This innovative program turns out to be a bargain at only about $3 million per year, or about 0.065 percent of Seattle's annual budget. It's funded through a property tax — the smallest in the city's history — at the time of passage around $7.76 per year on the average home.[203] Giving more people a voice in election campaigns for the price of a few coffees? Seattleites voted a resounding "yes."

For voters, Democracy Vouchers are simplicity itself. Early in an election year, all registered voters receive an envelope in the mail from the Seattle Ethics and

Elections Commission (SEEC) with an instruction sheet and four $25 Democracy Vouchers. Voters who already know which candidates they want to support can sit down and mail them their vouchers right away. Other voters who may wish to take more time can set the vouchers aside until a candidate knocks on their door or they get invited to a community event where they can hear candidates in person make their case for their votes and vouchers. Voters then hand over their vouchers, either physically to candidates or by mail, or through a secure electronic system.

Fraud? Unlikely.[204] Trying to buy or sell vouchers is a serious crime, like buying votes, and penalties include prison time. A candidate whose campaign participates in such fraud can be ejected from the program and required to repay public funds. Voucher donations, like any donations, are also public records; anyone can check the status of a voucher at any time online via the SEEC website. It's like a card game where everyone's cards are face-up — not terribly suspenseful but almost impossible to cheat at.

Success in the Emerald City

Two years after voters approved Honest Elections Seattle, during which time SEEC prepared to implement the program and various community organizations educated the public about it, Democracy Vouchers made their debut in Seattle's 2017 election. All four of the city council candidates who made it to the general election used the program.[205] Candidates who otherwise might not have been able to raise enough money to compete could run and win with vouchers. Notably, Teresa Mosqueda, a self-described "union advocate, woman, Chicana/Latina, renter, and fighter for social justice" with student loan debt[206] raised the maximum amount of voucher money, $300,000, and won a seat.

Democracy Vouchers freed candidates from having to rely on big money. Mosqueda and the other voucher candidates funded their campaigns entirely through donations of $250 or less and Democracy Vouchers. Of all the money raised in races where candidates could opt to use vouchers, 89 percent went to voucher candidates, all made up of $250-or-less donations and Democracy Vouchers. By contrast, in the 2013 elections before the implementation of Honest Elections Seattle, small donations accounted for less than half the money backing candidates for city council and city attorney.[207]

> **Democracy Vouchers free candidates from having to rely on big donors.**

And vouchers weren't just good for candidates; they were great for voters, too. Vouchers engaged more voters in the process, expanding the pool of Seattle-based donors by about 300 percent compared with 2013 (the last mayoral cycle).[208] More than 31,000 Seattle residents — a historic number — donated to candidates in the city's 2017 election cycle, nearly four times the roughly 8,200 residents who donated to candidates in 2013.[209] Incredibly, nearly 90 percent of 2017's voucher donors were new donors, or nearly 19,000 individuals who had not contributed to city candidates since at least the 2011 cycle.[210] They included more young people and women, and more people from poorer parts of Seattle, than had ever supported campaigns in the past.[211]

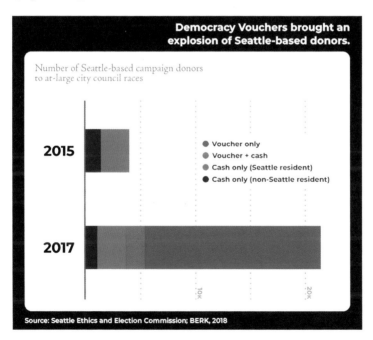

Figure 5.1: *Campaign donors in Seattle.*

The payoff: More voters meet more candidates

Through all this, it's important to keep in mind that vouchers mean more than money, too. They mean more voters meeting more candidates. They mean more people from all sorts of backgrounds feeling like they can run for office and win. They mean candidates feeling more invested in winning over a room full of Susan Lees than schmoozing a cocktail party of big-check writers. Ultimately, they mean a healthier, more engaged democracy that more people can believe in.

 # Make it happen: Vouchers across the United States

Democracy Vouchers can work for any level of government: city, county, state, or nation. As with many reforms, though, starting local with your city or county, and proving time and again the success of the program, will help make the case at those bigger levels. If you live in San Diego, California, you can connect with the Voters' Voice Initiative, which is working on implementing Democracy Vouchers there. Other organizations to help connect you with campaigns to make small-dollar donors work in your city or state include Equal Citizens, Mayday America, Common Cause,[212] the Campaign Legal Center, Democracy Policy Network, Demos, RepresentUs, Indivisible,[213] and the League of Women Voters.

Discussion questions

☐ Have you ever donated money to a candidate for public office? If yes, how did it feel? If no, why not?

☐ If you had $100 in Democracy Vouchers to give to qualifying candidates, what would you do? How would you decide whom to support?

☐ Have you ever thought about running for public office? Do you think you could raise enough money? Do you think you would have a better shot at raising the money if your city or state used Democracy Vouchers?

Summary: Amplify Small Donors' Power

- Candidates for public office spend the bulk of their time raising money from wealthy donors. This (a) privileges *candidates* with wealthy friends or family they can more easily raise money from and (b) privileges the *concerns* of those wealthy donors, since candidates spend a disproportionate amount of time talking with and trying to please them, rather than everyday people.

- A system of citizen-funded elections, like Democracy Vouchers, is a game changer. It means that candidates can spend more time with a broader range of voters instead of having to prioritize wealthy ones who can write big campaign checks. And it means that candidates themselves can come from a broader set of people — not just those who are wealthy or have wealthy connections.

- Democracy Vouchers are already working successfully in Seattle, Washington.

III. MAKE EVERY VOTE COUNT

ENSURE NO VOTE FEELS WASTED TO LIMITED CHOICES, GERRYMANDERED DISTRICTS, THE STATE-WINNER-TAKE-ALL ELECTORAL COLLEGE, OR THE MINORITY-RULE SENATE.

T his section is perhaps the most technical of the four in this book, but stay with me! Because the payoff is pretty great — I promise. In the following four chapters, we'll look at reforms that dismantle the hyperpartisanship and extremism that are tearing this country apart, making it hard for neighbors to connect on issues that matter to them and their communities. We'll discuss solutions that make all votes count, give voters more options beyond the two-party system, reward candidates who engage in solving problems, disarm the polarization that is infecting our institutions, and ultimately effect better policy outcomes for more people across the United States.

Specifically, we'll discuss these solutions for:

- Executive races: These are elections that can yield only one winner, like president, governor, or mayor (chapter 6).

- The presidential race: Okay, this is a type of executive race, but it's a unique case because voters don't directly elect the U.S. president, so it requires special treatment (chapter 7).

- Legislative races: These are elections that can yield multiple winners and send them to legislative bodies like the U.S. House of Representatives, state senates and assemblies, and city councils (chapter 8).

- The U.S. Senate: Another special case, because its undemocratic nature is deeply entrenched in the Constitution and resistant to the solution explained in chapter 8. Happily, there is something the states and Congress can do to make it better represent Americans and pass policies with majority support (chapter 9).

It's important first to understand a few terms, particularly "first past the post" voting systems that elect plurality winners, and we'll introduce the ideas of single- and multi-winner districts and how they relate to gerrymandering. In this section overview we'll also take a brief look at the origins of party primaries, the Electoral College, and the contemptible compromise that birthed the U.S. Senate.

Some votes matter more than others

Unfortunately, at the time that Americans were writing their second constitution in 1787,[214] the most recent innovation in election methods was a 1430 British law for electing a candidate with the most votes in a district: that is, a first-past-the-post system in which the candidate with the most votes wins, even if they don't have a majority of votes, and a single-winner district system in which each district can select only one person to represent all the voters in that district.

Nearly 250 years later, these inheritances from Americans' long-ago-overthrown colonial rulers, the British, are wreaking havoc on our democracy. Indeed, the only jurisdictions apart from the United Kingdom to still use first-past-the-post and single-winner districts are or were British colonies, like Canada or Kenya or India . . . and the United States. Any democracy that has updated its rules in the past century uses better methods. Perhaps it's time for a second revolution. No redcoats or George Washingtons fording the Delaware River this time, please. Just some good old-fashioned modernization.

First-past-the-post can leave a majority of voters behind

A president, governor, or mayor is supposed to represent an entire country, state, or city. That's a tall order. And unfortunately, most American election methods aren't up to the challenge. Almost all U.S. elections use a **first-past-the-post** or **plurality** system in which the candidate with the most votes wins. This sounds fair, but a candidate who needs to win only a plurality — more votes than any other candidate — doesn't have to win majority support. For example, when three candidates are running and two are similar to each other, together they might win support from the majority of voters while the third wins over only a minority of voters. But because the two similar-to-each-other candidates "split the vote," that third candidate can win with only a minority of the overall votes.

Single-winner districts aid two-party domination

A second hangover from British rule is that of **single-winner districts** to fill multi-member lawmaking bodies of government. In the United States today, this looks like each congressional district sending just one individual to the U.S. House of Representatives on behalf of all its 700,000-plus residents. How could one person fairly represent all the people in Denver, or more people than live in Boston, or twice as many people as live in Honolulu? This is anathema to fair representation, and it silences groups of voters with minority views. In addition, the difficulty inherent in choosing a single candidate to represent a huge group of people is what makes **winner-take-all** districts vulnerable to gerrymandering: enabling politicians to choose their voters.

Political scientists have known for nearly a century that single-winner districts aid two-party dominance. This finding is so consistent across countries and cultures that it is known as Duverger's law.[215] In sum: even if voters become disenchanted with the two dominant parties, the system itself dooms third parties to perpetual defeat.[216]

The United Kingdom and Canada have more robust regional parties that give them a bit more national party diversity than the United States, where parties are the same at the state and national level. But even so, in the UK and Canada, two parties dominate and win seats well out of proportion to their support from voters.

Gerrymandering: No one wins but incumbents

Everyone hates the **gerrymander**, a beast named after a salamander-shaped district authorized by Massachusetts governor Elbridge Gerry in 1812.[217] The term refers to the practice of drawing electoral districts to suit partisan ends. Most people agree that voters should choose their politicians rather than politicians choosing their voters[218]: TV news comedian John Oliver,[219] former U.S. attorney general Eric Holder,[220] and Republican former California governor Arnold Schwarzenegger[221] are all anti-gerrymandering.

These critics hope they can defeat the beast by taking the district line-drawing pen away from legislators and handing it to a commission or a computer — someone or something without a partisan stake in the game. Unfortunately, this move wouldn't be enough, particularly with the single-winner districts and plurality voting system that most jurisdictions use in the United States. No matter who holds the line-drawing pen, gerrymandered single-winner districts take power away from voters and put it in the hands of whoever draws the district lines. They sap voters' power to make a difference with their ballots, make some votes more powerful than others, and make it difficult or impossible for voters to hold elected officials accountable. You can learn more about gerrymandering in chapter 8.

Founders feared two-party rule, but fair voting methods had not yet been developed

At the time of the country's founding, some leaders worried about the zero-sum war that would result if two equally matched parties came to dominate politics. George Washington warned that "the alternate domination of one [party] over another, sharpened by the spirit of revenge . . . has perpetuated the most horrid enormities." He worried that two-party fighting could lead voters "to seek security and repose in the absolute power of an individual," allowing the leader of the winning party to become an authoritarian.[222] John Adams wrote, "[T]here is nothing I dread so much as a division of the republic into two great parties . . . in opposition to each other. This . . . is to be dreaded as the great political evil."[223]

James Madison particularly feared parties based on geography. He thought that while parties with individuals "intermingl[ing] in every part of the whole country" would strengthen the United States as a whole, parties "founded on geographical . . . distinctions" would clash against each other and weaken the country.[224]

Americans in 2020 watching the Democratic and Republican Parties, divided by urban and rural geography, fighting each other ferociously, while indeed some voters fulfill Washington's fear of the rise of a more authoritarian figure, can see that these founders' instincts were right. But in 1787, U.S. democracy was in its infancy, and election methods to help the founders avoid their worst fears had not yet developed.

Founding father John Adams believed the legislature should give all people "equal representation" and create "in miniature, an exact portrait of the people at large."[225] In other words, he believed that each vote should count equally, and each voter should have an equal chance at translating their vote into representation. But alas, his ideals outpaced the abilities of eighteenth-century electoral methods. In the nineteenth century, mathematicians began innovating proportional voting methods that could achieve John Adams's dream of equal representation, and in the twentieth century most robust democracies started using them. (You can learn more about them in chapter 8.) But the United Kingdom and its former colonies have mostly stuck with flawed single-winner districts clear into the twenty-first century. New Zealand is the standout former colony that managed to change its voting system and break free from two-party dominance.[226]

A Historical Note: How single-winner districts came to dominate American elections

The Constitution is silent about voting methods, leaving it up to the states. Most states first used a crude method called *block voting*,[227] which is the worst method for achieving fair representation. Block voting can award 100 percent of seats to the single party that wins the most votes, blocking all other parties and their voters from any representation whatsoever.

Over time most states recognized this method's inadequacy and switched to single-winner districts, in part to give voters in the minority a chance to win at least some representation.[228] In 1967, on the heels of the National Voting Rights Act, Congress mandated single-winner districts to protect African Americans from being completely shut out of elections, as they had been under block voting. Single-winner districts were an improvement over block voting, but they have serious drawbacks: they still silence minorities in all districts except the carefully gerrymandered majority-minority districts. They also lead to two-party domination and enable gerrymandering. Indeed, many Voting Rights Act lawsuits have found single-winner districts to be a poor solution to fair representation and have mandated **multi-winner districts** with a proportional or semi-proportional voting method.[229]

The Duopoly and its discontents

American parties recently sorted and realigned

For about 100 years after the Civil War, the United States had a four-party system hidden inside the moniker of two major parties.[230] Each party included conservatives and liberals, rural and urban dwellers, and people of different races, religions, and income and education levels. Voters had a mix of identities pulling them this way and that — they were like pickup sticks dropped on the ground pointing every which way, with some aspects of who they were or what they believed pulling them toward one party and some another, and lots of overlap and points of connection with other sticks.

In the 1970s, even though Congress was split between Democrats and Republicans, some Democrats were more conservative than some Republicans, and many members of Congress would vote across party lines. Voters approved of their representatives reaching across the aisle because they did the same all the time — when talking to neighbors, colleagues, and fellow churchgoers who shared that identity but labeled themselves a member of the other party. This gave the two-party system some of the flexibility of a multi-party system.

But in the past three decades, the parties have been sorting and realigning, a process commentator Ezra Klein says was completed in 2010.[231] All our identities are now aligned with our party identity. Americans who identify as Democrats tend to live around, work with, and socialize with other Democrats, and the same for Republicans — and never the twain shall meet. The recent sorting was like a magnet passing over metal pickup sticks, pulling them so they all point either north or south, running parallel and never crossing or touching. "Look who's coming to dinner" used to be about race, but now interracial marriage elicits a shrug,[232] while many Americans would be horrified if their little Democrat brought a Republican home for dinner.[233]

Like two continents drifting across an ocean, the two parties have pulled apart. Figure 03.0.1 below shows how, in 1969, there was a fair amount of overlap between Democrats and Republicans in Congress, and some Republicans were more liberal in some senses than some Democrats. In 2019, the parties had no overlap. Now, all Democrats are more liberal than all Republicans, and hardly anyone votes against their party. In addition, the center of gravity of the Republican Party has markedly shifted from centrist-right a few decades ago to far-right today.

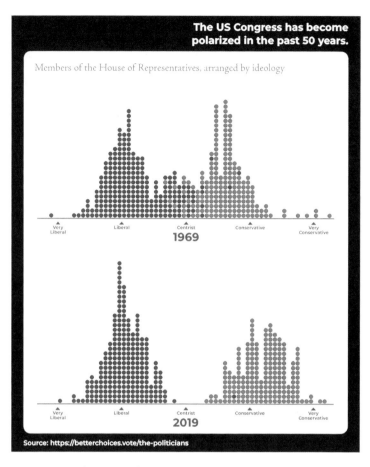

Figure 03.0.1: *Polarization of the U.S. Congress.*

Public primaries with partisan consequences

Figure 03.0.1 above shows that not only have the parties receded from each other, but congressional Republicans have lurched to the right. This move was, and continues to be, driven in part by party primaries. In 2010, the Tea Party vociferously opposed Republicans who had voted for the recession relief bill. In some districts that were safe for the Republican Party, a Tea Party candidate challenged and sometimes beat the more mainstream Republican in the primary to become the sole Republican candidate in the general election, and then won the "safe" general. The mainstream candidates were said to have been "primaried." The phenomenon struck fear into the hearts of other Republican candidates, pushing them to move rightward and oppose all Democratic proposals lest they too be primaried.

Ironically, this mechanism for polarization was enabled by a well-meaning reform at the turn of the last century. During the Progressive Era — a time of widespread hope and advocacy for a better democracy that flourished 100 years ago and delivered such victories as women's suffrage — American reformers agitated to move the candidate selection process out of smoke-filled rooms and into the sunlight of public elections.

In the nineteenth century, party bigwigs decided which candidates could appear on the ballot under the party banner. As the twentieth century dawned, progressive reformers, shunning the secrecy and exclusivity of this process, pushed for publicly funded party primaries in which voters, not bigwigs, could decide.[234]

These public party primaries had some unintended consequences, though. Where in the past party bosses may have been making decisions behind closed doors, they ultimately wanted their candidate to win the election, so they were mindful of choosing someone who would have broad voter appeal. Primary voters like Tea Party adherents, on the other hand, tend to be at the more extreme end of their party's issue stances and want to move their party in that direction, so they vote for more extreme candidates who will not have as much appeal to general election voters. As a result, candidates now have to be — or pretend to be — the extremists that primary voters want if they are to make it past the primary. And if they don't measure up to primary voters' expectations during their time in office, next time around they might lose the primary to a more "pure" competitor. Combine this with gerrymandered single-winner districts that are "safe" for one party, meaning that the primary winner for that district's dominant party is all but guaranteed to win the general, and the public primary becomes a mechanism for shifting lawmakers toward their most partisan voters, instead of representing the average voter in their district.

That's already a potent brew, but add in a serving of two parties with little in common, and you have a recipe for partisan war.

Two-party rule is war

The founders thought they could avoid the rise of political parties, so their famous "separation of powers" is designed to "check" and "balance" power across branches of government, not across two warring parties. The Constitution creates distinct power bases in the House, the Senate, the presidency, the courts, and the states. So long as the players within each power center want to keep the other power centers in check, no branch can acquire the King George–like powers the revolutionaries abhorred. Members of Congress kept the president in check, while state legislators reined in Congress, and so on.

The system is woefully ill-prepared for the modern era in which parties, not branches of government, are the important power bases. The system is designed to encourage members of Congress to jealously guard Congress's power, but it is breaking down at an alarming rate in the face of members of Congress whose goal is to enlarge their party's power, even if that means ceding king-like status to the president.

As some founders feared, two-party rule means war. And not war in the sense of healthy competition, where political parties and candidates put their ideas forward and voters choose the best and hold elected officials accountable for implementing their vision. No, war in the sense of a bloody battle that is tearing us apart, hobbling our ability to function as a nation, and wounding our democratic institutions. The two dominant parties are engaged in a war against each other instead of working together to solve the overwhelming problems facing our country.

The Electoral College

The delegates to the 1787 Constitutional Convention were in a quandary. How should the United States of America select the president?

One option would be to have Congress do it, analogous to the way many state legislatures selected their respective governors at the time. But many delegates didn't like that option because they feared that giving the legislative branch such power over the leader of the executive branch would violate the separation of powers.

The other obvious option was to allow people to vote directly for the president. But many delegates adamantly opposed this. Some feared that parochial voters, unfamiliar with candidates from other states, would vote only for local candidates. Others feared that voters would be vulnerable to the siren song of demagogues who appealed to people's prejudices but were not qualified for the solemn office of president.[235] And slave states were worried about being overpowered by non-slave states. Enslaved people made up a large portion of the South's population but were not allowed to vote, so in a popular vote contest for president, the South's small white population would have been at a disadvantage compared to the North's larger white population.

A measure to limit voter power, separate the branches of government, and appease slave-owning states

Deadlocked and running out of time, delegates hastily devised a way of sidestepping both congressional appointment and a popular vote.[236] They created the **Electoral College**, an unelected body assembled only for the purpose of selecting a president. Each state could appoint a number of electors equal to its number of congressional delegates — that is, a state's number of representatives in the House plus its two senators.

This arrangement gave Southern whites outsized power in the choice of president by extending the **three-fifths compromise** that applied to legislative representation to the presidency as well. Under the three-fifths compromise, nonvoting enslaved people counted as three-fifths of a person for purposes of determining each state's number of representatives in the U.S. House. The extension of this compromise to the presidency was very beneficial to the slave-holding South. For 32 of the United States' first 36 years, a slave-holding Virginian occupied the White House (John Adams from Massachusetts was the exception).[237]

Many founders thought the Electoral College would, in the end, usually give Congress the power to choose the president. They thought many candidates would run for president and split the electoral vote so that none would win a majority, leaving it to the House to decide. One delegate foresaw that the House of Representatives would choose the president "nineteen times out of twenty."[238]

That didn't happen.

Instead, the winner-take-all Electoral College system (in which all of a state's electoral votes go to whichever single candidate earns even a small majority of that state's popular vote) reinforced the two-party domination created by single-winner districts. Two-party domination means that there aren't a lot of candidates splitting the vote and that the Electoral College, not Congress, has decided all but two elections.[239]

States choose how to select their electors

State legislators have enormous power over presidential elections.[240] The U.S. Constitution mandates, "Each State shall appoint, in such Manner as the Legislature thereof may direct, a Number of Electors."[241] The Supreme Court has affirmed, too, that state legislatures have exclusive control of the electors.[242]

Early on, states used different methods of selecting electors. The three most common methods were selection by the legislature, popular vote by district, and statewide popular vote.[243] In 1800, 11 of the 16 states used some form of legislative choice, usually meaning that whichever party controlled the state legislature could deliver all that state's electoral votes to the candidate from that party. Some states chose electors by district; in some cases they drew special districts just for choosing electors, and in others they used the state's congressional districts to choose one elector each and chose the remaining two by some other method, such as letting the district electors choose the final two. District states tended to allow smaller parties to pick up a few votes. The third method was to award all the electoral votes to the winner of the statewide popular vote. This allowed the strongest party to make a clean sweep in each state, crowding out other parties. By 1836, all states but one (North Carolina) had adopted winner-take-all rules.[244] Today, almost all state legislatures require electors to cast their Electoral College votes for the candidate who wins the state's popular vote[245] — hence the several unpopular winners of late.

Would-be deliberators were really rubber stamps

When the founding fathers hastily wrote the compromise of the Electoral College into the Constitution, the best gloss they could put on that unique arrangement is the one often foisted on modern-day American elementary students: it is a well-informed super-committee, a select group of the country's most informed people tasked with deliberating carefully on the important question of who should be president. In *The Federalist Papers* (1788), Alexander Hamilton promoted this view of the Electoral College. It was "a small number" of "men most capable of analyzing" the "complicated" question of who should be president.[246]

In an era with no internet, TV, phone, or telegraph, when it took weeks to travel across the country, it was hard for presidential candidates to connect with voters across the country.[247] So it wasn't such a bad idea to make sure that the people selecting the president were actually familiar with the candidates and could deliberate on their strengths and weaknesses. Unfortunately, the Electoral College has never been the deliberative body that *The Federalist Papers* tried to sell it as. As soon as political parties came into play, the electors were a rubber stamp for their party's candidate.[248] As one Federalist proclaimed in 1796, electors were expected "to act, not to think."[249] That is still true today.

The Senate

If the founders shrugged at the slapdash Electoral College, many chafed at the bitter pill they were forced to swallow in the form of the undemocratic Senate. Alexander Hamilton wrote that giving each state the same number of senators, regardless of their very different populations, "contradicts the fundamental maxim of republican government," goes against "every rule of fair representation," and counteracts "justice and common-sense."[250] In other words, Hamilton hated the Senate. He believed in majority rule, and the Senate entrenches minority rule into the very heart of our federal government.

James Madison didn't feel any more warmly, but he drew the short straw and was assigned the task of writing the Federalist Paper lauding the Senate. Readers can practically hear his sigh of resignation as he wrote that we must accept the "lesser evil" of a Union with unfair representation rather than have no Union at all. You see, some smaller states were prepared to walk away from the Philadelphia Convention and form alliances with foreign nations if they did not get state-based representation in the new constitution.[251] After the Revolutionary War, each colony thought of itself as a sovereign nation and was treated as such under the ailing Articles of Confederation,[252] which gave each state a vote, much as each country in the European Union has a say. Smaller colonies would rather have risked further international war than give up their semi-sovereign status. Democracy-minded convention representatives such as James Madison and Alexander Hamilton weren't willing to risk it. The undemocratic Senate was born.

Hamilton thought that such an unfair institution could not last. He predicted that larger states would eventually "revolt" and demand that representation be based on people, not on historical colonial boundaries.[253] At the time of the revolution, the largest colony was 13 times larger than the smallest. Americans in the smallest resulting state had 13 times more representation in the Senate than those in the largest. Over the centuries, some states have swelled with the diverse ranks of city dwellers, young people seeking education and work, and people of color seeking new opportunities, while other states have remained tiny and mostly rural and white.

Americans in the least populous states now have a whopping 70 times more representation in the Senate than those in the most populous states. By 2100, that will have grown to 154 times. States with just 16 percent of the population will be able to elect a majority of the Senate, and barring filibuster reform, states representing 7 percent of the population will be able to block nominations and treaties supported by the remaining 93 percent. If Hamilton returned today, he'd be amazed to learn that the citizens of large states have not yet revolted against the excessive power of the statelets in America's upper house, even as the large states have become even larger than the small.[254]

Talkin' about a revolution

The United States uses outdated election systems that waste votes, limit voters' options, make some people's votes matter more than others just because of the state or district they live in, spawn deadly partisan gridlock, and entrench dangerous minority rule. The United States' presidential Electoral College is unique in the world.[255] The U.S. Senate is nearly unique. Only England and some former British colonies still use first-past-the-post voting and single-winner districts, with poor results for voters and institutions of democracy. Nearly 600 years after the Brits came up with this voting method, it's time for an update. Nearly 250 years after the revolution, it's time for the United States to fully throw off the King George yoke.

This section's chapters offer three game-changing solutions to the problems discussed above:

- Chapter 6 discusses **ranked choice voting**, a better way to vote that gives voters the option to rank candidates in order of preference. This gives voters more options and makes their voices matter more. Ranked choice voting is particularly great for executive-level races, and indeed, four states are already conducting their presidential primary elections this way.

- Chapter 7 introduces the **National Popular Vote Interstate Compact**, which if enacted would use the power the Constitution grants to the states to honor Americans' popular-vote preference for who should hold the highest office in their country. Seventeen states have already signed on.

- Chapter 8 describes **proportional representation**, a powerful reform for legislative races (for multi-member lawmaking bodies like the U.S. House, state legislature, or city council). Proportional representation would allow more than two parties to flourish, transforming our gridlocked, zero-sum, hyper-partisan politics into a positive-sum problem-solving game. Along the way it would give voters more options and de-fang the gerrymander beast for good.

- Chapter 9 proposes a way to make the **U.S. Senate** more fairly represent Americans by using the power the Constitution grants to states and Congress to form new states out of old.

These solutions might be new to you, but rest assured that numerous jurisdictions around the world have been using ranked choice voting and proportional representation for decades. Scholars and voters have learned from those experiences, so we Americans simply get to choose from among the best options. The National Popular Vote Interstate Compact, meanwhile, would merely enshrine in law what most Americans think should happen with the votes we cast for president anyway: the popular vote should prevail!

Chapter 6:
Give Voters More Choices in Executive Races

Use ranked choice voting to put more power in the hands of voters — where it belongs.

Jorge's story

In 2016, 28-year-old dockworker Jorge Ramirez was excited to vote for Marco Rubio for president. He was not excited come the general election, from which Rubio had been excluded, to see Donald Trump and Hillary Clinton as his only two options on the ballot. And the negative tone of the campaign, in both the primary and the general election phases, almost drove him from the ballot box completely.

"It's like all they can think about is how much they hate each other, not about what to do for us. What about my job, my health care? What are they gonna do about that? No, they just spend their time tearing each other down."

With Trump and Clinton as his two options, he voted for Trump but wished he could have had more candidates to choose from.

"Trump wasn't really my first choice. But I could only choose him," Jorge explained. "I wish I could have voted for Marco. I wish they could work together and get down to work."[256]

Politics are tearing Americans apart

Hyperpartisanship — the tendency to place party allegiance above everything else — plagues modern American politics, from the national to the state level. It dismisses the norms and traditions that hold communities together, mocks working together across party lines to solve important problems, and can even override opportunities to help one's own constituents. Ultimately, it disenchants people about the integrity of our shared system of governance and moves them to disengage, sometimes altogether.

Sadly, the election system that most U.S. jurisdictions currently use in executive races (for offices like president, governor, or mayor, where there can be only one winner) makes hyperpartisanship worse. **Plurality voting** (in which the person with the most votes but not necessarily a majority wins), combined with partisan primaries, drives this polarization. Potentially good candidates who don't sufficiently fit the mold of the two major parties get pushed out in the primary or don't run at all. Voters see only limited options on the ballot, or fear wasting their vote on a non-establishment candidate.

Candidates don't need a majority of votes to win, just more votes than anyone else — a plurality. This vote-for-one plurality system rewards major-party campaigns that attack the candidate from the other party.

A few voters and special interests determine election outcomes

A funny thing happened when the United States combined private party nominations with public elections. As discussed in the section overview, when political parties could choose their own candidates in private, they made an effort to choose people who could win elections and work with others to govern.[257] The parties put these candidates forward, and voters could choose between them in a public election.

Party primaries change that dynamic.[258] Rather than deciding who will run in the general election, primaries often *are* the election. In many jurisdictions, one of the major parties dominates, so whoever wins that party's primary is all but guaranteed to win the election. And in some local jurisdictions, the election literally ends with the primary. They don't even hold a general election if one candidate wins a majority of the (very small number of) votes in the primary. But very few people vote in primaries, making them vulnerable to special interests that can more easily swing a primary election than they could a general election.

Primaries reward special interests and extreme voters

Unfortunately, party primaries tend to drive hyperpartisanship by giving a few extremist voters and moneyed special interest groups an outsized voice in elections.

It works like this: primaries are low-turnout elections. Often just one in five voters participates, and the rest of us sit them out either by choice or by exclusion due to election rules requiring that primary voters affiliate with either of the two major parties. A much smaller group of voters wielding a potentially large amount of power in the election outcome is a tempting target for special interests. They get more bang for their buck in these races, and they engage accordingly. By the time the general election rolls around and many more voters are ready to vote, they find their choices have been restricted by these narrower interest groups.

Primaries can exclude non-establishment voters

Party primaries are supposed to help political parties choose their candidates. Under that reasoning, it makes sense to exclude voters who aren't affiliated with the party. In 14 states, only people registered with a political party are allowed to vote in the primary. In another 10 states, primaries can exclude nonpartisans if they choose.

But when the primary is the election, it makes less sense to restrict nonpartisan voters' voice. And with more and more people in the United States identifying as independent, unaffiliated, or of a minor party, choosing leaders in elections from which many Americans are excluded starts to seem downright undemocratic.

Primaries reward a party's most extreme candidates

Because candidates have to win over their party's primary voters in order to advance to the general, and because many voters vote party-line in the general, U.S. elections incentivize candidates to distinguish themselves not so much by what they stand for as by whom they stand against, and how strongly: the opposing party. Candidates and incumbents who don't weaponize every opportunity to disparage an opponent could face primary challenges by candidates who do. If they work across party lines to pass common-sense laws, they could face the wrath of purist primary voters and never make it to the general election, where they might have won. As a result, elected officials who want to be reelected — which is nearly all of them — hew tightly to what the most extreme voters in their party desire, rather than responding to what the average voter prefers.

A candidate vying to be the only person representing a whole city, state, or country should have broad appeal. Yet in the current system, a candidate who is unpopular with a broad share of the electorate can win with only a plurality of votes. Indeed, in three of the six most recent presidential elections, the victor earned less than 50 percent of the votes.[259] And even when someone does win a real majority, many voters might have been holding their noses while voting because there wasn't a better option on the ballot, their preferred candidate having been picked off during party primaries.

Negative partisanship takes over

In a two-party-dominated, vote-for-one plurality system, each party sees a winning strategy in making the other party look bad. They don't need voters to like their party so much as they need them to dislike the other party. Increasingly, that is exactly how American voters feel. A majority of both Democrats and Republicans have a "very unfavorable" view of the other party,[260] and around one-third believe the other party is a threat to the nation's well-being.[261] Voters are often voting *against* the party they oppose more than they are voting *for* the party they support. Political scientists call this "negative partisanship." This phenomenon was on Technicolor display in the 2016 presidential election: many voters didn't love Donald Trump so much as they hated Hillary Clinton and wanted to "lock her up"; other voters didn't love Hillary Clinton so much as they feared Donald Trump would usher in the end times.

The negativity comes out in each election, where negative campaigning, like attack ads and personal digs, works. Negative campaigning means voters don't hear their issues discussed as much, and they may find little reason to tune into campaigns and vote or engage in civic life.

These toxic campaigns have consequences after the election is over, too. Elected officials need to be able to work together to solve pressing issues, and generally speaking, they can devise better solutions working together across their different perspectives. But if they've just finished a monthslong campaign dragging each other through the mud and they might have to do so again in the next election, it can be hard to turn around and work together.

Plurality winners limit voters' options

Voters should be able to look at their options on the ballot and find at least one candidate they believe in. Instead, many Americans look at their ballot and are at best underwhelmed by the lack of options and at worst disgusted by the need to choose between the lesser of two evils. They cast a vote grudgingly rather than enthusiastically, throwing their support behind the least objectionable candidate they think has a real shot at winning — often one of two major-party candidates. There's no way to vote for a minor-party candidate without wasting one's vote, and no opportunity at all to vote for a major-party candidate who was eliminated in the primary.

In a country known for supplying consumers with endless choices, this system of voting restricts voters' options often well before they even see a ballot. Not surprisingly, this is disheartening to most Americans. When voters feel they don't have a chance to vote for somebody they support, they may not vote at all. And not voting at all can be as significant a move as casting a ballot. Vote-for-one plurality systems limit options and disenchant voters.

Established parties and special interests edge out non-establishment candidates

An embarrassment of riches: that's what the Republicans had in 2016 and what the Democrats had in 2020, in terms of presidential candidates in the primaries. Lots of candidates should be a good thing. With a voting system that can handle more than two parties, more candidates means that non-establishment candidates can enter the race and put the concerns of voters first rather than those of special interests. A diverse field gives voters a variety of policy positions to choose from and brings different issues and perspectives to light.

> **" In 2016, fewer than 7 percent of GOP voters actually cast a vote for Trump through Super Tuesday. "**

Our voting system, though, makes these additional candidates a bad thing. In what is sometimes called "vote-splitting" or "the spoiler effect," candidates who are similar to one another can fracture the votes of like-minded voters, and a candidate with support from a mere one-third of primary voters can easily become the party's standard-bearer. It can't handle having more than two candidates run; the system breaks down and elevates a less popular winner. Instead of being welcome options for voters, additional candidates become loathed spoilers. Left-leaning voters may think of the 2000 election, in which Al Gore could have won the presidency if the voters who supported Ralph Nader had gone to Gore instead; and right-leaning voters may remember the 1992 election, in which George H. W. Bush could have won if he had received the votes that went to Ross Perot.

For a more recent example, rewind just a few years and ask Republicans how they felt about Donald Trump leading the field of candidates in their Super Tuesday primary races in 2016. He garnered just one-third of Super Tuesday votes cast, with only one-fifth of registered Republican voters in Super Tuesday states even voting. Ultimately, that meant that less than 7 percent of GOP voters actually cast a vote for Trump through Super Tuesday. Yet Trump would go on to be the sole option for Republicans — or Democrats, for that matter — if they did not want to support Hillary Clinton.

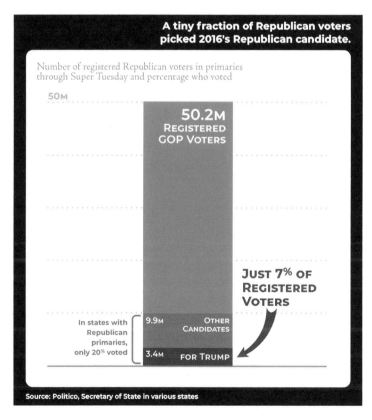

Figure 6.1: *Republican primary voters, 2016.*

The reform: Ranked choice voting gives voters more choices in executive races

Allowing voters to rank their choices — writing a "1" next to their favorite candidate, a "2" next to their second favorite, and so on, as in the sample ballot in figure 6.2 below — can circumvent many of the problems outlined above. **Ranked choice voting** (RCV), sometimes called **instant-runoff voting**, gives voters the option to rank candidates in order of preference. (If you want to vote for just one candidate, you can still do that.) If one candidate receives more than half the votes, they win. But if no candidate wins a majority, then less-popular candidates are eliminated and their votes get transferred to each voter's next-favorite candidate who is still in the running. Election officials continue this "instant runoff" process until one candidate receives a majority of votes and wins. The sample ballot in figure 6.2 imagines this setup for the Democratic primary candidates in 2020.

Ranked choice voting streamlines elections while giving voters more choice. How? Well, under our current plurality vote-for-one system, we have two elections: a primary and a general. Sometimes there's even a third special runoff election. If your favorite candidate doesn't make it out of the primary, even if it's close, too bad. You're stuck voting for just one of the candidates still left in the general. Maybe you're fine with one of them, maybe you're torn between two of them, or maybe you dislike all of them. Your only option is to vote for one of them or not vote at all.

A ranked ballot, though, can include all candidates, even the underdogs and non-establishment types, giving you more options in a single election. The ranked ballot and instant runoffs effectively combine a primary and general, and even a special runoff (if needed), in one election. Rather than narrowing the field over the course of several elections that eliminate fewer popular candidates, and then asking voters to come back and vote again among a smaller number of candidates, officials narrow the field in a single race by eliminating those who receive the fewest votes and then reassigning those votes to the candidates that voters ranked next. If your favorite gets eliminated in the first round of counting, you still get a chance to vote for your second- or third-ranked candidate if they make it to the next round, just like you would get a chance to vote for a candidate in the general under the current system, even if your favorite gets eliminated in the primary.

For example, in a 2018 House race, Maine voters saw four candidates on the ballot. No candidate won a majority, so the race went to an instant runoff between Democrat Jared Golden and Republican Bruce Poliquin. Voters who had ranked the Independent candidates first now had a chance to have a say between the Democrat and the Republican, if they had ranked them. For example, a voter who ranked Independent candidate Tiffany Bond first and Jared Golden second had a say equivalent to voting for Bond in the primary and Golden in the general. Without RCV, they would have voted for Bond and not had a say between Golden and Poliquin. Or, more likely, they would have felt pressured to not throw away their vote on Bond in the first place. Without RCV, Poliquin would have won with less than half the votes. But because of the instant runoff, Golden won with 50.5 percent of the final votes.[262]

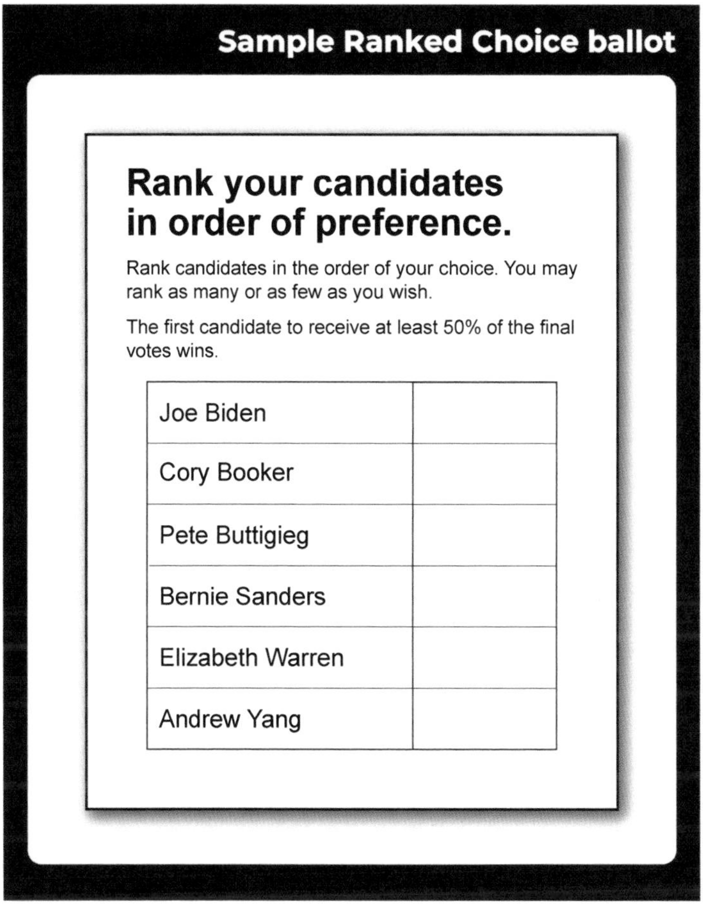

Sample Ranked Choice ballot

Rank your candidates in order of preference.

Rank candidates in the order of your choice. You may rank as many or as few as you wish.

The first candidate to receive at least 50% of the final votes wins.

Joe Biden	
Cory Booker	
Pete Buttigieg	
Bernie Sanders	
Elizabeth Warren	
Andrew Yang	

Figure 6.2: *Sample ranked choice ballot.*

RCV gives voters more choice and voice

Ranked choice voting makes it safe for more candidates to run. Because there is no longer a risk that similar candidates will split the vote, there is no reason to discourage additional candidates from running. Voters will hear more voices on the campaign trail and see more options on the ballot. Voters, in turn, don't have to fill in the bubble for the least-disliked-but-viable candidate. They can rank their true favorite first, because even if that candidate is eliminated, their vote can still transfer to their favorite candidate remaining in the race.

For example, in the 2020 Democratic primary, a voter forced to vote-for-one might like Andrew Yang best but be loath to "waste" her vote on him. Yang would get very few votes, and elected officials would see his policy platform as unpopular. But with a ranked ballot, that voter could rank Yang first and, say, Joe Biden second. If no one won a majority of first-choice votes and Yang were eliminated, then counting would go to the next round. Her vote would count for Biden, and it would also signal to the ultimate winner how many voters liked Yang's policy ideas.

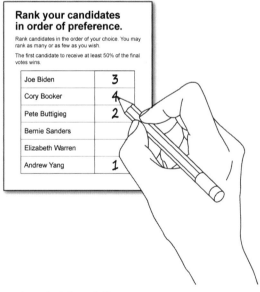

Figure 6.3: *Sample ranked choice ballot.*

Long-shot candidates might even encourage their voters to rank them first and the most like-minded major candidate second. That way, instead of being spoilers, third-party candidates could give voters more options without damaging the vote totals for the more popular side. For example, in Maine's 2020 Senate race, a more left-leaning independent candidate, Lisa Savage, encouraged her supporters to rank her first and the Democrat, Sara Gideon, second.[263] If more voters lean left, they won't split their votes between the Democrat and the left-leaning independent, throwing the race to the Republican. Instead, if Savage is eliminated, her voters who ranked Gideon second will be assigned to Gideon, giving a true accounting of her total support.

RCV can save money and empower voters by eliminating party primaries and shifting focus to general elections

If cities, states, or the United States as a whole used ranked choice voting to elect their executive leaders, they could eliminate party primaries entirely. Voters would just rank their choices in the general election. This would save counties money, because they wouldn't have to administer primary elections, and it could shorten the campaign season.

If officials are worried that the general election ballot may become over-whelming if too many candidates run, they could increase the barriers to declaring candidacy, say, by requiring would-be candidates to turn in signatures showing some threshold of support before they can appear on the ballot. Or officials could narrow the field with an open primary ("open" here meaning inclusive of all parties). For example, they could use a top-four open primary with a ranked choice ballot.[264] Each party could decide how to nominate their own candidate, and if four or fewer candidates total from all parties and all nonaffiliated candidates declared they were running, the race would go straight to the general with no primary at all. If more than four candidates declared, all would be listed on the same primary ballot with something indicating which party endorses them; voters would rank them; and the top four vote-getters would go on to the general ballot.[265] The real race would then in fact be the general election, where voters would see a variety of options and could rank as many or as few as they liked. (As of this writing, advocates in Alaska and Massachusetts are working on ballot initiatives to use a top-four open primary and a ranked choice general.)

Ranked choice general elections (with or without a primary to narrow the field) would put power back in the hands of voters, rather than special interests or small groups of more extremist partisan voters. The approach could also save money if it enabled jurisdictions to eliminate primaries entirely. And it could shorten the campaign season and lower campaign costs if candidates were running only in the general.

What's more, general election debate stages would have more candidates, bringing a diversity of views to the debates but still few enough for voters to get to know and be able to rank them. For example, in 2016 an open top-four primary for president might have sent Donald Trump, Hillary Clinton, Bernie Sanders, and Marco Rubio to the general ballot for voters to rank. Or, in 2020, an open top-four primary might have given voters the opportunity to rank Joe Biden, Donald Trump, Elizabeth Warren, and Bill Weld. The candidates with the fewest first-choice votes would be eliminated and his or her votes redistributed until one candidate had a majority.

A warning against top-two primaries

In an attempt to tamp down partisanship while also solving the vote-splitting problem, some states have adopted open top-two primaries,[266] in which all candidates, regardless of party, participate in a single primary and the top two vote-getting candidates advance to the general. Unfortunately, this doesn't give voters more choices, doesn't solve the partisan predicament, and occasionally eliminates more popular candidates through vote-splitting, giving voters in the general election even *fewer* good options than they would have had.

For example, in the 2016 race for Washington state treasurer, general election voters had no Democratic option on their ballots even though Washington voters lean Democratic. In the primary, most voters preferred a Democrat, but they split their votes among three Democratic candidates — Marko Liias garnered 20 percent, John Paul Comerford 18 percent, and Alec Fisken 13 percent. Only 47 percent of voters preferred a Republican, but there were only two Republican candidates, so their votes were not as split: Republican candidates Duane Davidson and Michael Waite got 25 and 23 percent of the vote, respectively. As a result, the less popular Republican viewpoint was the only option on the general election ballot. In contrast, sending all five candidates to the general election would have given voters more options, and the ranked choice ballot would have protected against like-minded voters splitting between similar candidates.

RCV shifts focus to the higher-turnout general election

About half of eligible voters vote in general elections, but only one-quarter or less participate in primaries. Primaries give those few voters an outsized voice, since they get to pick the candidates — often only two — for everyone else to choose between. Ranked choice voting could move the real contest to where it belongs, the higher-turnout general election, by either eliminating primaries or making them less important than the general, because they are open and advance, say, the four overall strongest candidates instead of just one from each major party.

Without a primary, or with a much less important primary, the campaign season would be shorter and focused on the higher-turnout general race. Not many races have more than four serious contenders, so the most popular candidates will most likely make it through the open top-four primary and save their money and energy to campaign closer to the general election.

RCV promotes discussion of issues over mudslinging

With ranked choice voting, the contest among candidates for votes is not a zero-sum game. Rather than winning by firing up core supporters and scorching the earth under opponents, victory in ranked elections depends on reaching beyond core supporters to win support from other voters. Often, those more tenuously supportive voters will be attracted to a civil candidate over a mudslinger.

Consider a race between candidates Progressive, Moderate, and Populist. If a core group of voters rank Candidate Progressive first, all is not lost for Candidate Moderate, because those voters could still rank her second if she reaches out to them. Further, if Moderate attacks Progressive, that might turn the progressive voter away from her, causing them to skip her altogether and instead rank Candidate Populist second. A candidate focusing her energy on promoting the issues she cares about and inviting voters into the conversation, rather than just bashing her opponents and turning voters off, is more likely to win a ranking.

Indeed, former Minneapolis mayor Betsy Hodges, after running in a ranked choice system, spoke about how she asked voters who preferred another candidate to make her their second or third choice. The incentive to seek second- and third-place rankings meant she spoke with voters she would have written off in a vote-for-one race. In that zero-sum model, there would have been no point in continuing to talk to voters who had already selected another candidate as their first choice.

Ranked choice campaigns focus more on positivity and policy issues and less on character attacks and mudslinging. Candidates in ranked choice races find that they

101

have something to gain by being positive about other candidates and something to lose by being negative. Mike Brennan, who was elected mayor of Portland, Maine, under ranked choice voting, explained: "You don't spend a whole lot of time saying things about your opponent that might be construed as being negative because whoever votes for them as number one might vote for you as number two."[267]

In San Francisco, candidates in ranked choice elections positively support other candidates, hoping to win second-ranked votes.[268] Candidates in Oakland also found there was a cost to mudslinging in ranked choice elections, and the fear of losing voters' second- or third-choice ranking motivated them to put down the mud and pick up the issues. Oakland mayor Jean Quan "ran a very focused campaign to be the second-place candidate for a lot of [voters]. She never spoke ill of anyone."[269]

Voters feel the difference in ranked choice campaigns, too.[270] In U.S. cities that use ranked choice voting, voters were more likely to report more civil campaigns, compared with voters in vote-for-one cities. Voters in vote-for-one cities were 70 percent more likely to say campaigns were more negative, with most voters in vote-for-one cities saying that candidates criticized each other some or a lot. Meanwhile, 81 percent of voters in ranked choice cities said candidates did not criticize each other much or at all. Across all demographic categories, voters perceived ranked choice campaigns to be less negative.[271]

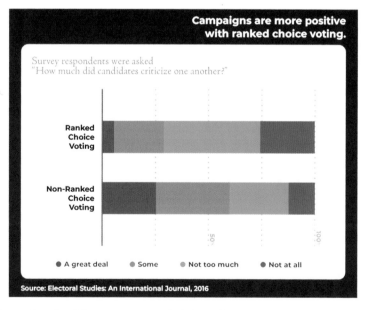

Figure 6.4: *Candidate criticism in ranked choice elections.*

RCV ensures winners have more overall support

Returning to the example of the Republicans' 2016 primaries, imagine if the Republican Party had used ranked choice voting in that race. Suppose that Marco Rubio was the second choice for many supporters of non-leading candidates such as Jeb Bush and Ben Carson. As it was, those voters cast their votes for their favorites, but then their votes were rendered worthless when their favorite was eliminated. They didn't get a chance to choose between front-runners Trump and Rubio.

With a ranked choice ballot, those voters would have ranked their favorite first and Marco Rubio second. When their favorite was eliminated, their vote would have transferred to Rubio. Like a primary within a primary, all Republican voters who ranked Trump or Rubio would have had a say between them. If this had played out, Rubio, not Trump, would have gone on to become the nominee and would have had more overall support from Republican voters than Trump had.

Some Democrats have learned from the Republicans' experience in the 2016 primaries and want to give voters more options without artificially narrowing the field. Democratic parties in six states (state party chapters being the administrators of primaries and caucuses) used ranked choice voting for all or some of their 2020 Democratic primaries or caucuses[272]: Alaska,[273] Hawaii,[274] Kansas,[275] and Wyoming[276] used only ranked ballots, while all early voters in Iowa[277] and Nevada[278] used them. National Democratic Party rules for the nominating convention required candidates to win at least 15 percent of the vote in a state to win pledged delegates from that state. The states using ranked choice voting eliminated last-place candidates and reassigned votes until all remaining candidates were above the 15 percent vote threshold. This ensured that voters who ranked a less popular candidate first still had a say in how many delegates the remaining candidates got at the convention.

For example, Alaska Democrats gave 50 percent of their first-choice votes to Biden and 39 percent to Sanders, with the rest divided between six other candidates. When those candidates were eliminated and their votes transferred, Biden had 55 percent and Sanders had 45 percent, and the delegates were divided accordingly.[279]

In these states, voters can be sure that a candidate won't advance to the general election just because the majority of voters split their votes between other, similar candidates. Instead, the winner will have strong overall support.

Better together: Ranked choice voting + Vote At Home

Voting at home with a ranked choice ballot would improve the process for both voters and election administrators. Voters might enjoy the chance to sit around the kitchen table or meet up with friends to learn more about the candidates and make informed rankings of one or more of them. Meanwhile, the state wouldn't have to worry about running any expensive special runoff elections, because ranked choice voting has an instant runoff built in.

In 2019, two cities in Utah did just this, using ranked choice voting for the first time in their fully Vote At Home elections. An overwhelming majority of voters ranked every candidate in the field, and almost all voters ranked more than two candidates. In Payson, Utah, 87 percent of voters ranked three or more candidates, and in Vineyard, Utah, 85 percent did.[280] Using ranked ballots at home gave these voters a better voting experience and a more nuanced voice in their elections.

Case study: Maine

In 2018, the state of Maine used ranked choice voting to elect its members of the U.S. Congress. All three elections — Senate, 1st congressional district, and 2nd congressional district — had three or more candidates on the ballot for voters to rank. In two of those three races, one candidate won over half of the first-choice votes, and the race was over.

The race for the 2nd congressional district, though, was closely contested between incumbent Republican Bruce Poliquin and Democratic challenger Jared Golden, with two independent candidates also participating. On Election Night, Poliquin led by a hair with just over 46 percent of first-choice votes, while Golden had just under 46 percent. Because no candidate had the majority required to win outright, Maine eliminated the two independent candidates and transferred their votes to those voters' next-choice selections. As described in the introduction to this chapter, most of those voters ranked Golden above Poliquin, so Golden beat the incumbent with just over 50 percent. Golden's victory showed how civility prevails in ranked elections: while Poliquin had publicly dismissed the independent candidates, Golden had found areas of agreement with them, encouraging their supporters to rank him next.[281]

Exit polls after that 2018 race showed that Maine voters support ranked choice voting. Nearly three out of four voters said that using the ballots was "very easy," and more than 60 percent wanted to either keep or expand their use of ranked choice voting. More than 70 percent thought it was important that candidates win with majority support, not just a plurality.[282] In 2020, Maine used ranked choice voting in the presidential general election.[283]

 ## Make it happen: From mayor to president

Nearly 20 U.S. cities already use ranked choice voting.[284] Most recently, voters in New York City overwhelmingly voted to adopt it.[285] At the state level, as mentioned above, Maine is already using ranked choice voting for congressional and presidential races, and six other states use ranked ballots for overseas voters.[286] In November 2020, voters in Massachusetts[287] and Alaska[288] voted on whether to approve ranked choice voting for county, state, and federal elections. As mentioned above, six states' Democratic parties used ranked choice ballots for all or some of their 2020 presidential nomination contests: Alaska, Hawaii, Iowa, Kansas, Nevada, and Wyoming.[289]

You could encourage ranked choice voting for your town or city to elect its mayor, your county to elect its executive, or your state to elect its governor. If you are a member of a political party, you could push your party to use ranked choice voting in its presidential primary.[290] If you are a student, you could advocate that your college or university use ranked choice voting to elect student government positions, as dozens of schools do.[291]

Some organizations that could connect you with like-minded advocates include FairVote, Unite America, Common Cause,[292] RepresentUs, Indivisible, Equal Citizens, the League of Women Voters, and Take Back Our Republic.

Discussion questions

- [ ] Have you ever used a ranked choice ballot? What did you think?

- [ ] If you are a Republican, did you worry about the crowded field in 2016? If you are a Democrat, did you worry about the number of candidates running in 2020? Would you feel more confident if you knew you could rank the candidates?

- [ ] Have you ever wished you had more options for president, governor, or mayor?

- [ ] Do you have any concerns about using ranked choice voting?

- [ ] Do you think your state should use ranked choice voting in presidential or gubernatorial elections? Whom could you contact to help make that happen?

- [ ] What do you think would be the biggest benefits of having more than two candidates in the race for governor or mayor and being able to rank them? What would be the drawbacks?

- [ ] Which four candidates do you wish had been in the running in the last few presidential elections? How do you think that would have changed the races?

Summary: Give Voters More Choices in Executive Races

- Most Americans use vote-for-one plurality systems to elect mayors, governors, and other executive offices. Voters can express support for only one candidate, and the winner doesn't necessarily earn majority support. This creates lots of problems.

- Ranked choice voting, abbreviated as RCV, is just what it sounds like: a voter writes a "1" next to her favorite candidate, a "2" next to her second favorite, and so on. If she wants to vote for only one candidate under a ranked choice system, she can still do that. An instant-runoff process selects the winner with the majority of votes, not just a plurality.

- Using ranked choice voting to elect a president, governor, or mayor would give voters more choices and make their votes matter more.

- Party primaries fuel the hyperpartisanship that is tearing Americans apart, but ranked choice voting can eliminate those primaries or make them less important, shortening the campaign season, giving special interests less power, allowing non-establishment candidates to run, and letting voters and candidates focus on issues and shared values.

- Ranked choice campaigns wouldn't get so ugly. Why? Because candidates would be vying not only for first-place rankings from their base but also for second-place rankings from independent voters *and* their opponents' voters. Mudslinging at their opponents only turns off crucial potential second- and third-ranking voters, and it takes time away from discussing the issues voters actually care about.

- With ranked choice ballots, voters aren't stuck choosing between the lesser of two evils in a general election, and they needn't worry about spoiling a race or wasting a vote on a candidate who can't win.

- Nearly 20 U.S. cities use ranked choice voting to elect their mayors and council representatives; Maine uses ranked choice voting for statewide elections and used it for the presidential election in 2020; and six states used ranked choice voting in their Democratic presidential primaries in 2020.

Chapter 7:
Honor the People's Choice
for President

––––––

Implement the National Popular Vote Interstate Compact to respect the will of the people in choosing their country's leader.

Ron's story

Ron Branston, 63, has lived in Mobile, Alabama, his entire life. He votes in every presidential election and follows the candidates avidly. But sometimes he feels discouraged.

"Why do I even bother?" he asks. "I keep voting, but all my state's votes always go to someone else."

As a Democrat in a reliably red state, under a state-winner-take-all Electoral College system, his vote has never helped a candidate win a single electoral vote.

"And they know it, too. They know it doesn't matter what I do. That's why they never stop here."

Ron has been waiting for a candidate to make a campaign stop nearby so he could go hear them talk in person. He's been waiting in vain. Alabama is a "safe" state for the GOP, which makes it a "spectator" state that candidates from both parties can ignore because its nine electoral votes are all sewn up, no matter what voters like Ron do. Ron and his fellow Alabamans, whether left or right, are relegated to the status of spectator, just watching the presidential race play out in the handful of battleground states.[293]

The state-winner-take-all Electoral College system makes many Americans' votes pointless

In two of the past five elections, and five times in the history of the United States, the candidate who won the most votes nationwide lost the presidential election. The fault, as discussed in the section overview, lies with the archaic Electoral College, an eighteenth-century compromise that still controls the elections of the twenty-first century's most powerful country.

Although Americans cast a vote for president every four years, their votes do not count directly for their choice for president, but instead are strained through a Constitution-mandated filter that inflates the importance of voters in some states and relegates others to irrelevance. The filter is this: each state gets electoral votes equal to the number of its congressional delegation, which equals the number of representatives it sends to the House of Representatives plus its two senators. At present, most states[294] award their Electoral College votes on a "winner-take-all" basis: the U.S. presidential candidate who gets the most votes in the state gets 100 percent of that state's electoral votes, no matter how many of its voters preferred a different candidate. This system creates a host of ills for the country, not least of which is overriding the will of the people.

The Electoral College

- gives almost all the political power to voters in **battleground states**. For example, because New York (with 29 electoral votes) is a reliably blue state while Florida (also 29 electoral votes) is a toss-up, candidates campaign fiercely in Florida and ignore New York.

- gives more numerical power to voters in smaller states. Wyoming, for example, with fewer than a million voters, and California, with nearly 40 million, both have just two senators, and each Senate seat gives each state one additional Electoral College vote.

- gives more effective power to white voters than Black voters. Black voters are concentrated in Southern states, which have consistently given all their Electoral College votes to the candidate that most Black voters voted against.

Problem 1: Overriding the popular vote

Counterintuitively, the candidate who gets the most votes does not necessarily win the U.S. presidency. In 2000, the state-winner-take-all system chose George W. Bush, despite Al Gore's half-million vote lead in the popular vote. While this stung for Democrats, the mismatch between people's votes and electors' votes may not always favor the Republican. There have been six other near-miss elections since World War II,[295] including in 2004, when a shift of just 59,393 votes in Ohio could have awarded the presidency to John Kerry, even though George W. Bush would have won the popular vote by nearly 3 million votes.

The chart below shows the percentage of the popular vote that Democratic and Republican candidates for president have won in the past six elections. When the election is clear-cut — that is, greater than a few percentage points' difference between the top two candidates — the Electoral College agrees with the people.

But when the election is close — within two percentage points — the Electoral College anoints the less popular candidate as president one time in seven.[296] Candidates can become president of the United States without support from a majority of voters (more than 50 percent), and they don't even need to win a plurality (more votes than any other candidate). A candidate *could* win just 22 percent of the popular vote and win the presidency,[297] and a candidate *has* won the presidency with just 31 percent of the vote.[298] That kind of result might make Americans wonder just exactly what "one person, one vote" really means.

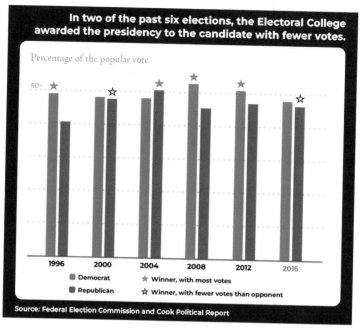

In two of the past six elections, the Electoral College awarded the presidency to the candidate with fewer votes.

Percentage of the popular vote

50%

1996   2000   2004   2008   2012   2016

● Democrat   ★ Winner, with most votes
● Republican   ☆ Winner, with fewer votes than opponent

Source: Federal Election Commission and Cook Political Report

Figure 7.1: *Votes for U.S. president, 1996–2016.*

 Problem 2: Campaigns and policies skew to favor battleground states

Under the current Electoral College system, presidential candidates ignore four-fifths of Americans[299] and spend all their time and money campaigning in just a handful of battleground states.[300] Voters in the other states are mere spectators in the election, watching it go by but not able to play an active role. Former Wisconsin governor Scott Walker, a Republican, bluntly summed up the current Electoral College system in September 2015: "The nation as a whole is not going to elect the next president. Twelve states are."

> ## The nation as a whole is not going to elect the next president. Twelve states are.
>
> ### – Former Wisconsin Governor Scott Walker

Before his inauguration in January 2017, President-elect Trump pointed out in a tweet that if he had needed to win the popular vote, he would have campaigned in states that the Electoral College allowed him to ignore.[301]

Donald J. Trump ✓
@realDonaldTrump

If the election were based on total popular vote I would have campaigned in N.Y. Florida and California and won even bigger and more easily

7:34 AM · Nov 15, 2016 ⓘ

♡ 149.7K   ♡ 57.5K people are Tweeting about this

Shortly after winning the 2016 election, he even reflected on how the Electoral College leaves **spectator states** out of the election, and he announced:

> *I would rather see it where you went with simple votes. You know, you get 100 million votes and somebody else gets 90 million votes and you win. There's a reason for doing this because it brings all the states into play.*[302]

To wit: in 2012, presidential and vice presidential candidates held post-convention public campaign events in only 12 states,[303] including 73 visits to Ohio alone.[304] They spent $463 million on TV ads in just 10 states.[305] Four years later, in 2016, candidates lavished 91 percent of their campaign stops on the 11 states with close margins.[306] They made two-thirds of their campaign stops in just 6 states with margins under 2 percent.[307] The map in figure 7.2 below shows the states sized according to their Electoral College votes. Candidates held at least 48 events in each of the four dark-blue battleground states but ignored most other states.

In 2016, presidential candidates concentrated campaign visits in battleground states.

Purple shows states sized by number of campaign visits.

Sources: National Popular Vote Interstate Compact; mapping and analysis by CORE GIS

Figure 7.2: *Presidential campaign visits in 2016.*

Candidates held almost no public campaign events[308] and spent almost no money advertising in **safe states**, or those they could safely assume would direct their electoral votes to one party or the other. Sure, they were happy to do quick stops in California, New York, and elsewhere to hold fundraising events and collect checks from large donors, but they usually left without holding any public events or listening to voters' concerns, and they whisked away the spectator states' money to enrich the economies of battleground states.

Favoritism toward battleground states doesn't stop after the votes are counted, either. By the time they are elected, presidents and their staff members have spent a lot of time listening to and thinking about the issues important to people in battleground states, but little to no time on the issues important to people in spectator states. Indeed, they might presume these issues to be the same.

Not surprisingly, the few battleground states receive more federal funds than the many spectator states.[309] For example, they receive 7 percent more presidentially controlled[310] grant dollars,[311] twice as many presidential disaster declarations, more Superfund enforcement exemptions, and more No Child Left Behind exemptions.[312] Their priorities also more influentially shape federal policies on economics and trade.[313] In short, elected officials never stop being candidates. They continue to have an interest in wooing voters in battleground states, either for themselves or for the next candidate from their party.

Problem 3: Battleground state votes count more than votes in spectator states

Under the current state-winner-take-all system, votes in battleground states are worth more. Because winning 51 percent of the votes in a state yields exactly the same number of Electoral College votes as winning 71 percent of the votes in that state, candidates ignore voters in safe states where the margin is greater than 5 percent and campaign only in the states where margins are close.[314] This means that they ignore the vast majority of American voters.

The logic of the winner-take-all Electoral College dictates that candidates treat millions of Americans as if they are not Americans, or at least not voters who matter in an election. Compare the map in figure 7.2 above, showing where candidates spent all their energy in 2016, to the map in figure 7.3 below, showing where Americans actually live, to see how the winner-take-all arrangement renders most Americans invisible to presidential campaigns.

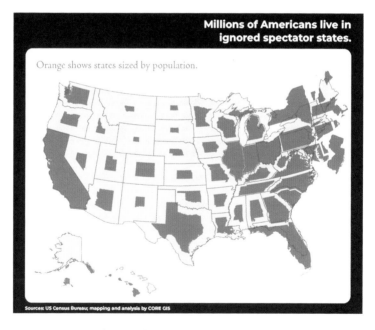

Figure 7.3: *States sized by population.*

Problem 4: Votes in some small states are worth more than votes in large states

A Wyoming voter has almost four times the power of a California voter to elect the president.[315] How? States get one electoral vote for each U.S. senator and one for each representative. And since every state has two senators no matter its size, Wyoming has three electoral votes for its half a million residents, one for each U.S. senator and one for its single representative. That works out to one electoral vote per 142,741 people. California's 40 million residents, on the other hand, represented by two senators and 53 representatives, have 55 Electoral College votes, which works out to about one electoral vote for every 720,000 people.

Problem 5: White votes are worth more than Black votes

As noted in the section overview, the aim of the political compromise behind the Electoral College was the same as the compromise behind the U.S. Senate and the infamous three-fifths compromise for the House: to give white Southerners outsized political power in order to keep the smaller Southern slave states in the new Union. Although the total populations of the North and South were roughly equal, about one-third of people in the South were slaves. In a popular vote for president in which only white people were allowed to vote, white Northerners would far outnumber white Southerners.

But white Southerners would not join the Union at a disadvantage. They leveraged their threat of breaking up the young country to gain an advantage in the House, via the three-fifths compromise,[316] and in the Senate, by making representation permanently based on state lines rather than population, no matter how disparate the state became in size. Then they combined the two to increase their power in selecting the president via the Electoral College. The result was that Southern states were punching above their voting weight by nearly 50 percent.[317]

This isn't just a historical curiosity. The Electoral College continues supporting the Southern strategy to this day.[318] By ignoring all the votes for the second-place candidates within a state, the winner-take-all Electoral College ignores most Black voters who live in red states. Five of the six states whose populations are 25 percent or more Black have been reliably red in recent presidential elections, though their Black voters are reliably blue.[319] Three of those states[320] have not voted for a

Democrat for president in more than four decades.[321] The Electoral College was designed in the eighteenth century, when Blacks weren't allowed to vote, and it continues working in the twenty-first century to drown out Black votes.

 ## Problem 6: Minority party votes in safe states do nothing to elect the president

Are you a Republican in New York? A Democrat in Idaho? Thanks for voting, but your vote means nothing in the presidential race. The current state-winner-take-all Electoral College system means New York will assign 100 percent of its electoral votes to the Democrat as long as you and your Republican friends are in any even-slight minority in the state's popular vote count. Idaho will do the same to its Democratic voters, in favor of the Republican candidate.

This is to say: you could vote . . . or you could stay home and watch Netflix. You could organize your like-minded friends to vote with you. Or not. Your down-ballot choices will matter, but when it comes to electing the president, it really doesn't matter what you and your fellow party voters do — which doesn't make for a motivating, inclusive race, does it? Which brings us to . . .

 ## Problem 7: The state-winner-take-all Electoral College depresses turnout in spectator states

Voters in spectator states correctly sense that their votes for president do not matter, and they engage accordingly. Voter turnout in battleground states is about 11 percent higher[322] than in less competitive states. Turnout often trends upward as a state gets more campaign attention and downward if a state gets none.[323] Even in states that have taken other measures to lead the way in encouraging their residents to vote, like Oregon,[324] being ignored by presidential campaigns hurts those efforts.

 ## Problem 8: It doesn't protect against demagogues

Alexander Hamilton's best argument in defense of the Electoral College may have been that it would protect us against a demagogue. In Federalist Paper No. 68, he wrote that electors would be immune to politicians with "talents for low intrigue, and the little arts of popularity."[325] Even if such a charlatan with "the desire in foreign powers" could manage to win over voters, they would not get past the Electoral College.

But as the section overview notes, electors have always been rubber stamps rather than thoughtful judges of what is best for the country. In a polarized two-party system, electors become even more unthinkingly loyal to their party and ill-equipped to make an independent assessment of whether a candidate has demagogic tendencies. The final justification for letting electors, not voters, select the president rings hollow.

 # The reform: The National Popular Vote Interstate Compact

The U.S. Constitution is notoriously hard to amend. Fortunately for voters, there's no need. The Constitution leaves the decision of how to select electors and how to distribute their votes completely up to states. Most state legislatures have *chosen* to give all their Electoral College votes to the candidate who wins in their state, but they could instead choose to cast their Electoral College votes for the candidate who wins the national popular vote. And if enough states *chose* to cast their electoral votes for the popular winner, U.S. voters would no longer see a mismatch between who wins the national popular vote and who wins the presidency. The Electoral College would always agree with the people: a national-winner-wins system rather than a state-by-state winner-take-all one.

Some states are already making moves to do just that. Sixteen jurisdictions have signed on to the **National Popular Vote Interstate Compact**,[326] pledging to assign their Electoral College votes to the popular winner once enough other states have also signed on, so that together those states have enough electoral votes to guarantee the popular winner. The Compact does not abolish the Electoral College — because again, the Constitution makes that very difficult — but instead uses it to execute the will of the people.

The National Popular Vote Interstate Compact is a binding agreement among states, but it isn't in effect yet. Why? Because part of the agreement is that it won't take effect until the Compact states' count of electoral votes amounts to a majority — that is, enough to ensure that the candidate who wins the popular vote will win the electoral vote — so it takes effect only after states controlling at least 270 electoral votes have signed on.

To sign on, the state legislature, or the people via a ballot measure, pass a bill approving the interstate agreement.[327] Once signer states meet the 270-electoral-vote threshold, the Compact takes effect for the subsequent presidential election. All signatory states cast their Electoral College votes for the presidential candidate who wins the most popular votes in all 50 states and DC, and that popular candidate wins the Electoral College and the presidency. By signing the Compact and acting together, state legislators are standing together for the principle that the presidential candidate who wins the most votes should win the presidency.

The threshold point is key, of course. When it comes to states casting their electoral votes for the national popular winner, it doesn't make sense to go it alone. For example, if a medium-sized blue state like Oregon had acted alone in casting its electoral votes for the popular winner in 2000, Al Gore, it wouldn't have changed anything because Oregon had already done so. If Oregon had cast its votes for the popular winner in 2004, George W. Bush, it again would not have changed the outcome; it would have only made Bush's Electoral College win larger (and would have really upset the majority of Oregonians who hadn't voted to support him). States will want to switch only if enough other states promise to do the same to ensure they are collectively electing the national popular winner. That way, if there is a mismatch between a state's popular vote and where it sends its electoral votes under the Compact, voters there can at least take comfort in knowing that any override of their state preference is in service of the national popular preference. The map in figure 7.4 below shows the 16 jurisdictions signed on so far and the 196 electoral votes they control, with states sized according to their respective numbers of Electoral College votes. The 15 dark-green states and DC have signed on to the Compact, and the nine light-green states have passed it through at least one house.[328]

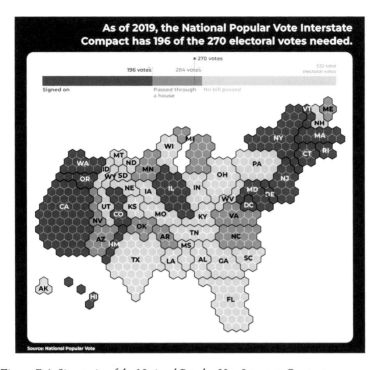

Figure 7.4: *Signatories of the National Popular Vote Interstate Compact.*

Astute readers will notice that most of the states that have signed on so far are safe blue states. Signatories New Mexico and Colorado are formerly purple states, but trending blue these days. Some safe red states are interested in the prospect of no longer being spectators in the presidential election: for example, Oklahoma passed a bill through its Senate in 2014. Voters in red spectator states want to matter in the presidential race, but they have also seen the Electoral College twice hand the presidency to a Republican candidate who lost the popular vote, causing them to fear that joining the Compact could hurt future Republican candidates' chances of winning the presidency. Formerly safe red Arizona passed a bill through its House in 2016, but may have become less interested in the popular vote due to the increased presidential attention it is receiving as a battleground state these days.

The closer the Compact gets to taking effect, the harder it may be to get states to sign on. But the more states sign on, the more attention the Compact will receive, moving the country toward the idea that the presidential candidate with the most votes should win.

The payoffs: Better representation, greater participation

A national popular vote would make every vote matter, regardless of safe or swing state residency, so everyone who chose to vote would benefit. States that protected and promoted their citizens' right to vote — say, by enacting the reforms in section I of this book — would get more individual votes counted in the presidential race and make the most of their electoral voting clout. But states that tried to prevent their citizens from voting via various voter suppression methods would lose out. Those states' citizens, overall, would have less say in who becomes president than they could have if all had been easily able to vote.

Make blue state conservatives' and red state progressives' votes count

Watching the map light up red and blue state by state on Election Night could make one suppose that California has no Republican voters and Texas no Democratic ones. Those voters exist, but they are silenced by the tyranny of the red-state-blue-state winner-take-all Electoral College system. Pushing past the trickery of the red and blue state maps to look at county-level voting, though, reveals masses of Republican voters in California and Democrats in Texas. Those Americans patriotically vote, but officials might as well throw their ballots straight in the trash for all they matter to the presidential race. With the National Popular Vote Interstate Compact, on Election Night we would instead watch a red bar and a blue bar build, vote by vote. Every single vote, no matter where it was cast, would add to that candidate's potential victory.

Encourage candidates to woo voters in all states, not just swing states

If every vote counted equally regardless of the state the voter lived in, a candidate would go to every place where there were persuadable voters. She would travel around the country to talk with voters because every voter she won over could push her to victory. No more of just 12 states enjoying (or enduring) all the candidate visits and media attention and ad buys and pundit analyses. Candidates — not to mention the entire political-industrial complex of campaign consultants and staff, special interest funders, and media commentators — would have to reach more voters throughout all states, not just the persuadables in Ohio, Florida, Wisconsin, and other battleground states perennially in the election spotlight.

The changed incentives to win over as many voters as possible, not just those in a handful of states, would transform campaigns. Rather than focusing all their polling and messaging and money on a sliver of the electorate, campaigns would be reaching out to more Americans. Republicans might look at the two recent elections where the Electoral College winner was the popular vote loser (2000 and 2016) and conclude that the popular vote is bad for Republican candidates. The truth, though, is that we can't really know, because those candidates were running Electoral College campaigns, not popular vote campaigns. With both candidates appealing to the most voters, campaigns will look very different, and vote totals might too.

Incentivize states to increase voter turnout, not suppress it

In the nineteenth century, as discussed in the section overview, states figured out they could wield more clout in presidential elections by assigning all their electoral votes to a single candidate, so one by one they adopted the state-winner-take-all system. If states instead adopted the Compact — a national-winner-wins system — the incentives would switch. States could then magnify their electoral power by boosting the total number of voters who cast ballots in the state. As a result, the rash of state voter suppression laws[329] might reverse course.

Increase turnout for down-ballot races

States encouraging — not suppressing — voter participation, plus presidential candidates paying attention to all voters, might create a new buzz of voter participation across the United States. Newly engaged voters might vote all the way down the ballot, increasing civic participation in state and local races and in turn inspiring more interest in state and local issues beyond the ballot box.

And no, the Compact would not disadvantage small states

One argument against the Compact is that it would disadvantage small states, reducing their outsized electoral power in presidential races. Not so. The current Electoral College system protects battleground states, not small states. Small states may have a disproportionate number of electoral votes, but this surplus doesn't translate into election power. Candidates make 94 percent of their campaign stops in 12 states and two-thirds of their campaign stops in just 6 states.[330] None of the smallest states are in those groups. The only small state to receive attention during the presidential campaign is New Hampshire, but that's because it's a battleground state.

Meanwhile, the other 12 small states, all of them spectator states,[331] together have 40 electoral votes, which is more than twice Ohio's 18 electoral votes. But battleground Ohio received fully 73 of 253 post-convention campaign stops in 2012[332] (29 percent!) and 48 of 399 in 2016,[333] while all 12 small spectator states received exactly zero visits in either year.

Another argument against the Compact purportedly made on behalf of small states is that the current state-winner-take-all system helps elect a president who is ideologically aligned with most small-state voters. Here again, though, the current Electoral College system fails the people. Small states don't have any single small-state ideology but are in fact ideologically divided, similar to larger states. About half of small states usually vote Republican[334] and the other half usually Democratic.[335]

Finally, one could look to the small states themselves to see what their voters think. In these states, too, voters on both sides of the aisle are chomping at the bit for a national popular vote.[336] Polls show that 69 to 77 percent of voters in small states favor a national popular vote for president.[337] It makes sense, then, that fully 10 of the 12 spectator small states have either signed the Compact,[338] passed a bill through one house,[339] or introduced a bill to join the Compact.[340] Defenders may claim the Electoral College status quo is for the good of small states, but small states seem to disagree.

 ## Better together: The Compact + RCV

The National Popular Vote Interstate Compact would ensure the candidate with the most votes wins. But alone, it wouldn't ensure the winner had a majority of votes. In three of the past six presidential elections, no candidate won a majority of the popular vote; the vote was split between more than two candidates, and in many states no candidate won a majority.

For example, in 1996, neither Bill Clinton nor Bob Dole won a majority in 26 states, yet each of those states gave their Electoral College votes to one of those candidates. States could choose to use ranked choice voting (see chapter 6) for their presidential races to ensure their votes went to the candidate with majority support in the state. In 1996, Libertarian Harry Browne, Green Ralph Nader, and Reformer Ross Perot would have been eliminated and those votes redistributed to the voters' second choices. Ranked choice ballots would have ensured that either Clinton or Dole won a majority of the votes, and the Compact would have ensured that the popular winner won the presidency.

Make it happen: Get your state to join in

If you live in a state that is not yet a signatory to the Compact, you could contact National Popular Vote to find out if there is an active campaign in your state to join. There might be a campaign urging state legislators to join, or a ballot campaign to put the issue directly before voters. These other organizations may also be able to connect you with the campaign in your state: Equal Citizens, Common Cause, the League of Women Voters, FairVote, and Indivisible.

 ## *Discussion questions*

☐ Do you think the candidate with the most votes should win?

☐ When the founders put the states in charge of the Electoral College, do you think they would have wanted states to be able to adopt reforms like the Compact?

☐ Do you think the founders needed to make the compromises they made to keep slave states in the Union? How do you think things might have turned out if they had not compromised? If you think compromises were necessary at the time, do you think it's time in the twenty-first century to undo some of those compromises?

☐ Do you think the Electoral College acts as a deliberative body? Or is it a rubber stamp?

☐ What unforeseen consequences has the current state-by-state winner-take-all Electoral College system created?

☐ What other effects might a popular vote for president have, besides just electing the candidate with the most votes?

Summary: Honor the People's Choice for President

- The Electoral College filters Americans' votes, making some of them matter more than others. Voters in battleground states have more of a say than do other Americans in electing the president.

- The state-winner-take-all Electoral College effectively limits the presidential race to a few battleground or swing states, rather than the whole country. Spectator or safe states don't matter.

- This has consequences for the election, but also for how policies are made and resources distributed — the voters that matter more during presidential elections also get rewarded between elections.

- The Constitution leaves it up to the states how to assign their Electoral College votes. By implementing the National Popular Vote Interstate Compact, states could use their power to change this dynamic and make every American vote matter without amending the Constitution or abolishing the Electoral College.

- State legislators choose how to appoint their state's presidential electors. Instead of awarding electors for the candidate who won the most votes in the state, they could award them to the candidate who won the most votes in the country. Once enough states sign on to the Compact to do this, the presidential candidates would have to campaign in every corner of the country because every vote would matter and count equally.

Chapter 8:
Break the Two-Party
Stranglehold

Usher in a multi-party system to
ensure that people's votes matter
and elected officials can work together
to get things done.

Jamie's story

"It feels very lonely out here," says Jamie Garner, a 52-year-old nurse in
Topeka, Kansas, who is frustrated with the political climate in the United
States. "You turn on the news, and they can't work on anything. They can't
even stay in the room and discuss. They storm out; it's tit-for-tat; you threw
mud and now I'm going to throw mud back. We've got real problems in this
country, but instead of solving them, they just keep telling me what's wrong
with the other side."

Jamie adds that it's hard to stay motivated to go out and vote when the
options are so lacking.

"Everybody is so right or left, it feels like there's no options where I am. I really
don't think anybody should be able to tell me what to do with my own body,
but I also don't think we should let just anybody into the country. Where's
the party for that?" In the past ten years she has voted for some Democrats
and some Republicans, but not felt great about any of them. In the last election, she voted for an independent candidate she was actually excited about.

"But of course they couldn't win. It makes me feel like I'm just not represented,"
she says, "like solving actual problems is almost irrelevant to the parties trying
to beat each other and cut each other down."[341]

Gerrymandered single-winner legislative districts disempower most voters

Many Americans are disgusted by political gerrymandering, a practice that allows politicians to draw district lines and rig elections in their favor. While you might hope we can simply fix gerrymandering and move on, it turns out gerrymandering is just a flashing warning alerting us to a fundamental problem with the way we vote. Sadly, we Americans are still working with "democracy 1.0," in which we use vote-for-one plurality voting in single-winner districts . . . and it's riddled with bugs and viruses. Gerrymandering isn't something that evil politicians have foisted on us voters, but rather an evil that our single-winner district system has produced over time and foisted on voters and politicians alike. We might even thank political gerrymandering for bringing attention to this otherwise submerged but sprawling problem: single-winner districts disempower voters. They systematically give an unfair boost to certain parties, at the expense of voters.

The bad news is that courts and computers can't fix a problem that's baked so deeply into the very architecture of the system. The good news is that upgrading the voting system will largely cure gerrymandering — and a bunch of related ills along with it. Most other democratic countries in the world have upgraded to "democracy 2.0," if you will. The idea behind the upgrade is simple: candidates win seats in proportion to the amount of support they have from voters. If Democratic Socialist candidates win 15 percent of the vote, they win 15 percent of the seats. This ensures that the 15 percent of voters who supported those ideas have a fair voice when laws are getting written. It's well past time for an upgrade, and proportional representation to populate our legislative bodies, from city councils to the U.S. House of Representatives, is just the thing we need.

Chapter 6 discussed ranked choice voting for executive offices. Here we'll discuss legislative offices, or those in which multiple people serve in the same role: representative or senator charged with writing and passing laws. First, we'll dig into the ways in which gerrymandered districts waste some votes and magnify others, and from there we'll explore the rest of the faulty operating system, from unaccountable elected officials to unstable policies.

Gerrymandering can "pack" and "crack" voter groups to waste the opposing party's votes

Single-winner districts guarantee just one type of representation: geographical. All voters know they have one representative in the legislature with a home address not too far from them. But in the modern world, that might not mean much. Living in the vicinity gives no guarantee that a candidate shares a voter's values, worldviews, and priorities. And the guarantee of geographical representation comes at a grievous cost: it often gives those drawing the lines more power than voters themselves have, and it gives some voters more power than others.

Gerrymandering — the idea that political parties draw district lines to give themselves an unfair edge in winning legislative seats — has gotten a lot of attention recently.[342] Many Americans are outraged at the idea that politicians can choose their voters instead of voters choosing their politicians. Some defenders of the status quo point out that skewed election results aren't just a product of partisan pen-wielding; they are a result of people moving to be near like-minded neighbors. That may be true (more on that later), but it does not excuse a system that dismisses some votes and yields unfair election results.

Under our current system, some votes matter and some votes don't. These are known as powerful and wasted votes, respectively. A **powerful vote** is one that a candidate needs to get elected and that succeeds in electing that candidate. You can use your powerful vote to hold elected officials accountable. If they don't represent you well, you can vote for someone else in the next election to take their place. A **wasted vote** is one a candidate doesn't need or that doesn't succeed: it is either unnecessary surplus to the candidate's margin (because she would have won the race anyway), or it is unsuccessful because the candidate loses the election. Either way, the winning candidate didn't need your vote and so doesn't need to worry about you withholding it the next time she is up for reelection. You, the voter, have no power over her.

In single-winner legislative districts, where only one person wins to represent the whole district, often the majority of votes are wasted. In our two-party system, this happens in one of two ways.[343] First, line drawers (partisans in charge of redistricting) can **pack the vote**, herding one party's voters into a safe district, where the winner has a huge surplus beyond what is needed to win.[344] Many of that party's votes are thus wasted on a candidate who is already a shoo-in because of how the district is drawn, when they might have made a neighboring district's race more competitive if applied there.

A second strategy used to waste votes is when the line drawers **crack the vote**, divvying up like-minded voters among districts in such a way that, despite their large numbers, they can't elect a fair number of legislators (see the red districts in figure 8.1 below).[345] In these competitive districts, nearly half of voters vote for the loser, but with their power diluted across districts, their votes are wasted on a losing candidate, and they fail to garner the representation they deserve. By drawing lines that just barely tip the advantage to their own party, line drawers ensure that the opposing party wastes close to half its votes in that district.

All this is to say that before any candidates have declared their candidacy and long before voters fill in their ballots, party strategists can call a race just by looking at the district lines[346] . . . which, conveniently, party representatives have often drawn themselves.[347]

If a party can draw district after district where the other party is either packed and winning in a landslide (wasting unnecessary surplus votes) or cracked and just barely losing (wasting unsuccessful votes), those lines become more powerful than the people living between them. They ensure that the line drawers' party gets more seats than it has votes. For example, in the gerrymandering case the U.S. Supreme Court heard in 2018, Wisconsin's Republican-drawn district maps[348] enabled the GOP to win more than 60 percent of seats in the state house despite earning less than 49 percent of the vote.[349]

People can also "self-pack"

Even without nefarious pen-wielding, simple demographic changes based on similar people choosing to live in similar places can make district lines all-important.[350] In the United States today, left-leaning voters have packed themselves into dense urban areas.[351] Researchers call it "the Big Sort" or "natural geographic sorting."[352] Journalists recognize "the two Americas."[353] Even the U.S. Supreme Court cites the difficulty in distinguishing intentional partisan manipulation from a "natural packing effect" as being at least partly behind its reticence to strike down gerrymandering.[354]

Some research concludes that *unintentional* self-packing plays a bigger role than intentional (political) gerrymandering in districts' "persistent pro-Republican bias."[355] Even when maps are drawn by supposedly nonpartisan courts or commissions, Republicans still win more seats than votes because Democratic voters have self-packed into urban districts.[356] A brief submitted by the Republican National Committee (RNC) to the Supreme Court in a recent gerrymandering case dedicates an entire section to this point, titled: "Research confirms that the geographic distribution of Republican and Democratic voters results in more Republican seats irrespective of partisan gerrymandering."[357] The RNC cites computer modeling showing that in single-winner districts, geographically concentrated voters can't win as many seats as geographically dispersed voters, even if they outnumber them,[358] so urban Democrats will consistently lose to suburban and rural GOP voters.

The RNC brief goes on to note that if the Court adopts a standard that requires districts to ensure the party that wins the most votes also wins the most seats, that standard would result in "bizarrely shaped districts of the kind this court previously rejected." In short, you can fix bizarrely shaped districts, or you can fix unrepresentative results. But with single-member districts, you can't fix both.

And no, computers and nonpartisan commissions won't fix this, either

Redistricting processes — including even California's, which was conducted by a well-designed independent commission[359] — often include an explicit goal of drawing compact districts to avoid the unsightly shapes that signal intentional gerrymandering. Sure, independent commissions or computer algorithms can draw compact districts,[360] but because of the "self-packing" explained above, those compact districts will disempower voters. They will be neither competitive nor representative, and in terms of geography will mean rural Republican votes count for more than urban Democratic ones. Another way to say this is that single-winner districts, by their nature, give one party a seat bonus — that party gets more seats than its share of votes warrants.[361] In recent years, Democrats' "self-packing" has meant the seat bonus goes to Republicans.[362]

A hypothetical can illustrate what the researchers cited by the RNC were pointing out: say a computer drew compact single-winner districts,[363] and one district encompassed an urban area that was 71 percent Democratic, while the surrounding four suburban districts were each 51 percent Republican and 49 percent Democratic. The map would look well proportioned and logical, but it would not be very fair, because when the numbers across all five districts were averaged, 53 percent of voters would have voted for Democrats, but their legislators would be 80 percent Republican. No nefarious partisan shenanigans needed — single-member districts' inherent flaws just result in legislatures that don't represent the voters.

And this isn't just a wild hypothetical. Researchers from Stanford University and the University of Michigan used actual votes in several states and modeled different ways of drawing district lines. They found that compact districts led to Republicans winning between 56 and 68 percent of the seats in Florida, though actual votes were split almost exactly 50-50.[364] They concluded that, because Democrats are concentrated in cities, they can expect to win fewer than half the seats when they win half the votes. A Democratic-leaning state will elect a Republican-leaning legislature from single-member districts even if a nonpartisan body draws compact district lines. This problem will only get worse with time as left-leaning Americans continue moving to cities.

Imagine a state with 100 voters, 54 of whom lean Democratic and 46 Republican. Voters elect an 11-member legislature. The graphic below shows districts carefully gerrymandered to be nearly homogenous. They may be funny-looking, but almost all voters would be members of the same party as their district representative, and the legislature would reflect the partisan split of voters overall: six Democrats (54.5 percent of the legislature) and five Republicans (45.5 percent).

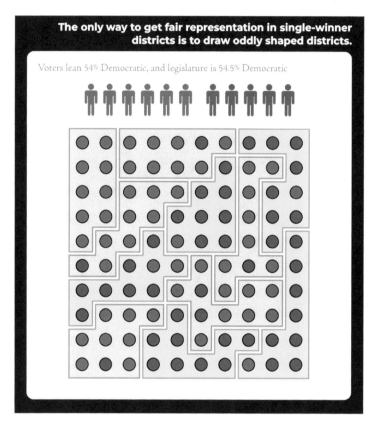

Figure 8.1: *Homogenous but oddly shaped districts.*

Compare that with supposedly "un-gerrymandered" districts where a computer or commission draws compact districts. Figure 8.2 below shows the same distribution of voters, but with tidily compact single-winner districts. Yet here too, in each district, up to half of the voters would not feel represented by their local elected official, and the legislature would not reflect the partisan split of the voters overall: five Democrats and six Republicans (even though 54 percent of voters chose a Democrat).

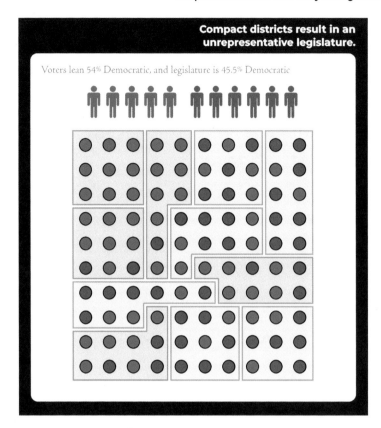

Figure 8.2: *Compact but unfair districts.*

Another criterion that independent commissions sometimes prioritize is competitiveness — drawing districts where each party has a shot at winning. But to do that in our sorted modern world, the line drawers would have to slice and dice cities into irregular, gerrymandered districts that clumsily mash together a bit of the city and a chunk of suburbia: pizza slices radiating out from downtown, or snakes cutting across a state to pick up a bit of a city and a bit of the countryside. Independent commissions are loath to draw districts like this — ones that at a glance seem to embody gerrymandering — so they end up drawing districts that are just as safe for one party as do partisan line drawers.[365]

Again, and it bears repeating: you can fix bizarrely shaped districts, or you can fix unrepresentative results. But with single-member districts, you can't fix both — not even with the purportedly unbiased help of computers, courts, or nonpartisan commissions.

Two parties dominate, leading to zero-sum gridlock

As the introduction to this book notes, many Americans are feeling disenchanted with our democratic system. It may be tempting to lay blame at the feet of the two major parties, who are engaged in a zero-sum, existential war, but what if the problem isn't parties per se, but rather that we have too few of them?

Here is the big secret that the two parties have been keeping from you: the way we vote perpetuates two-party domination.

It's not that Americans are more polarized than other peoples; it's that we use an outdated operating system — *democracy 1.0* — that enforces two-party domination.

The good news is that *democracy 2.0* works better and is within reach. We just need to scrap our flawed system — vote-for-one plurality voting in single-winner districts — and adopt a system that's designed to yield fairer results. Many more-modern voting systems ensure that legislators proportionally represent the voters. That is, if 30 percent of voters want lawmakers who support a certain kind of policy platform, then representatives who champion those policies will win 30 percent of the seats.

Single-winner districts disappoint

Say you are a conservative living in an urban area — a safe blue district. You vote for the Republican candidate. He doesn't get elected. Instead, a left-leaning candidate goes to the capitol as "your" representative, and she votes for a health-care bill you hate. The next time around, you (again) don't vote for her and she (again) gets elected anyway as "your" only representative.[366] Alternatively, say you are a Social Democrat or a Green Party enthusiast in an urban area. You consider your options and, seeing no viable Social Democrat or Green Party candidates on the ballot, you vote for the Democrat. You are incensed that he refuses to vote for universal health care, and you vow not to vote for him again. But the next time around, you again have to choose between a Democrat and a Republican, so despite your vow, you vote for the Democrat again.

Voters get frustrated, and politicians learn that they can safely ignore half their constituents. Indeed, they may *need* to in order to win their party primary. Elected officials aren't bad people or even bad representatives. It's just that their constituents have varied views, and they can't represent them all simultaneously. In a politically diverse district, one representative can't be all things to all people.

Right about now, you might be suspecting that wasted votes or complaints about gerrymandering are really just sour grapes from sore losers, like in sports matches: "One team wins, and the other loses. That's just life." This analogy might work when electing a president or governor: only one candidate can win, so many voters will have voted for someone who lost. But electing a legislature is more like ordering drinks for a group of friends at a restaurant. Some will want various kinds of alcoholic beverages, some soda or juice, and some just water. If each table is allowed to order only one kind of drink, half or more of the people won't get a drink they like. That's not "just life." It's a silly way to order drinks. Patrons in a one-type-of-drink-per-table establishment would get annoyed and likely stop patronizing that establishment.

Analogously, and more consequentially, voters in a one-representative-per-district (single-winner-district) system might start to get annoyed with their government and its elections. The futility of voting and never feeling that your one representative really represents you can cause people to stay home on Election Day or drop out of civic life altogether. Or they might rage against a system that seems rigged against them, voting for destructive candidates who promise to burn the whole thing to the ground. In our current system, voters can turn in their ballots year after year with no legislator to show for it . . . which in turn amplifies many of the problems we saw in prior chapters.

No room for minority parties . . . or minorities

In 2016 Libertarian candidates won 3 percent of the vote in Washington State,[367] despite the fact that single-member districts systematically exclude third parties from winning seats.[368] And more than 3 percent of voters likely wished to vote for a Libertarian or other third-party candidate, but they didn't want to throw their votes away on a candidate doomed to lose. All those voters have less power to elect a representative they like than do voters who truly prefer a major-party candidate.

The two dominant parties, particularly the modern Democratic Party, are so broad that even voters who identify as Democrats might not be getting what they want when a Democrat wins. For example, in 2016 Democrat Pramila Jayapal ran a campaign focused on a national agenda of racial justice and immigration reform, and won 56 percent of the votes in Washington's 7th congressional district. Democrat Brady Piñero Walkinshaw, who focused on more local issues of transit and housing, won the other 44 percent.[369] Even though both candidates were ideologically on the left, they had different priorities and some voters ended up with their priorities well represented and others less so.

Single-winner districts don't just exclude third-party voters or minority voters within a party. They exclude minorities of all sorts. Americans are racially, ethnically, culturally, and economically diverse. Yet elected officials at the federal, state, and provincial levels are disproportionately wealthy white men. Nationwide, white men make up 31 percent of the population and 65 percent of elected officials, while women of color make up 19 percent of the population but just 4 percent of elected officials.[370] The United States ranks number 100 in the world in the percentage of women who hold office in their national legislatures.[371] Rwanda, Nicaragua, Mexico, South Africa, Namibia, and others all have more than 42 percent women legislators, compared to just 19 percent in the United States. More than half the members of the U.S. Congress are millionaires,[372] while the average American family has 10 percent that much wealth.[373]

A big part of the reason for this lack of racial, class, and gender representation is that single-winner districts typically exclude voters in any minority, whether by party, income, race, or ethnicity. A single-winner district where fewer than half of voters are Black, for example, will likely consistently fail to elect the candidates preferred by its Black voters. Drawing lines to boost minority representation is imperfect, too. Supreme Court rulings against "racial gerrymandering" have made it much harder to establish **majority-minority districts** (districts where people in a racial or ethnic minority make up the majority of the population).[374] It goes the other way, too: gerrymandering can be used to draw racial and ethnic groups out of power.[375] Without the voices of people with different life experiences, lawmakers are sure to have blind spots and biases that shape their laws in harmful ways.

Elected officials play tug-of-war with important policies

A two-party war leads to unstable policies that seesaw between opposing sides.[376] When one party comes to power, it can push through a policy the other party hates. Because it has limited time in power, the party might grab the opportunity to ram through a slapdash policy rather than carefully working it out with many stakeholders. As soon as the other side comes to power, it strives to dismantle the policy and put in place its own narrow version. This leads to uncertainty about what the laws will be from one year to the next, and when those winning office are the ones holding more extreme policy views, that can result in massive policy swings from one legislative term to another, which is bad for businesses, families . . . well, basically anyone trying to plan for their future.

For example, renewable energy tax credits, which are key to growing the clean energy resources most Americans agree they want,[377] are constantly in jeopardy of being repealed, and that instability harms clean energy businesses trying to expand. As another example, Democrats passed the Affordable Care Act on pure party lines in 2010. Since then, the Republicans have spent huge amounts of time, energy, and political capital trying to tear it down, again creating uncertainty that has been costly both to the health-care industry and to the public.

When two parties play tug-of-war for control of the government, it's a zero-sum game: every inch that one party relinquishes is an inch the other party gains. And when the parties are as completely separated as Democrats and Republicans now are, having one party in charge is an existential threat to the other. The party in charge will fight with the fervor of a cornered animal to keep the other party out, or to trip them up at every turn if they win power. We've seen the results: government shutdowns, filibusters, a blocked Supreme Court nomination.

Part of why this happens is that, in a two-party system, the party out of power often bears no cost but stands to gain a lot when it throws bombs under the wheels of governance. If the government shuts down and can't get things done, voters tend to blame the party in power, not the party out of power.

Worse, majority control of the legislature doesn't equal support from a majority of voters, so these haphazard policies often don't even have majority support. Because single-winner districts are vulnerable to gerrymandering, one side might gain power in any given year with only a minority of votes. Voters for the losing side, even if their side actually won more votes, can be locked out of government until the next election, so the party in power may be pushing through policies with mere minority support. The resulting policies are not only unstable but also unpopular.

Voters can't hold elected officials accountable

With only two parties on offer, each party has near-monopoly control over the voters who lean its way in a given district. What are dissenters going to do — vote for the other party? When voters have just two viable options, candidates don't really have to compete for their support. They just have to be marginally more attractive than the other party.

Worse, safe districts mean candidates don't even have to compete with the other major party. In districts that are safe for one party or the other, whichever candidate wins the party primary can just coast to victory in the general. So an incumbent running in the primary is almost guaranteed to win. For example, in Oregon more than 90 percent of state house incumbents face no primary challenger. In a safe district, members of the weaker political party know they have no chance to win, so they may not even bother running a candidate, leaving general election voters literally without any power to choose who wins. In more than one-third of races, one of the two major parties doesn't even bother running a candidate.

Forget about going beyond two-party domination — many American voters don't even have two options on the ballot!

Here, the wasted and powerful votes described above come into play. In single-winner districts, whether packed or cracked or somewhere in between, the majority of votes don't matter, so elected officials seeking reelection don't have to worry how most people feel about them and their policy choices. The district lines have already delivered their next victory. Which may make it less surprising when …

Voters grow cynical and opt out entirely

Many Americans don't realize that two-party dominance is baked into the heart of the voting system, but they do know they are sick of the two-party duopoly, and they are registering their objections to it by opting out entirely. People who don't identify with one of the two major parties are the biggest and fastest-growing group of U.S. voters. More Americans identify as independent than as Democrat or Republican.[378] At last count, 40 percent of Americans considered themselves independent,[379] and nearly half of millennials did, too.[380] Yet almost every member of a state legislature or U.S. Congress is a member of one of the two major parties.

 # The reform: Proportional representation

Back to that drinks-with-friends example at our weird one-drink-per-table restaurant, surely to go out of business soon if it doesn't change its ways. Fortunately, based on patron feedback, it does. So now imagine instead that each table or group of tables could order four or five kinds of drinks. All restaurant patrons would have access to a cold one they like, no matter which table they're at. That's the promise of this chapter's reform, proportional representation. Because in a country with 535 legislators, or a state with 200 lawmakers, or a city with 15 city council members, nearly all voters should be able to cast a vote for someone they support and have a chance of seeing that person win one of the many seats in the running.

With **proportional representation**, often shortened to "ProRep," candidates and parties win seats in legislative (that is, multi-member) bodies in proportion to the votes people cast for them. Forty percent of the vote, for example, equates to 40 percent of the power. ProRep comes in many varieties, but the basic idea is to let voters elect more than one representative at a time in a way that ensures the mix of elected officials reflects the mix of the voters in their district.[381] The result is multiple political parties, usually three to five, that represent more voters, bring more ideas into the political mix, and work together to solve problems. Most of the advanced democracies around the world elect officials using proportional representation. Why? It's democracy, upgraded.

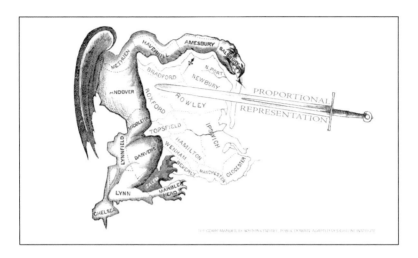

Options for implementing ProRep

There are many different ways of achieving proportional results. Here are three options for a race that aims to fill five seats in a legislative body, such as a city council, state legislature, or Congress.

Ranked choice ballots.[382] Instead of seeing (probably) just two candidates on the general election ballot and filling in a bubble for one of them, voters see several more candidates on the ballot, perhaps ten, and get to rank them. Then vote counting works much as it does for other ranked choice voting elections (see chapter 6). But instead of one candidate winning after hitting the threshold for a one-winner race, five candidates win when each hits the threshold for a five-winner race. This is simply *multi*-winner ranked choice voting.

Sample Ranked Choice ballot

Rank your candidates in order of preference.

Rank candidates in the order of your choice. You may rank as many or as few as you wish.

The first candidate to receive at least 50% of the final votes wins.

Maria Moderate	
Fiona Free-Trade	
Leroy Left	
Henry Hawk	
Rex Rural	
Rachel Right	
Elijah End Corruption	
Bai Better Way	
Sal Safety Net	
Felicia Fun College	
Steven Silicon	
Chen Cut Taxes	

Figure 8.3: *Sample multi-winner ranked choice ballot.*

Open list ballots.[383] Ten to twelve candidates are listed on the ballot by party. Voters can vote once for any candidate. The top five candidates win, and each party wins a share of seats proportional to its share of votes.

Sample Open List ballot

Vote for one candidate.
Your vote counts for both the candidate and their party.

Democrat		Republican		Independent		Progressive		Libertarian	
Maria Moderate	○	Henry Hawk	○	Elijah End Corruption	○	Sal Safety Net	○	Steven Silicon	○
Fiona Free-Trade	○	Rex Rural	○	Bai Better Way	○	Felicia Fund College	○	Chen Cut Taxes	○
Leroy Left	○	Rachel Right	○						

Figure 8.4: *Sample open list ballot.*

Mixed member proportional. Voters can cast one vote for their favorite individual candidate and one for their favorite party. Two individual winners win two of the seats, and candidates from the most popular parties fill the other three.

Figure 8.5: *Sample mixed member proportional ballot.*

Case study: Cambridge, Massachusetts, enjoys more diverse leadership and higher voter turnout thanks to ProRep

Cambridge, Massachusetts, has used proportional representation in its city and school board elections for nearly a century. Though Cambridge is similar to, say, Portland, Oregon, in its demographics and overall political leanings, the differences in the two cities' election results are striking.

Like Portland, Cambridge elects its city councilors from the city as a whole rather than from districts. But in Cambridge, all candidates run in a single pool, and voters get to rank their choices.

From the voters' perspective, Cambridge's multi-winner ranked choice system makes it much more likely that their vote will help put someone they support on the city council. Over 90 percent of voters are able to elect their first- or second-choice candidates to the nine-seat council.[384] Compare that to Portland, where up to half of voters didn't vote for the councilor who supposedly represents them. Not surprisingly, Cambridge boasts better voter turnout compared to similar cities.[385]

In Portland, winner-take-all elections have helped white men to almost entirely dominate the city council. From 1993 to 2018 in Cambridge, whose population is over one-third people of color,[386]

- 17 white men (including a Muslim man whose parents were immigrants) collectively served during 57 percent of the years,

- 8 white women collectively served during 26 percent of the years,

- 2 men of color collectively served during 10 percent of the years, and

- one woman of color served during 7 percent of the years.

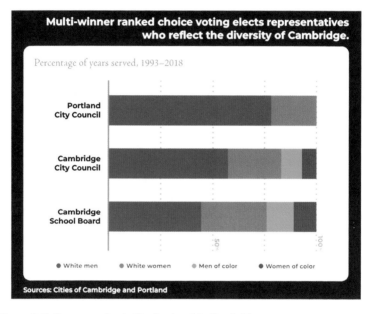

Multi-winner ranked choice voting elects representatives who reflect the diversity of Cambridge.

Percentage of years served, 1993–2018

Portland City Council

Cambridge City Council

Cambridge School Board

● White men   ● White women   ● Men of color   ● Women of color

Sources: Cities of Cambridge and Portland

Figure 8.6: *Representation in Portland and in Cambridge.*

While these numbers still don't reach parity with the population makeup, they are an improvement over Portland, where winner-take-all elections have helped white men to almost entirely dominate the city council for that same span of time.

Cambridge also uses multi-winner ranked choice voting to elect its school board, which is even more diverse than the city council.[387] Figure 8.6 above shows that Portland's city council did not reflect its voters during this time period, whereas Cambridge's city council and school board came closer.

The payoffs: Power to voters and good policy ideas, not to parties and district lines

Break two-party dominance

Legislatures in proportional systems end up with more parties, better representing a broader range of voter viewpoints.[388] We do have to look abroad for examples of these successes, but for instance, in Ireland's Dáil Éireann, the 158-member lower house of that country's legislative body, voters who believe in "People before Profit" have six legislators representing them, while the isle's independents have four. In Australia, the Greens have nine representatives in the country's 76-seat Senate.

Empower voters to elect representatives and hold them accountable

In proportional systems, one winner doesn't take control; instead, power is divided based on the share of votes each candidate or party receives. A minority of votes doesn't mean total lockout. Above a minimum threshold, it means a minority share of seats — but still seats at the table. Twenty percent of the vote means 20 percent of the seats.

This proportionality creates healthy competition between political parties. If a party starts losing voters' trust, an alternative party will rise up to give voters another option. Because smaller parties have a shot at a fair share of seats, even small shifts in voter preferences can shift power. As a result, voters aren't held hostage to the party closest to them; they have the power to make a difference in who wins and who loses.

Proportional results guarantee that almost every voter wields the power to help elect a representative they like. When voters have real options and know their votes matter, they also know candidates and parties can't take them for granted, so they engage at a higher rate. Research bears this out: more people turn out to vote in countries using proportional representation than in winner-take-all countries.[389] This participation, in turn, incentivizes leaders to be responsive to everyone in their district, not just to their typically more dogmatic primary voters.

Break up partisan gridlock

A proportional voting system might yield, say, five American parties. This would give voters more options on the ballot and the chance to vote for someone they really like, instead of just voting against the one party they hate.

The chart below maps American voters on the issues of cultural change versus traditional values (x axis)[390] and business profits versus anti-capitalism (y axis),[391,] based on political typology developed by the respected Pew Research Center.[392] Clearly, voters have more groupings of views that two parties can capture. But ProRep might surface, for example, the following five types of parties:

1. a Conservative Party that wants to retain traditional values and not regulate business interests (upper right in the graph below; it might encompass Senator Mitt Romney and the voters Pew calls "Core Conservatives");

2. a Nationalist Party that wants to retain traditional values but rein in trade and globalization (center right, perhaps encompassing supporters of President Trump and "Market Skeptic Republicans");

3. a Labor Party whose focus is improving the lot of workers (lower left, Senator Bernie Sanders and "Disaffected and Diverse" voters; it might bring in the "Market Skeptic Republicans");

4. a New Socialist Party that wants to remedy historical oppression (far lower left, Representative Alexandria Ocasio-Cortez and "Educated White Liberals"), and

5. a Liberal Party that embraces cultural changes and seeks to regulate markets (central lower left, Senator Joe Biden and the "Comfortable Democrats").[393]

These parties would have different areas of overlap, allowing them to build coalitions and pass broadly popular policies. They would not be stuck in a zero-sum war in which if they are against each other on one thing; they are against each other on everything. Instead, they could find areas of agreement on some policies and agree to disagree on others. For example, the Labor, New Socialist, and Liberal Parties (and maybe even the Nationalist Party) could work together on laws that would rein in runaway inequality and benefit American workers. The Conservative, Liberal, and New Socialist Parties might work together on immigration reform.

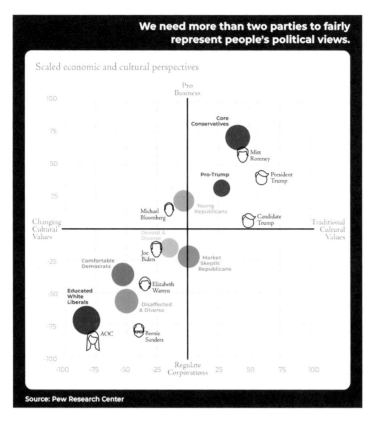

Figure 8.7: *Matrix of American voters.*

Produce better policy outcomes

This isn't all hypothetical. Experience from countries that use proportional systems — including New Zealand, Germany, and Sweden — shows that more diverse viewpoints and robust minor parties foster innovative and durable policy solutions. Having more parties competing for votes brings new ideas to political debates, both on the campaign trail and in the halls of power.

For example, many proportional representation countries adopted marriage equality faster than single-winner-district countries because smaller parties brought the then "radical" idea into campaigns and political discussions. The idea worked its way into the mainstream. In the United States, neither of the two major parties wanted to risk being first to adopt a new position, so it took much longer for Congress to take the topic seriously.

Having more parties working together also means the policies that pass will better stand the test of time, because they must be more durably popular. Lawmakers have to consider many views instead of just steamrolling whichever party is not in power at the moment, only to see the policy rolled back once the other party comes to power.

Enact stronger environmental protections

No electoral system can guarantee certain outcomes, but the record shows that ProRep countries have stronger environmental protections.[394] One reason: with proportional representation, voters have more influence. When voters matter, the system has to be more responsive to the people who often suffer from pollution than to moneyed interests that often benefit from environmental exploitation.

ProRep countries were quicker to ratify the Kyoto Protocol, an international agreement to limit greenhouse gas pollution, and have slowed their carbon pollution more than four times as quickly as winner-take-all countries.[395] Proportional representation countries are more likely to have Green Party representation in their legislatures, too.[396] Once they win seats, Green Party officials can introduce innovative policy ideas, some of which steadily work their way into the mainstream. Often, Greens make coalition partners for bigger parties, helping set a pro-environment agenda.

Boost economic equality and empower low-income voters

Countries that use proportional representation have less inequality and more equality-enhancing policies compared with winner-take-all countries such as Canada and the United States.[397] Because candidates in winner-take-all countries have to answer only to certain voters, they are more likely to protect the wealthy at the expense of lower-income people. A recent analysis of 24 democracies found that proportional electoral rule reduces underrepresentation of the poor.[398] Representatives in ProRep countries reflect a broader swath of society, and the record shows they spend more on public education, health care, and other policies that reduce inequality. Overall, proportional representation countries are more economically equal than winner-take-all countries.

De-fang gerrymandering

Replacing single-winner districts with proportional voting would largely bypass the gerrymandering mess. That switch would eliminate safe seats, diminish the power of cracking and packing, and render partisan redistricting battles irrelevant. It is difficult or impossible to gerrymander the lines in proportional districts.[399]

When voters elect multiple candidates, one winner can't take all the power. Instead, multiple candidates represent each district according to how many votes each gets. Even if 80 percent of voters in a district favor one party, the 20 percent minority electorate isn't shut out — they still keep 20 percent of the power. No matter how the district lines are drawn and no matter how party voters are distributed among districts, almost all voters have a say in sending representatives they support to office.

Elect more women and people of color

Proportional representation has a history of putting more women in office.[400] In countries that use it, women are almost twice as likely to get elected to office compared with winner-take-all systems.[401] In a comparative study of 36 countries, the share of women elected to the legislature was eight percentage points higher in proportional representation countries.[402] All the ProRep countries in western Europe have at least 20 percent women in parliament.[403]

And multi-winner districts with seats elected proportionally would mean that any group in the minority, no matter where they live within the district, would have a good chance of electing someone to represent them.[404] For example, if Green Party voters compose 20 percent of the vote, they could elect at least one of the five seats.

Same for communities of color, if they tend to vote together in a given community.[405] In fact, well over 100 jurisdictions in the United States, mostly cities, counties, and school districts, have switched from winner-take-all to semi-proportional methods such as cumulative voting to remedy the vote dilution that winner-take-all elections can cause for communities of color.[406] Cumulative voting — in which each voter has a fixed number of votes and can cast more than one vote for one candidate — is called semi-proportional because it achieves more proportional results than winner-take-all, but not as much as the fully proportional methods described above.

Jurisdictions that have switched have seen immediate and sustained representation for people of color. For example, one study examined 62 jurisdictions where almost no Black or Latino candidates had been elected under winner-take-all. After cumulative voting was adopted, Latino candidates won seats in 70 percent of the cases in which they sought representation, while African American candidates won at least one seat in 96 percent of the elections in which one or more were on the ballot.[407] Electoral system reform is a more robust solution to the problem of underrepresentation of people of color than redistricting in single-winner districts.[408]

Rein in the far right

In an era of worldwide far-right ascendance like today's, two-party systems are vulnerable because there is a chance the far right can polarize voters, take over one of the two major parties, and gain power over the entire government.[409] The risk isn't just that the far right will be in charge for a while but also that they will feed on the polarization to cement their power by undermining democracy.[410] Proportional systems protect against this, awarding radical parties a few seats in proportion to their popularity, but preventing minority factions from taking over the government.

Some critics worry that faithfully translating votes into seats will put the far right in power. Well, that would be true only so far as far-right views have real voter support. By forcing far-right extremists to run on their own platform rather than hide inside a big-tent party, proportional systems ensure that extreme candidates get only as much representation as their platform actually has among the public. Because they are staking out a unique position, they aren't able to pull center-right parties to the far-right, and they definitely aren't able to take over the big-tent party. If, for example, 10 percent of voters support a nationalist party, then those candidates will hold just 10 percent of seats. But with their views out in the open and in real competition with more mainstream views, extreme parties will likely repel most voters. In contrast, the Tea Party has been able to move the entire Republican Party to the right, even if that's not where most voters are.

In the United States, we see that far-right elements have gained control of the Republican Party[411] and that more moderate Republican voters (and politicians!) feel trapped, not liking what they see happening under the Trump administration but having no other viable conservative option on the ballot.

 ## **Better together:** *Proportional representation + ranked choice voting*

As mentioned in chapter 6, nearly 20 U.S. cities already use single-winner ranked choice voting. They are just one step away from using multi-winner ranked choice voting and achieving a multi-party system. Multiple parties would work well with the proposal in chapter 6 to use ranked choice voting and eliminate primaries (or maybe use an open top-six primary to narrow the field). More parties would be able to field a candidate in executive races, and voters would have a chance to hear what each party is all about and how to rank them in order of preference (or just vote for one). The combination of a ranked choice ballot for the executive races and a functioning multi-party legislature would create positive, issue-based campaigns in which candidates would find out what they have in common during the campaign and work together toward shared solutions once elected.

Make it happen: From city hall to the U.S. Capitol

Proportional representation and multi-winner districts may be unfamiliar to many Americans, but they are well-tested democracy upgrades elsewhere. Most advanced democracies in the world use some form of proportionality, and these systems are well liked; nobody switches back![412] Consider New Zealand, which opted for a proportional system in the 1990s, for example.[413] Immediately, New Zealanders saw a more diverse, representative parliament.[414] They haven't looked back.

In fact, from school districts to counties and state legislatures, more than 300 jurisdictions in 30 U.S. states already use proportional or semi-proportional systems such as cumulative and limited voting.[415] The reform is gaining momentum, with two new cities — Eastpointe, Michigan, and Palm Desert, California — adopting multi-winner ranked choice voting in 2019.[416] It's time the rest of us had our fair shot, too.

> **New Zealanders voted for a proportional system in the 1990s and immediately saw a more diverse, representative parliament.**
>
> **They haven't looked back.**

You could urge Congress to pass the Fair Representation Act, which (bonus!) requires zero changes to the difficult-to-change U.S. Constitution.[417] This law would allow voters to elect all members of the U.S. House of Representatives from multi-member districts that are drawn by an independent commission. Districts would elect between three and five representatives each.

For example, in a less populous state like Kansas, which has just four representatives, the entire state would be a four-winner district. Ohio, with 16 representatives, might be broken up into two five-winner and two three-winner districts. This would shift the disproportionately Republican representation in both Kansas[418] and Ohio[419] to a mix of candidates that better reflected those states' mix of voters. Meanwhile, California's 50 districts would become ten districts electing five members each. Its congressional delegation would change from a disproportionately Democratic representation to a fairer mix.[420]

Aside from sending a more balanced delegation to DC, this change would also dramatically affect individual voters and candidates. Almost every voter would be able to vote for and elect a candidate they felt more closely represented them. And every candidate would have to reach out not only to their base of supportive voters but also to those voters they need to persuade, all of whom would hold them accountable over the course of their term. So, bonus: broader civic engagement beyond Election Day.

Closer to home, you could encourage your city or county to use ProRep to elect the council, and your school board to use it to elect its members. You could point to Cambridge and Eastpointe, where voters have more choices on the ballot and more voice in their local governance. You could urge your state representatives to adopt it or band together with others to run a ballot initiative implementing a state version of the Fair Representation Act.

FairVote is pushing for the Fair Representation Act. The League of Women Voters, Equal Citizens, Campaign Legal Center, and Ignite could also help you get involved.

Discussion questions

☐ Do you feel your vote matters? If yes, what does that mean to you? If no, what would it mean for your vote to matter?

☐ Do you feel your state or federal legislators represent you? Do you affiliate with the same party as your representatives? If you do, how do you think you would feel if you lived in a district that always voted in the other party?

☐ Do you strongly affiliate as a Democrat or a Republican? Would you like the option to vote for a different kind of candidate?

☐ What do you think American politics might look and feel like with more parties? How might things be better? What concerns would you have?

☐ What do you think it looks like when lawmakers are doing their job well? How do you feel your local, state, and national representatives are doing?

☐ Do you think gerrymandering is a problem in your district or in your state? Do you think it is intentional or self-packing?

Summary: Break the Two-Party Stranglehold

- The United States uses democracy 1.0 — single-winner districts and plurality voting. This system leads to two-party domination, wasted votes, and unrepresentative legislatures made up of fierce partisans locked into a zero-sum game.

- Most advanced democracies use democracy 2.0 — proportional representation. The legislature reflects the voters, lawmakers work together to craft durable policy solutions, and all voters feel they matter.

- Gerrymandering is a feature of single-winner districts and can't be completely solved by independent commissions or algorithms. Proportional representation isn't vulnerable to gerrymandering because the results reflect the diversity of the voters no matter where the lines fall.

Chapter 9:
Level the Slanted Senate

It's time for U.S. senators to represent people, not states.

Michael's story

"I'm an American, and I've spent my life serving my country," says Michael Ada, a veteran of the Iraq and Afghanistan wars and a resident of Guam. "It's a family tradition. My dad, my brother, my sister, we are all proud to serve.

"But there's no one to stand up for us in Washington. We have no senators, no congressmen, we can't vote for president. And it shows — the Senate has cut funding for the VA here. My sister is sick and should be able to get Social Security income, but she can't because she lives here. We're Americans, we're patriots, but we get ignored because we don't have representation. If we could elect someone to go fight for us, to tell our stories, I think we wouldn't get treated like second-class citizens anymore."[421]

The most powerful undemocratic body in the world

The U.S. Senate is arguably the most powerful undemocratic public body in the world. It represents a minority of Americans but has the power to block policies supported by the majority. The Senate's slant matters profoundly for our country: our unusual Senate has contributed to the United States' shameful historical protections for slavery, our outsized inequality, and our singular refusal to sign on to international climate accords.

That's no accident.

Malapportioned from the start

The Senate was explicitly designed to be undemocratic. It does not represent people; it represents states. But some of those states are the size of cities, while others are the size of large countries. If the entire state of Wyoming were a city, for example, it wouldn't even make the list of America's top 25 largest cities. California, on the other hand, is home to more people than either Canada or Australia. Nevertheless, both Wyoming and California each get exactly two U.S. senators, meaning some American voters have 70 times more representation in the Senate than others simply based on their happening to live in a particular state. Even after the Supreme Court upheld the principle of "one person, one vote" in the early 1960s and struck down undemocratic state rules that gave rural voters disproportionate representation,[422] the principle could not touch the Senate, whose "one person, 70 votes" design is enshrined in the Constitution.

The skew isn't random, either. White Americans are overrepresented in the Senate, while Hispanics and Blacks are underrepresented.[423] Where white Americans have, on average, 3.5 senators per 10 million people, Black Americans have only 2.6 and Hispanics only 1.9.[424] That's right: Hispanic Americans have only about half as much representation in the Senate as white Americans. How can this be? States that are large and growing, like California, Texas, New York, and Florida, are racially and ethnically diverse, while many of the states that are staying small, like Wyoming, the Dakotas, Maine, and Vermont, are overwhelmingly white.[425] Of the ten smallest states, seven are also in the top ten whitest.[426]

And it matters. Wyoming residents, 89 percent of whom are white, receive federal expenditures 50 times higher per capita than their Californian compatriots, only 40 percent of whom are white.[427] Rutland County, Vermont, receives about $2,500 per person in federal largesse, while just across the way similarly sized Washington County, New York, receives just $600.[428] Vermont has about 600,000 people, 94 percent of whom are white, and two senators, while New York has more than 19 million people, 58 percent of them white, and two senators. It matters for policy, too. The Senate's slant toward smaller, whiter states skews its views on policies such as gun control, minimum wage, and immigration.[429]

The malapportionment is only getting worse, too. As some states continue to grow, American people get even more unequal representation in the Senate. Already today, more than half the U.S. population lives in just nine states.[430] Think about that: just 18 senators represent more than half the U.S. population, and fully 82 senators throw their weight around for the other (less than) half of us![431] The concentration is likely to worsen. In 20 years, six senators will represent nearly one-third of Americans.[432]

151

Let's look at the same pattern another way. If we consider the least populous states instead of the most populous, we see that the 26 smaller states are home to just 18 percent of the U.S. population. A minuscule 18 percent of Americans elect 52 of this country's senators, which is a majority of the Senate.[433]

The map in figure 9.1 below gives you a visual sense of the imbalance: each state is sized by its population. When looked at as a function of people, not acres, California and Texas dominate. One-fifth of Americans live in those two states alone, but those nearly 70 million people have just four senators. Many western and northeastern states all but disappear, but each one of those specks of population enjoys two senators. Put the ten smallest specks together and you still have fewer than 10 million people (less than live in the state of Michigan), but they have 20 senators.

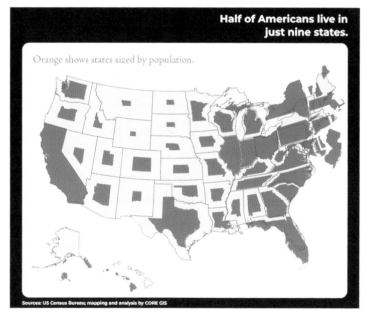

Figure 9.1: *States sized by population.*

As if this extreme imbalance weren't bad enough, the filibuster makes the Senate even more extremely undemocratic. Today, senators representing as few as 11 percent of Americans can block bills from passage.[434] In 20 years, that figure is projected to have shrunk to 9 percent.[435]

Although a few other advanced economies also have undemocratic upper houses, none is so malapportioned as the U.S. Senate's 70:1 skew. Only Switzerland and Canada are even in the same ballpark, with 40:1 and 21:1 respectively, while

Belgium and Austria have mild 2:1 and 1.5:1 skews.[436] In the world, only Argentina, Russia, and Brazil have more malapportioned legislatures than the United States, and those are hardly the bastions of democracy to which we should aspire.[437]

Uniquely powerful

No other advanced democracy hands as much power to an undemocratic and racially skewed upper house as we Americans do. In countries that have undemocratic upper houses, those houses are usually less powerful than the lower house: often they serve as a rubber stamp for the laws created by the lower "people's house,"[438] and in most they have no or only weak veto power.[439] The Senate, in contrast, has complete veto power and exerts near-total control over American lawmaking: when legislation passed by the Senate differs from that passed by the House, the Senate gets its way totally or partially 82 percent of the time.[440]

Not only that, but the Constitution itself gives the Senate complete power over treaties and veto power over all federal court nominations, including the Supreme Court. As partisan gridlock has brought the business of the legislature to a crawl, the judiciary has enlarged its role. And the Senate, conveniently, is also the gatekeeper to the judiciary. Where other countries either select fairly representative democratic bodies or neuter their unrepresentative bodies, the United States has a grossly unrepresentative body and gives it the keys to the kingdom.

The malapportioned Senate also leads to a malapportioned Electoral College, again allowing a party with minority support to exert power over not just the legislative and judicial branches but the executive, too. If smaller states skew toward one party (as they currently skew toward the Republican Party), then that party can dominate in both the Senate and the presidency, even if only a minority of voters support it.

Polarization breaks the checks

You probably learned in high school civics about the carefully designed system of "checks and balances" that keeps any branch from overstepping its bounds. Unfortunately, that system assumes that each branch wishes to keep the other branches in check. In the modern era, extreme two-party polarization means that party loyalty trumps branch loyalty, and the system of checks and balances falls apart. Rather than the presidency keeping the Senate in check, for instance, whichever party controls the Senate uses its power to keep the other party in check, even if that means bringing lawmaking to a halt or usurping another branch's power because it is controlled by the other party.

The U.S. Constitution gives the president the power to appoint justices to the Supreme Court with the "advice and consent" of the Senate. The president is supposed to have the power to choose justices, while the Senate is supposed to act as a check in case of bad behavior or poor judgment. In 2016, the Republican Party took the power of advice and consent to an extreme, using it to deny Democratic president Barack Obama — who won both the Electoral College and the popular vote *twice* — the power to appoint a Supreme Court justice, with nearly a quarter of his term in office still remaining. Even though Republican senators had won fewer votes and represented 20 million fewer Americans than Democratic senators, they turned this constitutional "check" into a partisan weapon.[441] Instead, the three newest members of the Supreme Court were nominated by a president who lost the popular vote and confirmed by a bloc of senators who represent less than half of Americans.[442]

The filibuster breaks the balance

Some apologists for the filibuster claim that it protects against majoritarian excesses. But one of its actual impacts seems to be that it empowers the other two branches. Think of political power like water flowing through a pipe. The founders created a fork where the pipe divides into three, with some power flowing through the legislative branch, some through the executive, and some through the judicial. No branch gets all the power. The filibuster is a clog in the legislative pipe, blocking all but the most uncontroversial policies from flowing through. That pipe gets backed up, overflowing into the other two available channels. Because Congress is paralyzed, presidents have gotten creative looking for ways to do things that rightfully should be in the province of the lawmaking branch. Courts have also gotten some of the diverted lawmaking power, further raising the stakes on Supreme Court nominations.

Slavery, inequality, climate inaction, and other "contemptible compromises"

The Senate's representative bias isn't a harmless oddity; it has enormous negative impacts on American life. In Federalist Paper No. 22,[443] Alexander Hamilton presciently anticipated that if a minority of voters were able to control a majority of votes, it would lead not only to "tedious delays; continual negotiation and intrigue" and "inaction" but to "*contemptible compromises of the public good.*"

How right he was. It starts, of course, with the contemptible compromise at the very root of the Union: slavery. Between 1800 and 1860 eight antislavery measures passed the House. All were killed in the Senate.[444] After the Civil War,

Southern senators continued to exert untoward influence on national policy, blocking federal laws passed by the House to protect the most basic human rights of African Americans.[445]

> **Between 1800 and 1860 eight antislavery measures passed the House**
>
> **All were killed in the Senate.**

The Senate's veto power is partially to blame for America's outsized inequality. **Veto points** are places in the lawmaking process where someone can block the law, preserving the status quo. Countries with more veto points tend to have higher inequality. The United States has the most veto points of 23 advanced democracies and the highest levels of social inequality as measured by the Gini index (a summary measure of income inequality) as well as the highest rates of poverty. Some 60 percent of children of single mothers in the United States live in poverty, compared with 10 percent or fewer in Germany, Sweden, Denmark, Finland, Belgium, and Luxembourg.[446] The Senate is not solely responsible, of course, but it does consistently block policies that the House passes, and that other advanced countries have enacted, to address poverty and inequality.

For example, in response to the financial crisis in 2009, the House passed financial reform and consumer protection bills that were then watered down to be able to pass in the Senate. The Senate also neutered health-care reform until it became ineffective and vulnerable to legal challenge. On climate change, the Senate has so far blocked passage of major legislation and ratification of international treaties, making the United States an outlier among Organisation for Economic Co-operation and Development (OECD) countries.[447] In 2009, the House passed a climate action bill. It died in the Senate. A majority of senators also oppose policies that most Americans would prefer concerning gun control and the minimum wage.[448]

In the overview of section I, I mentioned that in the 2013 decision *Shelby County v. Holder*,[449] the Supreme Court effectively disabled section 4 of the Voting Rights Act, instead charging Congress with devising a new formula to determine which jurisdictions require preclearance from the federal government before making changes that could disenfranchise voters of color. In 2019, the House answered the Court's call and passed a bill with a new formula for preclearance. It died in the Senate.

And in 2020, to address the economic devastation of the COVID-19 pandemic, the House passed a bill to extend aid to people who had lost employment, families at risk of eviction and food insecurity, and struggling local governments providing key services to their residents, among other things. It, too, died in the Senate.

This incomplete list of the ways in which the Senate blocks action that Americans want also shines a light on why many Americans are so disenchanted with the government. If you keep voting for candidates who promise certain policies, and they keep failing to deliver, you conclude that they are corrupt, disingenuous, or just ineffective. But what if it isn't them, but rather the system? The Senate is explicitly designed to frustrate voters' will.

Imagine what our country could be if we had one — just one! — truly representative lawmaking body. If the House could pass laws without the Senate's veto, we might have eradicated slavery sooner; we would be taking action on climate change; we would be protecting rather than impeding Americans' voting rights; and we might even have less poverty. The Senate was supposed to serve as a teacup where the hot ideas coming out of the people's House could go to cool. Instead, it serves as a drowning pit where the voices of more than half the American people go to die.

Any plausible rationale is now moot

Apologists for the undemocratic Senate put forth a few weak rationales, all of which depend on a premise of state primacy over collective national interest.

We're all Americans, now

At the time of America's founding, there was not yet a collective U.S. identity. Instead, people identified with their specific colony and saw the new country as simply a conglomeration of the colonies, now states. Grammatically, "United States" was used as a plural noun: people would say "the United States are beautiful." State legislators, not voters, selected U.S. senators because senators represented the states, not the voters.

But over time, Americans came to think of this country as unified. During and after the Civil War, Americans started using "United States" as a singular noun: it's one thing, like the pledge of allegiance says, "one nation." We now say "the United States is beautiful." We vote for our senators and expect them to represent us. Indeed, even state and local politics now seem to revolve around national politics rather than the other way around.[450] The Senate's role of representing states has faded. It now just overrepresents some voters and underrepresents others.

The Senate doesn't balance interests, but rather exacerbates divisions

During the 1787 convention, delegates were trying to balance the blocs of small states versus big states and to mediate between Southern slave states and Northern non-slave states. The compromises in the House (representation by population, but including enslaved people as three-fifths), the Senate (representation based on states, not people), and the Electoral College (importing the previous two compromises into the selection of the president) balanced the competing interests of small and big, North and South, to bring them together into one Union.

But now the Senate doesn't balance these interests; rather, it tilts the system toward the Republican Party. As the Democratic Party has come to dominate in urban areas and among more diverse voters, the Republican Party has increasingly been able to win a majority of senators representing a minority of more rural, more white voters.[451] Delaware need no longer fear (as it did in the country's early days) that Pennsylvania might invade, but Democratic voters there have seen how the dilution of their votes has blocked action on policies they desperately want and stacked the Supreme Court against them.[452] Rather than seeing a compromise that balances the score so they win some and lose some, diverse, urban, progressive voters are seeing the system is rigged only against them.

States are just as internally split as the country is

Imagine that some states pursued strong social safety nets, providing paid leave, health care, childcare, and wage protections. Other states pursued strong individual freedoms, allowing unfettered gun rights and laws to limit unions. Over time, these cohesive agendas would bear fruit. People could clearly see the pros and cons of the different approaches and perhaps migrate to the state that suited them best or else push their state in a direction that had proved to work better. The clearly differentiated states could serve as models demonstrating how different approaches worked in practice.

That's the dream of states as "laboratories of democracy"[453] — but it's just a dream. States are sprawling and diverse and just as internally divided between blue, urban voters and red, rural voters as is the country as a whole. Blue states attempt to pursue progressive agendas but are held back by their many conservative voters, while red-state legislators spend their time quashing the rules that blue cities within their borders try to pass for themselves.

For example, supposedly solid-blue Oregon has failed for a decade to take climate action that voters in the state's more urban parts are urgently demanding, because legislators from the rural parts of the state are just as adamantly blocking it. To the south, cities in reliably red Texas have adopted minimum wage increases, plastic bag bans, fracking bans, and transgender restroom protections, all in contradiction of their state legislature's agenda.[454] And farther east, North Carolina's Republican state legislators have prevented their state's cities from honoring their urban residents' policy priorities, like regulating fracking, destroying guns confiscated by the police, and passing local minimum wage and nondiscrimination laws.[455]

These sharp internal divisions exist in part because many states are just really big. In 1790, fewer than 4 million people lived in the entire United States.[456] Now, 27 states are each home to more than 4 million people. These aren't local laboratories so much as nations within a nation. Some local activists want to make states smaller and more cohesive. For instance, there is a movement in Illinois to let urban Cook County, where Chicago is located, be its own state and the more rural areas be a separate self-governing state.[457] Activists in other parts of the country have advocated for full secession from the United States of single states, like California or Texas, or groups of states, like Cascadia. These are long shots, though, or at least far-off possibilities. For now, taking a good hard look at the Senate and making high-impact changes there will serve more Americans sooner.

The most intractable problem in American democracy

The most elegant solution to all this would be to eliminate the Senate altogether. In fact, that's what former U.S. representative John Dingell, of Michigan, the longest-serving member of Congress ever, thought we should do.[458] The House is perfectly capable of formulating and passing legislation without a whole other group of legislators thwarting them, and in ridding ourselves of the Senate, we would join numerous other successful countries that have fewer veto points and so are able to get more done for their people. In this century, we desperately need our lawmakers to address complex threats such as climate change and economic inequality. But the odds of passing an amendment to strike the Senate from the Constitution are . . . well, low.

The second-best solution would be to make the Senate represent people, not states. But to do that, we'd have to get rid of the whole U.S. Constitution.[459] Not only is the Constitution the "most difficult to amend or update of any constitution currently existing in the world today,"[460] but even an amendment couldn't alter the Senate's basic undemocratic structure.[461] Here too, then, the outlook is dim.

This book, though, is about practical steps we can take right now to address problems with our democratic systems. That means we can't depend on long shots like abolishing or reforming the Senate by constitutional amendment. So while the ideas below can't remedy the Senate snafu, they can effect important changes to rein in the obscenely undemocratic Senate so that it better represents the American people and does its job of passing needed laws and confirming Supreme Court justices, rather than just blocking legislation from the House and blocking the initiatives of the president if he or she is from the other party. And those are priorities most Americans should readily embrace.

The first reform: Bust the filibuster

Our veto-heavy federal system can be likened to a fussy old car that requires many steps before it will run. You need to not only do the regular things like turn the ignition and put your foot on the gas but also turn the windshield wipers on and roll down the passenger-side window to get all the circuits to connect. It's plenty hard to enact policy. The filibuster is the equivalent of always having the emergency brake on. Now it's nearly impossible to go.

Yet defending the filibuster is one thing that Democrats and Republicans can agree on these days. The hyperpartisan environment makes both sides terrified of what could happen if the other side were able to pass laws.[462] They'd rather keep the emergency brake on than risk the car going in the wrong direction. But is it really true that the risks stemming from the U.S. Congress passing laws are greater than the risks from Congress being frozen?

We face myriad, urgent challenges. Climate change. Inequality. Global pandemics. Child poverty. In each of these cases, and others, *inaction is not safe.* Inaction is not neutral; it is a choice to stay the course. And in each of these cases, staying the course would be disastrous. Sure, poorly thought-out or wrongheaded policies can be disastrous too, and the filibuster may have blocked some of those. But its clearest legacy is of blocking civil rights. A recent report concludes:

> From the late 1920s through the 1960s, the filibuster was primarily used
> by Southern senators to block legislation that would have protected civil
> rights — anti-lynching bills; bills prohibiting poll taxes; and bills prohibiting
> discrimination in employment, housing, and voting. . . .

> Some of the most notorious filibusters in American history were against
> the Civil Rights Acts of 1957 and 1964. During the filibuster of the 1957
> Civil Rights Act, then-Democratic Sen. Strom Thurmond set a record by
> holding the Senate floor continually for 24 hours and 18 minutes. Seven

years later, the ultimately unsuccessful effort to obstruct the Civil Rights Act of 1964 lasted a total of 74 days and received major ongoing news coverage — ultimately helping to galvanize the public and break through the Southern opposition to civil rights.[463]

In his eulogy for civil rights leader and Representative John Lewis in 2020, President Barack Obama called for passage of many of the solutions in this book, including Automatic Voter Registration (chapter 1), expanded Vote By Mail (chapter 3), and statehood for DC and Puerto Rico (this chapter). But, he noted, to pass any of these, senators first need to eliminate the filibuster.[464]

The second reform: Right-size the states

The only way to make the Senate even faintly resemble a democratically representative body within the constraints of the Constitution would be to reduce the dramatic difference between state populations. Article IV, section 3, of the Constitution allows us to add new states, divide existing states, or join two or more states or parts thereof into a new state as long as Congress and the state legislatures agree.[465] This gives Congress and the states three options.

1. Adding new states, is the most straightforward, time-tested, and ready to roll.

2. Breaking up big states, has happened before, but not on the scale needed to level the Senate.[466]

3. Combining small states, is unprecedented. A "great redraw" of all states' boundaries and sizes has never occurred before in the United States, and it is hard to envision small states giving up their advantage in the Senate. But if even more Americans grew frustrated, perhaps there would come a day when our leaders agreed to a collective redistricting to make states better unified in their political makeup.

These all sound pretty far-fetched, I know. But unlike other far-fetched ideas, such as abolishing the Senate, these reforms do not require a constitutional amendment. They require building the right alignment of political movements and a series of ordinary majority votes in state legislatures, the House, and the Senate. It would surely be a long and perhaps tortuous path, but it's plausible.

Right-size option 1: Add new states

Nearly two and a half centuries after American revolutionaries fought for representation, more than 4 million Americans don't have any representation in the Senate. These American citizens live in DC, Puerto Rico, Guam, the U.S. Virgin Islands, and the Commonwealth of the Northern Mariana Islands (CNMI).[467] Adding those territories as new small states would be fair to those Americans. It would also help ease the Senate's racial bias because most Americans in the new states would be people of color, balancing out the disproportionate representation that existing small states give to white Americans.

Washington, DC

Even Strom Thurmond, the famously conservative U.S. senator from South Carolina, recognized the problem, saying, "The residents of the District of Columbia deserve the right to [full] representation in Congress if for no other reason than simple fairness."[468] With more than 700,000 people, DC is home to more Americans than Wyoming and Vermont and not much smaller than Alaska and North Dakota. DC has been advocating for statehood for decades, and in 2020 the U.S. House finally passed a bill (along party lines, with Republicans opposed) to make it a state.[469] But nearly half of DC residents are Black, and the Republican-controlled Senate scoffs at the idea of adding a deeply blue, majority African American state, so it has refused to take up the issue.

> **The residents of the District of Columbia deserve the right to (full) representation in Congress if for no other reason than simple fairness.**
>
> **– Former South Carolina Senator Strom Thurmond**

Puerto Rico

Farther south, with more than 3 million people, Puerto Rico would be a middling-size state, bigger than 20 existing states, and nearly all Hispanic. People there, too, desire statehood: in a 2017 referendum, a whopping 97 percent of voters there supported being recognized as a state.[470] Unfortunately, that was a nonbinding referendum in a low-turnout election due to Hurricane Maria, so lawmakers have put the statehood question on the ballot again in November 2020. If Puertorriqueños say yes, their governor will appoint a commission to negotiate for statehood and develop a transition plan.

Guam, the CNMI, and the U.S. Virgin Islands

Guam, the CNMI, and the U.S. Virgin Islands are also full of American citizens with no representation in American government, many of whom serve in the U.S. military. Congress has found that, on a per capita basis, residents of these territories have died at higher rates in U.S. wars and conflicts since World War I. Most residents are people of color. In Guam and the CNMI, they are mostly Asian American and Pacific Islander, and in the U.S. Virgin Islands, they are mostly Black. They would be tiny states, with fewer than 200,000 residents each, and it's unclear whether their people would ultimately choose statehood, but Congress could offer it.

A history of adding new states

Some might consider adding new states to be a power grab by the Democratic Party. But it's an American tradition the Republican Party has happily exercised when it has been in charge. In 1864 the party of Lincoln added Nevada to the Union, adding three antislavery votes to the Electoral College just days before the presidential election. In 1889 and 1890, Republicans added a whopping six new small Republican-leaning states. They broke the Dakota Territory into North and South Dakota to maximize the number of small states, and they bypassed normal procedures to add Wyoming and Idaho, each of which had fewer people than a single district in Massachusetts.[471] (Notably, those four states are still some of the smallest, whitest, and most reliably red, giving Republicans more power in the Senate to this day.) On the other hand, although New Mexico had been clamoring for statehood for some time and had a much larger — and more Hispanic — population than any of these new Republican states, it leaned Democratic, so Republicans successfully kept it out of the Union for several more decades, until 1912.[472] In fact, New Mexico was the fourth-to-last recognized state. Only Arizona, Alaska, and Hawaii were added later.

During bipartisan eras, the parties sometimes agreed to add states in pairs, with one state adding to the power of one party and the other state weighing in for the other. In 1812 Maine, previously a part of Massachusetts, entered as a free state together with Missouri as a slave state.[473] The most recent states to join the Union followed the same paired pattern: Alaska and Hawaii entered as a blue-and-red pair in 1959.[474] (Interestingly, they have since reversed their colors.)

Adding small states would slightly improve the undemocratic nature of the Senate, inching the needle toward fairer representation for Americans of color.[475] But to make it a body that represents a majority of Americans, we would also need to break up the biggest states and combine the smallest states, so all states have populations that are at least in the same range.

Right-size option 2: Break up the biggest states

The problem at the heart of the Senate is that it gives equal representation to every state, regardless of how many people live there. As some states continue to attract more residents while others remain stable or even shrink, the Senate skews even further toward ignoring the voices of the hundreds of millions of Americans living in larger states. Breaking up big states could help remedy that.

One way to do this would be for Congress to pass an act giving blanket permission for any state with more than 13 times the population of the smallest state (the original ratio between the largest and smallest colonies) to break into smaller states as long as no resulting state is any smaller than the smallest state (which is currently Wyoming, population about 580,000). It could extend the blanket permission into the future too, saying that anytime a state grew larger than 13 times the population of the smallest state, it could subdivide.[476] Thirteen times the population of Wyoming is 7.5 million, a figure that in 2020 would comfortably accommodate more than three new states in a subdivided Texas[477] and more than five in California.[478]

Imagine if in the 13 largest states, each with more than 7.5 million people,[479] state legislators agreed to take this opportunity to create smaller, more internally cohesive states. The map in figure 9.2 below posits one way of doing this so that there are 95 continental states, each with no fewer than 570,000 and no more than 7.3 million people. Based on party votes in the 2016 presidential election and using a cutoff of 54 percent to make that state safe for one party's candidates, this particular map leads to a country with 35 safe red states, 28 safe blue, and 33 purple. More Americans would have a senator they believed in, and half the senators would represent about half the American population.

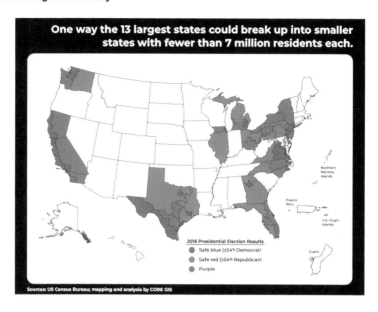

Figure 9.2: *One way the 13 largest states could subdivide.*

What's more, this is just within a two-party system! If we implemented proportional representation for the House (see chapter 8) or expanded the Senate and used proportional representation (see the section in this chapter, below, fleshing this idea out a bit more), that would free us from this limited red-blue-purple vision of ourselves. States would not be one color but many, and more Americans would feel represented in their halls of government.

Right-size option 3: Combine the smallest states

Congress could also give blanket permission for any state with less than 1 percent of the national population to join an adjacent state or part thereof. Right now, that would apply to the 21 states that are each home to fewer than 3.3 million residents.[480] Several of them sit side by side, creating an opportunity to join together into a single, less tiny state.

For example, Maine, New Hampshire, and Vermont together would make one state with 3.3 million people — still a small state. Idaho, Montana, and Wyoming together would make a state of 3.4 million people. North and South Dakota (which were originally one territory but split in 1889 so the Republicans could gain more senators) plus Nebraska would still have fewer than 3.6 million. Even these combined figures are minuscule in comparison to America's largest states' populations, but they do go some way toward addressing the wild imbalance currently in play.

Right-size option 4: Follow Americans' own "Big Sort" to guide a "Great Redraw"

If we really want to dream, we can imagine that Congress grants all states the opportunity to participate in a collective redrawing of boundaries to better align with tighter communities of interest, a sort of "Great Redraw." Any state that wished to participate would opt in by the next national census, at which time an independent redistricting commission would take into account history, culture, and communities of interest to draw state lines that made more sense to the people living there and that resulted in more equally sized states, say, all within a range of 1 to 5 million people.

For example, the current Oregon-Idaho border is a random historical accident, and many residents of eastern Oregon are already eager to join Idaho,[481] which matches them in geography, economy, and culture much better than coastal Oregon. And Congress could even give permission for historically disadvantaged groups, such as the Navajo Nation, to be their own state.[482] States resulting from this process would have more unified sets of values and policy priorities, and their residents would then feel better represented by their leadership.

The payoffs: A more functional legislative branch, more laboratories of democracy, and greater legitimacy

These four options for right-sizing our states, plus abolishing the filibuster, may sound ambitious, but the severity of the Senate's skew and the urgency of our country's challenges demand bold thinking. As long as we stick with our 1787 Constitution, we are stuck with an unusually undemocratic and powerful Senate. But eliminating the filibuster would at least allow Congress to creak into gear and pass some laws. As the legislative branch starts working again, it could restore a sense of legitimacy to the federal government as voters start to see some of the agendas they voted for actually getting implemented. It could also relieve some of the pressure for the executive and judicial branches to enlarge their roles, again enhancing feelings of legitimacy that the branches are better balanced and each playing their own roles.

Adding DC and Puerto Rico, and possibly Guam, the U.S. Virgin Islands, and the CNMI, would add some relief that, at long last, all American citizens had achieved the goal of no taxation without representation. And it would bring the Senate slightly more in step with the diversifying populace.

The greater benefits, though, would come from the harder-to-achieve goal of right-sizing the states. If states were within a closer size range than the current 70:1, a majority of senators would come closer to representing a majority of voters. These senators would look and act more like their counterparts in the House and might be more responsive to the needs of voters, passing into law the sorts of policies that the House is willing to pass, such as climate action, economic aid to those hit hardest by the coronavirus pandemic, and voting rights protections for all Americans.

More cohesive states resulting from a Great Redraw would experience less deadlock in their state legislatures, and we might see more clearly how different agendas play out over time — a return to the "states as laboratories" concept. And redrawn state lines could lead to other innovations, such as interstate compacts to share regulatory infrastructure among smaller states, offer universal health care to state residents, limit climate pollution and invest in equitable green jobs, or provide universal preschool. More rural states would not have to offer their residents any of these benefits and could keep their taxes low.

Feeling better represented and effective at the state level might also help restore Americans' faith in government and belief in the legitimacy of our democracy. Legitimacy is the feeling that the authority being wielded over us is being exercised fairly and justly, and it's a critical ingredient in any healthy system of government. A sense of legitimacy at the state level could filter up to apply to the federal level, too, and not just in a general sense. Seeing better representation in practice could help some people shed the myth they've internalized that the undemocratic Senate, and by extension the Electoral College, are essential to protect the rights of people in small states. If they experienced how a nation with more and smaller states better honors the will of the people — all people, more equally — and squared that with the belief most Americans hold in majority rule, which the Senate does not uphold, then their satisfaction with the federal level of government would also improve.

Can you imagine? Faith in the federal government, restored? (Or at least improving?) I know: it seems like a long way off from where we now sit, but I'm an optimist, and so are many Americans. And anyway, if Americans who live in Wyoming have the right to live in a state with fewer than a million people and two senators, why shouldn't all Americans?

Make it happen: End the filibuster and add new states

The first step is to turn off the emergency brake of the filibuster. A majority of senators can do this.[483] The Senate will still be undemocratic, but at least it won't be stuck. If you want to get involved, you can contact the organizations Fix Our Senate or Indivisible.

The second step is to give representation to Americans living in DC. Its leadership and the House have already agreed; they just need the Senate to pass the bill and the president to sign it, and it's done. If you want to see that happen, get in touch with the organization 51 for 51.

Next up, Puerto Rico. If Puertorriqueños say yes to statehood in November 2020, it would just be up to Congress to honor those Americans' clearly voiced opinion. Congress could also extend an invitation for statehood to Guam, the U.S. Virgin Islands, and the CNMI, and if those legislators voted for statehood, they would have it. Each of these additions would be a small step toward alleviating the Senate's racial bias.

But then comes the truly hard work: reimagining the states so that the Senate more proportionally represents the people. This will require a huge new political movement and the working out of some details to incentivize each state to participate. For example, states could form interstate compacts so that bigger states can retain their central governing infrastructure while smaller states can gain from their larger neighbors' more developed infrastructure. Or big blue states might agree to divide first, knowing that seeing many new progressive senators added to Congress could push big red states to divide as well.

Discussion questions

☐ Do you think the founders made the right decision when they gave all the states equal representation in the Senate?

☐ Do you think states or people should have equal representation in the Senate now? Why?

☐ Do you think of yourself first as an American or as a resident of your state?

☐ Do you think your state is as divided as the country, or is it a more cohesive community?

☐ If all states were redrawn to be more similar in size, do you think your area would be part of a bigger or smaller state than it is now?

☐ If you live in a big state, what do you see as the pros and cons of your state dividing into smaller states?

☐ If you live in a small state, do you think it is fair for your state to have the same number of senators as larger states? How do you feel about big states getting smaller? How would you feel about combining with a nearby small state?

Summary: Level the Slanted Senate

- The colonies saw themselves as semi-sovereign nations, and the smaller ones demanded equal representation in the Senate, regardless of population.

- Over time, as some states have grown, the undemocratic malapportionment of the Senate has worsened. By midcentury, half of Americans will live in just eight states, meaning the majority of voters will have only 16 percent of the representation in the Senate.

- The Senate is unusually powerful; it has complete veto power over legislation, treaty-making powers, and final say on federal court appointments, including the Supreme Court. And it contributes to the undemocratic nature of the Electoral College, which picks the president.

- The Senate matters a lot. If the House were able to pass laws without opposition from the Senate, the United States would have made faster progress on issues such as outlawing slavery, and at least some progress on issues like taking action against climate change and reducing wealth inequality.

- To make the Senate represent voters rather than states, we would need to ditch the Constitution.

- But within the mandates of the Constitution, Congress and state legislatures could lessen the imbalance by adding new states, breaking up the biggest states, and combining the smallest states. Or they could redraw the whole map to make more cohesive, more similarly sized states.

- Smaller, more cohesive states would also better enact the principles of local rule and local experimentation, in turn hopefully restoring Americans' sense of their government's legitimacy.

IV. BEYOND DEMOCRACY

ASK NOT WHAT YOUR COUNTRY CAN DO FOR YOU ... BUT WHAT YOU, SERVING ON CITIZENS' ASSEMBLIES, CAN DO FOR AMERICA'S THORNIEST POLICY ISSUES.

Chapter 10:
Citizens' Assemblies

Maggie's story

One day, Maggie McDonald, a retiree in Dublin, Ireland, received a letter inviting her to take part in Ireland's Citizens' Assembly. Over the course of six months, she met with other people from all over Ireland and all walks of life to listen to experts, read comments, and discuss in depth the topic of that country's constitutional ban on abortions.

"Going in, I didn't really know all that much about it," she said. "But after it all, I felt empowered and informed. It gave me the language and skills to have difficult discussions." She and her fellow citizens diligently dug into the complexities of the fraught topic and the need to engage and learn about all viewpoints.

"We were proud to have been given an important task, so we took the learning seriously and tried to find things to agree on and to discover common ground. I learned about points of view I hadn't considered before. Together, we made solid recommendations that reflected many different views."[484]

Whose house?

In a nation of more than 300 million busy people, it is impossible to get everyone together in a room to have a say. That's why we have a representative democracy: a smaller number of people representing all of us gather in a room to talk with each other and hash things out. James Madison wrote, in Federalist Paper No. 10, that representative democracies should "refine and enlarge the public views, by passing them through the medium of a chosen body of citizens, whose wisdom may best discern the true interest of their country."[485]

171

In other words, representative democracies select a group of citizens and ask them to apply their wisdom to come up with policies that are in the best interests of the country as a whole. But how to select a wise group of citizens? Elections are one method. But they aren't the only way, and indeed the group that they do select could still benefit from some complementary processes that bring complex policy issues closer to the people.

Voters often can't identify with their elected officials

Every solution in this book so far has assumed we need to use elections to choose representatives. To be sure, the work of directing this country's far-reaching policies is and should be many people's full-time job, so it is crucial that we make our elections work better. But elections select only people who feel equipped and entitled to run. Often, these people don't have life experiences that are similar to those they represent. Elected officials at every level of government in the United States are more white and more male than Americans as a whole (see chapter 8).

In addition, the process of running for office itself shapes candidates. The rigors of raising money (see chapter 5) and the pressures of partisan politics (see chapter 8) guide who is elected and what they do once in office. As one example, the typical American household has a net worth just below $100,000,[486] but their congressional delegates look nothing like them. One-third of the members of the U.S. Congress have a net worth over $1 million.[487] This financial gap exists at the state level, too, and it could be part of why President Donald Trump's call to "drain the swamp" resonated with so many voters in 2016. They felt the politicians in DC didn't really reflect them.

In some states, voters try to prevent elected officials from becoming rich by paying them nothing or only a pittance. Forty-three states pay their legislators[488] less than the median American income.[489] Oh, the irony! Who can afford to take a job that doesn't pay much? People who already have money. By withholding fair pay from their representatives in an attempt to keep them humble, these states are actually *requiring* would-be representatives to have some other source of income, such as a trust fund or a business that makes money whether or not they work at it. Such a system excludes anyone who needs to work for a living.

Elected officials themselves don't have time to dig into complex issues

This book so far has also assumed that elected representatives can get in a room together, talk about the issues of the day, and come up with informed and sensible solutions. But the reality is that the work of legislating (and fundraising to continue to legislate — again, see chapter 5) means many elected lawmakers don't have time to be as informed as they might like to be about every bill they vote on.[490]

In the meantime, special interests that would be affected by the proposed law or regulation have huge amounts of resources to throw at the lawmaking process through lobbyists and other means. Our elected officials often end up relying on lobbyists to guide their decisions about bills, especially those that are extremely important to the affected private companies but less so, or less immediately so, to the busy public.[491] Indeed, lobbyists often write the laws themselves and hand the text to elected officials to enact. And while voters hope their representatives are engaging with their colleagues to fully understand the issues and come up with solutions that work for everyone, partisan politics can mean that officials merely parrot the party line rather than really listen and deliberate on issues.

 ## This reform: Citizens' assemblies

If we are trying to get a small number of people who represent the rest of us into a room together to discuss policy, then elections are not the only option, or necessarily always the best option. Fortunately, there is another way to select representatives in a representative democracy. We can use a curated lottery to ensure that those selected truly reflect all the people they are representing.

Aristotle argued that elections are not the best way to run a democracy. He believed that elections create oligarchies, with wealthy elites finding ways to dominate elections and elected bodies. He thought the only way to maintain a true democracy was to select lawmakers by lottery.[492] Indeed, that's how democracy worked in ancient Athens. American juries also use a lottery. More recently, jurisdictions in the United States and around the world have improved upon the lottery model with **citizens' assemblies.**

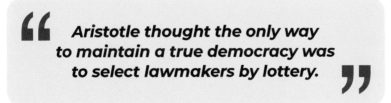

> **Aristotle thought the only way to maintain a true democracy was to select lawmakers by lottery.**

First, instead of running elections to select the small group of representatives, we can select a random sample of representative citizens through a curated lottery. Because it doesn't involve elections, this selection method would immediately render moot all the other problems and solutions in this book because they all revolve around elections. Rules to ensure that everyone can vote in elections, that big money doesn't dominate elections, and that election methods make every vote matter aren't necessary if representatives are selected randomly. To be sure, there are similar concerns around making sure the selection method works as promised, but if it does, then the group of representatives will bring the voices and perspectives of all kinds of Americans into the room.

Second, to ensure that a truly random sample of people are able to participate and not just those who can afford to engage, we can pay them for their time and travel.

Third, we can put these citizens in a room together with the time and resources to really deliberate on a particular issue. We can give them a chance to question leading experts on the topic, hear partisan perspectives, and engage with their fellow citizens in facilitated small- and large-group discussions to understand other people's views and experiences. Through intense engagement on one issue over time, regular citizens can come to understand the nuances better than politicians who have only minutes to spend on each topic, and may feel pressured to conform to their party or please their donors.

This method holds the promise of true representative democracy: a small group of people who are like the rest of us and who can talk with each other and come up with solutions.

How does random selection work?

Many representative democracies throughout history have used **sortition** to ensure that representatives are just like the people they represent. Sortition simply means to choose by random sample, like a lottery.[493] Modern citizens' assemblies curate the lottery to ensure the random sample is in fact a microcosm of the people. This is more representative than a group of self-selected politicians. It's also better than the supposedly random process that populates juries presiding over criminal trials in U.S. courts, which also suffers from some selection biases and so rarely gathers a truly random sample of the defendants' peers.

The curation works like this: say a committee is selecting a 20-member citizens' assembly for a city. It first gathers data on the population of the city: the number of people of different ages, race or ethnicity, income and education levels, and where residents live geographically. It then sends out invitations to a random sampling of residents. Of the people who respond to the invitation, a computer program evaluates them and selects 20 who, together, closely reflect the full diversity of the city in terms of their age, race, income, and location.

Because these ordinary people's participation is limited to a particular instance, they are relatively immune to outside influence.[494] They are not worried about reelection or about securing a lucrative job with a lobbying firm after serving their term. They don't have to take into consideration the views of donors, lobbyists, or political parties in the way that elected politicians do. They just get to be particularly engaged and informed citizens for a few days.

 Case study: *Oregon Citizens' Initiative Review*

The Oregon Citizens' Initiative Review periodically brings together people from across the state of Oregon to study a controversial ballot measure and advise fellow citizens how to vote. Their summary and recommendations are then included in the official voters' pamphlet mailed to all the state's voters prior to an election.

An oversight committee sends invitations to a random sample of 10,000 registered voters in Oregon and uses an algorithm to select 24 representatives who are an accurate cross-section of the state's demographics in terms of age, race, gender, geography, educational attainment, political party affiliation, and voting frequency.[495] To ensure that people can participate no matter their income, distance, or family situation, participants are paid a stipend equal to the average daily wage in Oregon and reimbursed for transportation and childcare or elder care as needed. These measures remove as many barriers as possible to participation so that members can assemble together to learn about and address a single issue and then return to their regular lives.

Participants in the Oregon Citizens' Initiative Review find it empowering, rigorous, and fair.[496] Oregon voters consistently find the review's description of the ballot measures in their voter pamphlet to be informative and helpful.[497] In 2010, the review helped reveal possible unintended consequences of a ballot measure to increase punishment for certain crimes.[498]

What could citizens' assemblies do?

Citizens' assemblies could play an important role in solving some of the most challenging problems we face. Specifically, we could use citizens' assemblies for the following endeavors.

Agenda-setting

Citizens' assemblies could consider possible topics for elected lawmakers to address and help prioritize them — a sort of "agenda council" to tell the elected body which issues to take up this year.[499] For example, in 2017 Mongolia's elected legislature identified 18 possible constitutional amendments for the 3-million-person country landlocked between China and Russia. A citizens' assembly of 669 randomly selected citizens then spent three days studying the 18 proposals and hearing arguments for and against each one. The assembly rated the proposals, giving elected lawmakers an idea of which would garner the most support from an informed random sample of their citizens. Interestingly, nine of the ten proposals the assembly rated most highly were directed at protecting the civil service and judiciary from political interference or corruption. The two proposals that lost the most support over the three days of deliberation were the most partisan ones.[500]

Another example of agenda-setting could be city charter review commissions. Many charter cities[501] ask a political body to review the charter every decade and propose changes. The city council could ask a citizens' assembly to first compile and prioritize a list of topics for the charter review commission to consider amending.

A citizens' assembly could also gather before each state legislative session to help ensure the elected body takes up the issues of the greatest importance to the public that year. It would deliberate over a list of possible issues and rank them in order of urgency for state lawmakers to address. An assembly could also filter ballot proposals to make sure the most important ones reach the ballot.[502]

Policy-making

If the elected legislature becomes gridlocked on an issue, or if it feels unable to broach a topic that is important but politically fraught, it could refer that topic to a citizens' assembly to address. For example, some state legislatures might be relieved to pass off the problem of public pensions to a citizens' assembly. The U.S. Congress might be happy to let a citizens' assembly try its hand at shaping a health-care bill.

This model could work well not just for legislature-referred issues but also for voter-referred ones. Each election cycle, a city, state, or country could allow voters to pick an important issue they feel their lawmakers have failed to address and send it to a citizens' assembly. For example, Americans might want a citizens' assembly to find a sensible way to act on climate change; in fact, the UK has just such an assembly currently underway.[503]

When voters see that a group of their fellow citizens, talking with experts and with one another, are able to cut the Gordian knot, they might demand more opportunities for citizens' assemblies to address persistent policy problems.

Policy alternatives

Twenty-seven states give their residents the opportunity to vote on laws directly through tools like a **citizens' initiative**. Advocates in these states can gather signatures to put a proposed law on the ballot, or the legislature can refer a law to the ballot for voters' approval. In theory, this adds a direct democracy backstop for those instances when a representative democracy fails on a given issue. For example, if state legislators fail to pass a law to rein in soaring public pension costs, voters could step in with a solution at the ballot. In practice, though, it is expensive to run a citizens' initiative campaign and relatively easy to defeat one. Say the initiative is for more apple pie, a presumably popular mandate. Opponents can run TV ads saying, "I'm all for apple pie, but unfortunately *this particular proposal* is poorly written and fatally flawed." Sow enough seeds of doubt, and voters will vote no rather than risk a poorly thought-out law. And sometimes those criticisms are valid. Someone, or a few someones, might have dashed off the legal language without consulting other interest groups or considering unintended consequences — for instance, they might have written an initiative creating a new tax to fund public education, but because they knew more about education than about taxes, they missed key negative implications of their tax design. The initiative could fail, and schools would still need money.

Citizens' assemblies could beef up this citizens' initiative process, though. If an initiative on an important topic qualifies for the ballot, the state legislature could convene a citizens' assembly to consider the issues and put the citizens' proposal, the ballot proposal, and the current law on the ballot as alternatives. Possibly, the legislature might want to put their own alternative on the ballot, too. Voters would then see three or four possibilities and could rank the options in order of preference, with instant-runoff processing eliminating less popular options. The first proposal to pass 50 percent approval would become the law (or stay the law, if voters chose the status quo).

All this is to say that if voters wanted action on an issue, they would have several proposals to choose from instead of just one. If voters liked the current law, or at least liked it better than any of the proposed alternatives, they would need to affirmatively select it — likely in the process learning more about what that current law was. In this way, important issues couldn't get swept under the rug just because the initiative language was lacking, and voters would see an option crafted by ordinary but well-informed and deliberative fellow citizens. This would require states to allow ranked choice voting for ballot initiatives, and to provide a mechanism for convening a citizens' assembly and putting its proposal on the ballot.

Rules and oversight

It's best not to put the fox in charge of the henhouse, or elected officials in charge of the rules by which they can win elections or enjoy cushy gifts from lobbyists. Reviewing, updating, or reforming rules governing elections, lobbying, and compensation for officials could be a good fit for an impartial citizens' assembly. For example, a citizens' assembly convened in November 2019 to consider whether the volunteer stipend paid to city councilors in Milwaukie, Oregon, should be increased.[504] For obvious reasons, the public may not have trusted the councilors to vote impartially on a raise for themselves, but the considered opinion of fellow citizens who will not benefit from an increase in pay? Sure. After several days of deliberation, the group of citizens recommended a modest increase to the stipend.

Apart from rules governing elected officials, especially in a local context, giving a group of regular people some say in a discrete aspect of an agency could improve that agency's responsiveness to the community it's supposed to serve. For example, a citizens' assembly might consider the question of police brutality in a community with a history of problematic relations between police and citizens. Or it might consider the question of opening up public lands to drilling or forestry. This kind of engagement could more thoughtfully inform the debate and the ultimate decision on the issue.

 # Case study: Ireland

In 2016, Ireland's parliament established a citizens' assembly to deliberate on a number of gridlocked issues, including abortion. The effort was modeled after a successful Irish constitutional convention that met between 2012 and 2014 to consider eight constitutional topics, including marriage equality. That convention led to a 2015 national referendum that garnered a strong win for marriage equality, with 62 percent voting in favor.[505]

The 2016 assembly consisted of 99 ordinary citizens randomly selected so as to represent Ireland in terms of age, gender, social class, and geography. Members met five times over the course of six months in 2016 and 2017, hearing from 25 experts and reviewing submissions from members of the public and interest groups.[506] By the end of the deliberations, an overwhelming 87 percent of assembly members agreed that the constitutional provision outlawing abortion should be amended or replaced.[507] This was a surprising conclusion in the heavily Catholic country. The assembly's findings were published in a report at the end of 2017 and debated in parliament in 2018. Eventually nearly three-quarters of the Irish people had heard about the assembly.[508] Later in 2018, Ireland held a referendum, and fully 67 percent of the Irish public voted to repeal the constitutional abortion ban.[509]

Case study: America in One Room

In September 2019, as part of a project called America in One Room, 523 Americans from around the country gathered in Dallas, Texas, to discuss some of the most pressing issues of the day: immigration, health care, the economy, the environment, and foreign policy.[510] This was not a citizens' assembly but rather a "deliberative poll," which bears some similarities to an assembly. The poll did not give citizens a specific agenda-setting or law-writing task, but asked them simply to discuss general topics among themselves.

The results of the gathering showed what can happen when random citizens gather in person and discuss complex issues. The opportunity to learn more about the issues, including hearing from experts and fellow participants, caused many to change their partisan views. For example, deliberation brought about the following shifts: Republican participants dropped from 66 to 34 percent support for "reducing the number of refugees allowed to resettle in the U.S.," while Democratic participants dropped from 54 to 39 percent support for "increasing the federal minimum wage to 15 dollars an hour."[511] This indicates that giving regular people the chance to truly deliberate can "refine and enlarge" public views, just as James Madison hoped.

The payoffs: Greater trust in decision-making, more civic engagement, and less gridlock

More young people are growing sour on democracy. In a recent poll, one-third of young Americans said that non-democracies may be preferable to democracies.[512] Citizens' assemblies could help restore faith that lawmakers are responding to the wishes of ordinary people over special interests. If the "lawmakers" are randomly selected regular people who can completely focus on the issue at hand, rather than politicians who must constantly balance between fundraising and campaigning on the one hand and policy-making on the other, they can more fully and earnestly engage with each other. Arming regular people with the resources to deliberate over weighty issues, as well as the power to influence policy agendas and laws, could restore faith that democracy can be of the people and work for the people.

By offering ordinary Americans the chance to engage in agenda-setting and law-writing, citizens' assemblies could enhance people's civic engagement and pride in their democracy. And once people have the opportunity to engage in a citizens' assembly, they are often more likely to want to participate in other civic opportunities, too.

Citizens' assemblies could also break partisan gridlock. If politicians became too entrenched on an important topic to be able to agree on a law, they could hand it off to a citizens' assembly unencumbered by partisan baggage and campaign pressures. Seeing citizens' assemblies thoughtfully engage and come up with compromises might also make voters less tolerant of posturing and stonewalling by their elected officials.

> **Citizens' assemblies could also break partisan gridlock. If politicians became too entrenched on an important topic to be able to agree on a law, they could hand it off to a group of regular people, unencumbered by partisan baggage and campaign pressures.**

 ## Make it happen: Put a citizens' assembly to work in your city

Of all the solutions in this book, citizens' assemblies are admittedly the least tested. They are also the most *testable* — that is, their potential applications are numerous across local, state, and national levels of government. If you live in a **charter city**, you could encourage the municipal government to use a citizens' assembly to review its city charter and recommend updates or improvements. Zooming out to the state level, you could urge your state legislature to use a citizens' assembly to prioritize issue areas, as described under "agenda-setting" above. Or you could encourage your state representatives to pass a law requiring a citizens' assembly to formulate alternatives to high-profile ballot measures, as described under "policy alternatives" above. Zooming out further (and further escalating the impact), you could urge the U.S. Congress to use a citizens' assembly to tackle a sticky policy issue on which Congress is gridlocked. If you are a member of a political party, you could encourage party leadership to use assemblies made up of people registered with that party to help formulate or hone its policy platforms.

You could reach out to Healthy Democracy,[513] the Jefferson Center,[514] Policy Jury Group, or Extinction Rebellion[515] to find out more about how to engage.

 ## Discussion questions

☐ Would you trust a citizens' assembly to pick priority issues for elected legislators to address? Why or why not?

☐ Would you trust a citizens' assembly to craft a new law? Why or why not?

☐ Would you like to serve on a citizens' assembly? Why or why not?

☐ What sort of information would you like to see about how a citizens' assembly works that would help you understand and trust its process and results?

☐ Is there a policy issue that your local, state, or federal government has failed to address that an *agenda-setting* citizens' assembly could take on?

☐ Is there a policy issue that your local, state, or federal government has been gridlocked on that a *law-writing* citizens' assembly might be able to address?

Summary: Citizens' Assemblies

- Of all the solutions in this book, Americans have the least experience using citizens' assemblies for decision-making, but they hold huge promise.

- Elections for public office select representatives from among politicians who have already self-selected to run for office. Citizens' assemblies select representatives from among all citizens.

- The members of citizens' assemblies are regular people who become highly informed as they engage and deliberate on a topic.

- The regular people who participate in citizens' assemblies don't have to raise money for reelection or answer to party bosses. Because of this, voters may trust the decisions of citizens' assemblies as much as or more than the decisions of elected legislatures.

- Citizens' assemblies could engage in agenda-setting, helping point elected lawmakers toward issues of highest importance.

- Or they could serve as lawmakers on a particular topic. If legislators are gridlocked on an issue, they could refer it to a citizens' assembly.

Glossary

Amendments to the U.S. Constitution:

- **14th Amendment (ratified 1868), section 2:** "But when the right to vote . . . is denied . . . or in any way abridged, except for participation in rebellion or other crime . . ."

- **15th Amendment (ratified 1870):** "The right of the citizens of the United States to vote shall not be denied or abridged by the United States or by any state on account of race, color, or previous condition of servitude."

- **19th Amendment (ratified 1920):** "The right of the citizens of the United States to vote shall not be denied or abridged by the United States or by any state on account of sex."

- **24th Amendment (ratified 1964):** "The right of the citizens of the United States to vote . . . shall not be denied or abridged by the United States or by reason of failure to pay any poll tax or other tax."

Automatic Voter Registration: An "opt out" system in which eligible voters are automatically registered to vote whenever they interact with government agencies (e.g., departments of motor vehicles). Eligible voters are registered by default, although they may request not to be registered.

battleground state (aka "swing state"): A state where voters are evenly split in their preference for the two dominant presidential candidates, meaning their Electoral College votes are up for grabs and they receive more attention in the presidential race than do **spectator states**.

charter city: A city that is governed by its own charter document rather than the general law of its state.

citizens' assembly: A political body, formed by a random selection of citizens who are insulated from the pressures of campaigns and elections and given access to information, experts, and mediators so that they can deeply understand, discuss with their fellow citizens' assembly members, and deliberate about a challenging policy issue.

citizens' initiative: A petition proposing a law that, after garnering a minimum level of support through signature gathering, is submitted to a public vote. If it passes, it becomes law.

Citizens United v. Federal Election Commission (FEC) (2010): A U.S. Supreme Court case decided in 2010, in a 5–4 decision. The Court held that corporate funding of independent political broadcasts in candidate elections cannot be limited, because doing so would violate the First Amendment. The Court's decision struck down a provision of the McCain-Feingold Act that banned for-profit and not-for-profit corporations and unions from broadcasting electioneering communications in the 30 days before a presidential primary and in the 60 days before the general election. The decision overruled *Austin v. Michigan Chamber of Commerce* (1990) and partially overruled *McConnell v. Federal Election Commission* (2003). But it upheld the requirements for disclaimer and disclosure by sponsors of advertisements and the ban on direct contributions from corporations or unions to candidates.

continual enfranchisement: Continually being allowed to vote, even if convicted of a felony.

crack the vote: A gerrymandering tactic in which partisan redistricting draws district lines to split the voters of one party across more than one district, preventing them from attaining a majority in one district.

Crosscheck: A software system that aggregated voter registration records across states to identify voters registered in multiple states. This had the effect of disenfranchising voters who otherwise should have been eligible to vote, and it disproportionately disenfranchised voters of color. The **Electronic Registration Information Center** is an improved version of Crosscheck.

Electoral College: The political body that elects the president and vice president of the United States. It composes 538 electors: each state has a number of electors equal to its number of U.S. senators and representatives, and DC has three electors. The Constitution decrees that each state's legislature chooses how to award its state electors' votes. Most states award all their electors' votes to the candidate who receives the most votes in their state, but Maine and Nebraska award only two electors (representing their senators) to the statewide vote winner and the remainder on an individual basis to the winner in each congressional district.

electoral vote: A vote cast by a member of the Electoral College for the president of the United States. The candidate who wins at least 270 electoral votes is elected president.

Electronic Registration Information Center (ERIC): A modern, secure voter registration system that searches for and corrects duplicate voter registrations, updates addresses when voters move across state lines, and removes deceased people who remain on the voter rolls. It is an improvement from the **Crosscheck** system.

first-past-the-post: See **plurality voting**.

fundamental right: A legal distinction defining rights that are so important that legislators should not be allowed to encroach on them except under the most dire circumstances. When lawmakers are accused of encroaching on a fundamental right, courts apply the **strict scrutiny** legal test. Examples of fundamental rights in the United States include those in the Bill of Rights, the right to privacy, and the right to marriage.

gerrymander: To manipulate the boundaries of an electoral district so as to favor one party.

Hispanic: A person who is from, or whose ancestors are from, a Spanish-speaking country.

Husted v. Randolph (2018): A Supreme Court case concerning the legality of the state of Ohio's voter registration laws under the **National Voter Registration Act of 1993**. In a 5–4 decision, the Supreme Court upheld Ohio's voter registration laws even though they resulted in the purging of thousands of voters from the rolls. The majority argued that since voting inactivity was one of two reasons Ohio removed voters from the rolls (the other reason being failure to respond to a postal notice), the law did not violate the NVRA of 1993.

hyperpartisanship: An extreme level of partisanship, in which the parties have polarized and oppose compromise, and in which voters loyal to one party become hostile to the other.

independent expenditure campaign: A campaign in support of a candidate or a cause funded by individuals or groups that are not in coordination with the candidate or cause's official campaign. Independent expenditures are not classified as contributions and are not subject to limits.

instant-runoff voting: See **ranked choice voting**.

Latino: A person who is from, or whose ancestors are from, Latin America.

literacy test: A barrier to voting ostensibly designed to ensure that voters had some degree of education, but in practice used to deny voting rights to African Americans and non-English-speaking American citizens. Literacy tests were prohibited following the Voting Rights Act of 1965.

majority-minority districts: A district in which the majority of the residents are members of a minority racial or ethnic group, such as African American or Hispanic people.

McCutcheon v. FEC (2014): A 5–4 Supreme Court decision that struck down aggregate limits for individual contributions. Aggregate donations comprise all donations an individual makes to any candidate or cause in a given two-year election cycle. The Supreme Court held that limiting the total amount of money an individual could donate imposed a restraint on their political communication.

multi-winner districts: An electoral district in which two or more candidates are declared the winners and all winners represent the district in the governing body. See also **single-winner districts**.

National Popular Vote Interstate Compact: An agreement between states to award their **electoral votes** to the winner of the national popular vote. This agreement would take effect only when the signatory states hold a majority of votes in the **Electoral College**. As of March 2020, 15 states and the District of Columbia, representing 196 electoral votes, have agreed to this compact.

National Voter Registration Act of 1993: The purpose of this act was to increase the number of registered voters, enhance the participation of voters in elections, protect the integrity of the election process, and ensure maintenance of accurate voter registration information. This act required states to offer voter registration opportunities to eligible individuals when they applied for or renewed a driver's license at the DMV, or when they applied for public assistance. Six states are exempt from this act because either they do not require registration to vote in federal elections or they offer same-day registration for federal elections. This act also bars states from removing someone from the voter rolls for not voting.

pack the vote: A **gerrymandering** tactic in which partisan redistricting draws district lines in such a way as to concentrate the other party's voters in one district where that party wins with an overwhelming majority, leaving nearby districts available for the party drawing the lines to win. See also **crack the vote, wasted vote.**

people of color: People who identify as Black, African American, Indigenous, Native American, Hispanic, Latino, Asian American, or Pacific Islander.

plurality voting: An electoral system in which the winner of an election is the candidate that received the highest number of votes. The candidate need not win an outright majority to be elected. This system is sometimes referred to as **first-past-the-post** or **winner-take-all.** This is the most common voting system used in the United States. Most other wealthy democracies use some form of proportional representation for legislative races, not plurality voting.

political action committee (PAC): An organization that raises and spends money to influence candidates and elections. PACs contribute directly to candidates and parties. See also super PAC.

poll tax: A payment required before a registered voter can exercise their right to vote.

powerful vote: A vote that a candidate needs to get elected, typically held by voters in battleground, or "swing," districts or states. Officials are more responsive to voters holding powerful votes. Contrast with **wasted vote.** See also **battleground state.**

proportional representation: A representation system in which candidates and parties win legislative seats in proportion to the percentage of the vote they received. For example, if a party received 40 percent of the vote, it would receive 40 percent of the legislative seats.

ranked choice voting: An electoral system in which voters rank their preferences among candidates for the same office. Candidates must receive 50 percent + 1 vote to win. If no candidate receives a majority in the first count, an **instant runoff** occurs in which the candidate who received the fewest first-choice votes is eliminated and those votes are reassigned to those voters' second-choice candidates. This process is repeated until one candidate receives at least 50 percent + 1 vote and is declared the winner.

rational basis, legal test: The most permissive form of judicial review test that courts use to determine the constitutionality of a law. To pass this test, the Court must determine that the law enforces a legitimate state interest and that there is a rational connection between the law's means and those legitimate state goals.

re-enfranchisement: The process of restoring voting rights to individuals after they have been unable to vote due to a felony conviction.

safe state: See **spectator state.**

Shelby County v. Holder (2013): A landmark Supreme Court case in which the Supreme Court struck down a key provision of the **Voting Rights Act of 1965, section 4.** After this decision, several states, including Texas and Mississippi, enacted voter suppression laws such as **Voter ID laws,** which the federal government had previously blocked them from enacting.

single-winner districts: An electoral district in which only one candidate is declared the winner. Contrast with **multi-winner districts.**

sortition: Selecting a group of people by lottery. Sortition means to choose — to "sort" — by the use of lots; that is, by random sample.

spectator state (aka "safe state"): A state where a majority of voters are certain to choose one or the other of the presidential candidates, so there isn't really a contest. As a result, these states receive little attention from presidential campaigns and generally less federal funding in non-election years, too. Contrast with **battleground state** (aka "swing state").

strict scrutiny, legal test: The highest form of judicial review test that courts use to determine the constitutionality of a law. To pass this test, the court must determine that the legislature passed the law to further a compelling government interest and that the law was designed specifically to achieve that interest.

super PAC: A specific type of **political action committee (PAC)** created following the *Citizens United v. FEC* **(2010)** U.S. Supreme Court decision. While super PACs may raise and spend unlimited amounts of money, their actions must be independent from the campaigns they support, and they are prohibited from contributing directly to candidates or parties.

swing state: See **battleground state.**

three-fifths compromise: At the 1787 U.S. Constitutional Convention, delegates from Southern states wanted their large slave populations to count for purposes of representation but not be allowed to vote. Counting slaves would give Southern states a big boost in representation in the new House of Representatives. Northern states argued that if Southern states didn't consider slaves to be people for other purposes, they shouldn't get to count them for purposes of representation. The two factions eventually reached a compromise: slaves counted as three-fifths of a person for purposes of determining each state's number of representatives in the U.S. House.

Vote At Home: A voting system in which election officials mail ballots to all registered voters. Voters fill out their ballots on their own time and send the ballot back either through the mail or by dropping their ballot off at a designated drop box.

voter fraud (in-person): Also known as voter impersonation, this is a type of voter fraud in which a person pretends to be someone else so that they can vote more than once or vote in a district where they are not registered to do so.

Voter ID law: A law that requires voters to present some form of official identification prior to casting a ballot. Especially in their stricter forms, these laws tend to disproportionately disenfranchise poor people, young people, and people of color.

voting-age population: In the United States, the number of residents at least 18 years of age.

voting-eligible population: The number of voting-age residents who are eligible to vote because they are U.S. citizens and have not been convicted of certain kinds of felonies (depending on state law).

Voting Rights Act of 1965: Passed at the height of the civil rights movement, this landmark law banned racial discrimination in voting nationwide. It required the federal government to enforce the rights enshrined in the **15th Amendment**. It prohibits any state or local government from implementing a voting law that has the effect of discrimination based on race or language.

Voting Rights Act of 1965, section 4: This section identified counties and states with a history of voter discrimination. Section 5 then required those jurisdictions to receive preclearance from the federal government before making any changes to their electoral laws. In Shelby County v. Holder (2013), the Supreme Court found section 4's formula for determining which counties and states tended toward voter discrimination to be outdated, effectively eliminating section 5's preclearance requirements until Congress came up with a new formula. To date, Congress has failed to do so.

wasted vote: A vote that was not necessary for the candidate to receive in order to win because it was a surplus beyond the 50 percent + 1 threshold needed to win. Or a vote that does not succeed in electing a representative because the candidate lost. Contrast with powerful vote. See also pack the vote.

winner-take-all: See **plurality voting.**

Appendix: Organizations Taking Action on the Solutions in This Book

Below you'll find a chart listing some of the leading organizations working on the ten solutions outlined in the chapters of this book. All are nonprofit and welcome volunteers and support from people like you. The descriptions below the chart include abridged language from their mission statements as well as links for you to learn more and get involved.

	AVR	ERIC	VAH	Reen-franchise	Vouchers / Match	RCV	NPVIC	ProRep	Senate	Cit Assems
League of Women Voters	●	●	●	●	●	●	●	●		
Indivisible	●	●	●	●	●	●	●		●	
Common Cause	●	●	●	●	●	●	●			
Represent.Us	●		●	●	●	●				
Let America Vote	●		●	●						
I Vote for America	●									
Brennan Center for Justice		●		●						
Campaign Legal Center			●			●		●		
Unite America			●				●			
National VAH Institute			●							
Rock the Vote			●							
Demos				●	●					
ACLU				●						
Forward Justice				●						
NAACP				●						
Prison Policy Initiative				●						
The Sentencing Project				●						
Equal Citizens					●	●	●	●		
Democracy Policy Network					●					
Mayday America					●					
FairVote						●	●	●		
Take Back our Republic						●				
National Popular Vote							●			
Ignite								●		
51 for 51									●	
Fix Our Senate									●	
Extinction Rebellion										●
Healthy Democracy										●
Jefferson Center										●
Policy Jury Group										●

League of Women Voters

For 100 years, the League has been an activist, grassroots organization promoting a democracy where every person has the desire, the right, the knowledge, and the confidence to participate. And no, you don't have to be a woman to participate.

The heart of the League is its hundreds of local chapters. In towns and cities across the United States, local chapters host events and meetings where you can learn more about civic issues and push for changes at the local, state, and national levels. The League is membership-based, so you join a local league as a member, and your membership dues also support the state and national leagues. Learn more at *lwv.org*, and find your local league at *lwv.org/local-leagues/find-local-league*.

Indivisible

Indivisible is a progressive grassroots movement of millions of activists across every state, fueled by a partnership between thousands of autonomous local Indivisible groups and a national staff. Indivisible's national team offers strategic leadership, movement coordination, and support to Indivisible activists, and also directly lobbies Congress, builds partnerships, runs media campaigns, and develops advocacy strategies. Together they fight to defeat the right-wing takeover of American government and build an inclusive democracy. Enter your zip code to find a local group at *indivisible.org/groups*.

Common Cause

Common Cause was founded in 1970 to serve as the people's lobbyist. It is nonpartisan and works for a pro-democracy agenda by, among other things, advancing legislation designed to reduce the influence of money in politics, expand voting rights and voting access, and end gerrymandering. It has local chapters in 30 states and DC. Join its action team at *actionnetwork.org/forms/join-the-action-team*.

RepresentUs

RepresentUs brings together independents, conservatives, progressives, and everyone in between to stop political bribery, end secret money, and fix our broken elections. Building on America's long tradition of pursuing federal reform through the states, it helps pass transformative anti-corruption laws in cities and states, on issues from gerrymandering and ranked choice voting to ethics and transparency. RepresentUs has local chapters throughout the country working on reforms and looking for volunteers like you. Find yours at *represent.us/what-is-a-represent-us-chapter*.

Let America Vote

Extreme voter suppression laws that disproportionately affect people based on their race or ethnicity, gender, age, or income are popping up all over the country at an alarming pace. Let America Vote believes that if people don't fight back, more and more Americans will become disenfranchised and lose their voice in our democracy. When politicians make it hard to vote, Let America Vote makes it hard for them to get reelected. You can join their mobile action team at *letamericavote. wpengine.com/action.*

I Vote for America

I Vote for America is singularly focused on securing voting rights for all Americans. Its strategy is to go on offense by working to pass Automatic Voter Registration in every state in the country. It also works to elect Democratic candidates to state-level secretary of state offices, especially in swing states. Learn more at *ivoteforamerica. org/about.*

Brennan Center for Justice

The Brennan Center for Justice is a nonpartisan law and policy institute. It advocates for the values of democracy, stands for equal justice and the rule of law, and works to craft and advance reforms to make American democracy work for all. You can get involved at *brennancenter.org/get-involved.*

Campaign Legal Center

Campaign Legal Center advances democracy through law, fighting for every American's right to participate in the democratic process. It uses tactics such as litigation, policy advocacy, communications, and partnerships to win victories that result in a more transparent, accountable, and inclusive democracy. Its long-term goal is a government responsive to the people. You can stay informed by signing up at *campaignlegal.org/get-updates.*

Unite America

Unite America is a nonpartisan organization dedicated to bridging the partisan divide. It argues that the central challenge facing our political system is a series of warped incentives, specifically primary elections that are closed to centrists and independents and low voter participation due to disenfranchisement and institutional obstacles between voters and their ability to cast a ballot. Unite America believes in creating better incentives through nonpartisan election reforms, such as making voting more accessible and eliminating gerrymandering. Its philanthropic Unite America Fund supports pro-reform candidates who commit to putting country over party. Learn more at *uniteamerica.org/strategy*.

National Vote at Home Institute

National Vote at Home Institute is dedicated to making sure every American can vote in secure, safe, accessible, and equitable elections by expanding Vote At Home systems in all 50 states. It works with election officials to optimize their administration processes and governing laws for both mail-in-ballot and in-person voting methods; to remove legislative and administrative barriers to Vote At Home systems; and to educate the public on the benefits of voting at home while preserving the ability to vote in person for those who may want or need it. Learn more at *voteathome.org*.

Rock the Vote

Rock the Vote works to increase voter turnout among millennial and Gen Z voters. Since 1990, it has leveraged media, technology, and culture to register over 12 million young voters. Today, Rock the Vote is focused on empowering young people through registration, education, and mobilization. Learn more at *rockthevote.org*.

Demos

Demos is a dynamic "think-and-do" tank that powers the movement for a just, inclusive, multiracial democracy. Get updates on its democratic reform work at *demos.org/our-issues/democratic-reform*.

American Civil Liberties Union

For nearly 100 years, the American Civil Liberties Union (ACLU) has defended the civil rights of all Americans. It spoke out against Japanese internment during World War II and helped the NAACP challenge racial segregation in public schools. Today, the ACLU's commitment to civil rights is exemplified as it defends the rights of unpopular groups and individuals. Learn more at *aclu.org*.

Forward Justice

Forward Justice is a regional nonpartisan organization dedicated to advancing racial, social, and economic justice in the American South. It contributes legal, policy, and strategic support to advocates and movement leaders with the goal of changing the South and, ultimately, the entire country. Learn more at *forwardjustice.org*.

NAACP

The National Association for the Advancement of Colored People is one of the oldest, largest, and most-respected civil rights organizations in the United States. It works to build an American society in which all individuals have equal rights without racial discrimination, including political, educational, social, and economic equality. Learn more at *naacp.org*.

Prison Policy Initiative

The Prison Policy Initiative is a think tank focused on criminal justice reform. It researches and produces national- and state-level data analysis to show how mass incarceration harms American life. Learn more at *prisonpolicy.org*.

The Sentencing Project

The Sentencing Project is a research organization that advocates for reforming the U.S. criminal justice system, with an emphasis on racial justice, including removing restrictions on voting for individuals with felony convictions. Taken as a whole, it works to change the way Americans think about the criminal justice system. Learn more at *sentencingproject.org*.

Equal Citizens

Equal Citizens has one simple but incredibly important mission: to fix democracy by establishing truly equal citizenship, thereby empowering us to take on all the other challenges facing us. You can join the movement by signing up at *equalcitizens.us/get-updates*.

Mayday America

Mayday America works to elect politicians at the local, state, and federal levels who commit to fixing gerrymandering, securing voting rights, and reforming the campaign finance system. It seeks to achieve national reform by first building momentum through systemic reforms at the city and state level. It also works to defeat sitting elected officials who stand in the way of systemic democracy reform. Volunteer at *mayday.us/take-action*.

Democracy Policy Network

Democracy Policy Network is an interstate policy infrastructure for the growing movement of trailblazing politicians working to deepen democracy in statehouses across America. By helping people to gather, package, organize, and champion the movement's policies, it develops a supportive network for state leaders. You can join its work at *democracypolicy.network*.

FairVote

Founded in 1992, FairVote believes that American politics is broken and the way to fix it is to fix how we choose our politicians. It is a nonpartisan organization driven by three principles: fair representation, fair elections, and fair access. FairVote has proposed and helped pass ranked choice voting legislation in cities around the country, supported legislative efforts to enact the National Popular Vote plan for electing the U.S. president, and drafted constitutional amendments for an explicit right to vote. It has local chapters across the country and welcomes volunteers like you. Learn more at *fairvote.org/volunteer_with_fairvote*.

196

Take Back Our Republic

Take Back Our Republic is a nonpartisan organization focused on educating the public on conservative solutions to fix our electoral system. Its leaders are deeply concerned about the undue influence of money on American politics, and they work to reform campaign finance laws and advocate for ranked choice voting. Learn more about their approach and advocacy at *takeback.org/about/our-mission*.

National Popular Vote

National Popular Vote is dedicated to enacting the National Popular Vote Interstate Compact. It can help you contact your state legislators to voice your support for the Compact at *nationalpopularvote.com/tell-your-legislators-support-national-popular-vote*.

Ignite

Ignite is a nonpartisan organization founded in 2010 to address the lack of proportional representation of women in elected office by building a pipeline of the next generation's leaders. It hosts training, networking, and mentoring to help young women build leadership skills, policy expertise, and confidence. Ignite has chapters at colleges in 25 states, all working toward its mission of electing more women. Learn more about its college chapters at *ignitenational.org/college_programming* and its legislative advocacy at *ignitenational.org/advocacy*.

Fix Our Senate

Fix Our Senate is a campaign committed to fixing the broken Senate. Its highest priority is the elimination of the legislative filibuster. Fix Our Senate coordinates work with allied organizations and advocates, serves as a resource for research and messaging guidance, communicates to key audiences directly and through the media, and educates and persuades senators, candidates, and the public about the need for reform. Learn more at *fixoursenate.org*.

51 for 51

The organization 51 for 51 urges full representation for the more than 700,000 residents of the District of Columbia, who have all the same responsibilities, but not the same rights, as their fellow Americans. Learn more at *51for51.org*.

Extinction Rebellion

Extinction Rebellion is a decentralized, international, nonpartisan movement using nonviolent direct action and civil disobedience to persuade governments to act on the climate and ecological emergency. It has three demands:

1. **Tell the truth**. Governments must tell the truth by declaring a climate and ecological emergency, working with other institutions to communicate the urgency for change.

2. **Act now**. Governments must act now to halt biodiversity loss and reduce greenhouse gas emissions to net zero by 2025.

3. **Beyond politics**. Governments must create and be led by the decisions of a citizens' assembly on climate and ecological justice.

Local and national groups are the core of Extinction Rebellion. Connect with yours, learn about trainings, and get involved at *rebellion.global/groups/us-united-states*.

Healthy Democracy

Healthy Democracy is a nonpartisan organization that designs and coordinates deliberative democracy programs such as citizens' assemblies. In the late 2000s, it pioneered the Oregon Citizens' Initiative Review process, in which a curated group of Oregonians evaluates active ballot measures and produces a statement to voters containing the best reasons to vote for or against each one. Healthy Democracy wants to bring this kind of deliberative process to states across the nation. Learn more at *healthydemocracy.org/about*.

Jefferson Center

With over four decades of experience, the Jefferson Center partners with citizens, communities, and institutions to design and implement informed, innovative, and democratic processes to address today's toughest challenges. It pioneered the use of citizens' juries in the United States. Learn more at *jefferson-center.org/projects*.

Policy Jury Group

The Policy Jury Group is dedicated to exploring when, how, and why policy juries can be implemented by state and local governments for the long-term benefit of society as a whole. Its goal is to put forward well-tested and fully evaluated policy jury programs for use by fellow reformers interested in making positive democratic change. Learn more at *policyjurygroup.org*.

Endnotes

Section 1

1. Tim Elfrink, "The Long, Racist History of Florida's Now-Repealed Ban on Felons Voting," Washington Post, November 7, 2018, *https://www.washingtonpost.com/nation/2018/11/07/long-racist-history-floridas-now-re-pealed-ban-felons-voting/?utm_term=.5dec91b79f6d.*

2. Matt Ford, "The Racist Roots of Virginia's Felon Disenfranchisement," Atlantic, April 27, 2016, *https://www.theatlantic.com/politics/archive/2016/04/virginia-felon-disenfranchisement/480072.*

3. German Lopez, "Mass Incarceration in America, Explained in 22 Maps and Charts," Vox, October 11, 2016, *https://www.vox.com/2015/7/13/8913297/mass-incarceration-maps-charts.*

4. E. Anne Carson, "Prisoners in 2014," U.S. Department of Justice Bureau of Justice Statistics, September 2015, *https://www.bjs.gov/content/pub/pdf/p14.pdf.*

5. Matt Ford, "The Racist Roots of Virginia's Felon Disenfranchisement," Atlantic, April 27, 2016, *https://www.theatlantic.com/politics/archive/2016/04/virginia-felon-disenfranchisement/480072.*

6. The other states whose constitutions permanently disenfranchise people with a past felony conviction are Iowa and Kentucky.

7. Very belatedly, the United States added three amendments stating that the right to vote "shall not be denied or abridged" for particular reasons — because of race (15th Amendment, ratified 1870), because of sex (19th Amendment, ratified 1920), and because of failure to pay a poll tax (24th Amendment, ratified 1964).

8. Joshua A. Douglas, "Is the Right to Vote Really Fundamental?," Cornell Journal of Law and Public Policy 18(1):143–201 (Fall 2008), *https://uknowledge.uky.edu/law_facpub/10.*

9. Harper v. Va. Bd. of Elections, 383 U.S. 663, 670 (1966).

10. Kramer v. Union Free Sch. Dist. No. 15, 395 U.S. 621, 622 (1969); Dunn v. Blumstein, 405 U.S. 330, 362 (1972).

11. Lassiter v. Northampton County Bd. of Elections, 360 U.S. 45, 51–53 (1959).

12. Rosario v. Rockefeller, 410 U.S. 752, 761 (1973).

13. Burdick v. Takushi, 504 U.S. 428, 430 (1992).

14. Crawford v. Marion County Election Bd., 128 S. Ct. 1610 (2008).

15. "List of Jurisdictions Subject to the Special Provisions of the Voting Rights Act of 1965," Wikipedia, last modified October 2, 2019, *https://en.wikipedia.org/wiki/List_of_jurisdictions_subject_to_the_special_provisions_of_the_Voting_Rights_Act_of_1965.*

16. Shelby County v. Holder, 570 U.S. 529 (2013), *https://www.supremecourt.gov/opinions/12pdf/12-96_6k47.pdf.*

17. "Shelby County v. Holder," Brennan Center for Justice, August 4, 2018, *https://www.brennancenter.org/our-work/court-cases/shelby-county-v-holder.*

18. H.R. 4, a bill creating a new formula, passed the U.S. House in 2019 but died in the Senate.

19. "The Effects of Shelby County v. Holder," Brennan Center for Justice, August 6, 2018, *https://www.brennancen-ter.org/analysis/effects-shelby-county-v-holder.*

20. Jonathan Brater, Kevin Morris, Myrna Pérez, and Christopher Deluzio, "Purges: A Growing Threat to the Right to Vote," Brennan Center for Justice, July 20, 2018, *https://www.brennancenter.org/our-work/research-re-ports/purges-growing-threat-right-vote.*

21. Husted v. A. Philip Randolph Institute, 584 U.S. 16-980 (6th Cir. 2018), *https://www.supremecourt.gov/opin-ions/17pdf/16-980_f2q3.pdf.*

22. Ibid., Sotomayor dissent, 3-4, *https://www.supremecourt.gov/opinions/17pdf/16-980_f2q3.pdf.*

Chapter 1

23 This is a composite of several true stories from Americans. See Zachary Roth, "Texas Keeping Thousands from Registering, Voting Group Alleges," MSNBC, May 27, 2015, *http://www.msnbc.com/msnbc/texas-keeping-thousands-registering-voting-group-alleges*; Marnie Eisenstadt, "Many People Turned Away from the Polls Thought They Registered through the DMV," Syracuse.com, November 8, 2016, *https://www.syracuse.com/politics/2016/11/many_people_turned_away_from_the_polls_thought_they_registered_through_the_dmv.html*; and Sarah Sarder, "Turned Away Twice from Her Polling Place, Dallas Teacher Fought Back," Dallas Morning News, November 6, 2018, *https://www.dallasnews.com/news/2018/11/06/turned-away-twice-from-her-polling-place-dallas-teacher-fought-back-and-then-voted*.

24 "Why Are Millions of Citizens Not Registered to Vote?," Pew Charitable Trusts, June 21, 2017, *https://www.pewtrusts.org/en/research-and-analysis/issue-briefs/2017/06/why-are-millions-of-citizens-not-registered-to-vote*.

25 "Pew: One in Eight Voter Registrations Inaccurate; 51 Million Citizens Unregistered," Pew Charitable Trusts, February 14, 2012, *https://www.pewtrusts.org/en/about/news-room/press-releases-and-statements/2012/02/14/pew-one-in-eight-voter-registrations-inaccurate-51-million-citizens-unregistered*.

26 Alexis Chemblette, "These Countries with Nearly 100 Percent Voter Participation Put the U.S. to Shame," Vice, October 25, 2017, *https://www.vice.com/en/article/ne3n9b/these-countries-with-nearly-100-percent-voter-participation-put-the-us-to-shame*.

27 P. R. Lockhart, "Tennessee Passed a Law That Could Make It Harder to Register Voters," Vox, May 3, 2019, *https://www.vox.com/policy-and-politics/2019/4/25/18516777/tennessee-senate-voter-registration-drives-legislation-fines-lawsuit*.

28 Kira Lerner, "Texas Is Poised to Make It Easier to Jail People for Voting Errors," Appeal, April 12, 2019, *https://theappeal.org/texas-is-poised-to-make-it-easier-to-jail-people-for-voting-errors*.

29 "History of AVR and Implementation Dates," Brennan Center for Justice, June 19, 2019, *https://www.brennancenter.org/our-work/research-reports/history-avr-implementation-dates*; "Automatic Voter Registration," National Conference of State Legislatures, April 14, 2020, *https://www.ncsl.org/research/elections-and-campaigns/automatic-voter-registration.aspx*.

30 "Connecticut Secretary of State and the Department of Motor Vehicles Sign First-of-its-Kind Automatic Voter Registration Pact," State of Connecticut Department of Motor Vehicles, May 17, 2016, *https://portal.ct.gov/DMV/News-and-Publications/News-and-Publications/Connecticut-Secretary-of-the-State-and-DMV--Sign-First-of-its-Kind-Automatic-Voter-Registration-Pact*.

31 "Auto Registration Requirements," H.B. 161, 62nd Leg., 1st sess. (Utah 2018), *https://le.utah.gov/~2018/bills/static/HB0161.html*.

32 In 2020, New York passed a bill that does a piece of what other states do — it will automatically update a voter's registration when they move within the state and update their address with the U.S. Postal Service. "Relates to Voter Registration Transfers," New York State Assembly, A.B. A775, 2019–20 sess., *https://www.nysenate.gov/legislation/bills/2019/a775*.

33 The original Motor Voter Law, also called the National Voter Registration Act of 1993, was a federal law requiring states to give citizens the option to register to vote at the DMV — so still an opt-in system. Oregon distinguished its opt-out system by calling it the New Motor Voter Law.

34 Rob Griffin, Paul Gronke, Tova Wang, and Liz Kennedy, "Who Votes with Automatic Voter Registration?," Center for American Progress, June 7, 2017, *https://www.americanprogress.org/issues/democracy/reports/2017/06/07/433677/votes-automatic-voter-registration*.

35 Emily Stewart, "2018's Record-Setting Voter Turnout, in One Chart," Vox, November 19, 2018, *https://www.vox.com/policy-and-politics/2018/11/19/18103110/2018-midterm-elections-turnout*.

36 Stanley Dunlap, "Georgia Elections Offices Swamped with Voter Registrations," Telegraph, May 1, 2017, *https://www.macon.com/news/local/article147934484.html*.

37 Kevin Morris and Peter Dunphy, "AVR Impact on State Voter Registration," Brennan Center for Justice, April 11, 2019, *https://www.brennancenter.org/sites/default/files/publications/2019_04_AVR_Report_Final_0.pdf*.

38 Mark Niesse, "Voter Registration Surges in Georgia Ahead of 2020 Elections," Atlanta Journal-Constitution, October 1, 2019, *https://www.ajc.com/news/state--regional-govt--politics/voter-registration-surges-georgia-ahead-2020-elections/NVKOTit4KEtsTHoXtd6ddN*.

39 Ibid.

40 Ibid.

41 "Georgia Breaks All-Time Voting Record," Georgia Secretary of State, accessed February 8, 2020, *https://sos.ga.gov/index.php/elections/georgia_breaks_all-time_voting_record*.

⁴² George Pillsbury, "America Goes to the Polls 2018: Voter Turnout and Election Policy in the 50 States," Nonprofit VOTE and U.S. Elections Project, March 2019, *https://www.voteathome.org/wp-content/uploads/2019/03/america-goes-polls-2018.pdf* (p. 10), *https://www.brennancenter.org/sites/default/files/publications/2019_04_AVR_Report_Final_0.pdf*.

⁴³ "Securing Fair Elections: Challenges to Voting in the United States and Georgia," Scholars Strategy Network, December 2019, *https://scholars.org/sites/scholars/files/12.10.19_Securing_Fair_Elections_Report_FINAL.pdf*.

⁴⁴ Mark Niesse, "Georgia Purge List Scrutinized for Voter Registration Removals," Atlanta Journal-Constitution, November 4, 2019, *https://www.ajc.com/news/state-regional-govt-politics/georgia-purge-list-scrutinized-for-voter-registration-removals/WCDFmhn9P9oFgnVKHAQHoJ*; Mark Niesse, "Legislators Asked to Change Georgia Voter Purge Law," Atlanta Journal-Constitution, January 9, 2020, *https://www.ajc.com/news/state--regional-govt--politics/legislators-asked-change-georgia-purge-law-after-court-upheld/C2cxuC65N9umd2Wg8bKO7J*.

⁴⁵ Mark Niesse, "Voter Registration Surges in Georgia Ahead of 2020 Elections," Atlanta Journal-Constitution, October 1, 2019, *https://www.ajc.com/news/state--regional-govt--politics/voter-registration-surges-georgia-ahead-2020-elections/NVKOTit4KEtsTHoXtd6ddN*.

⁴⁶ Bills have been introduced in the legislatures of Alabama, Arizona, Arkansas, Connecticut, Florida, Hawaii, Idaho, Indiana, Iowa, Kansas, Kentucky, Louisiana, Minnesota, Mississippi, Missouri, Montana, Nebraska, New Hampshire, New Mexico, New York, North Carolina, Oklahoma, Pennsylvania, South Carolina, Tennessee, Texas, and Wisconsin. "Automatic Voter Registration Bills, 2015–Present," Brennan Center for Justice, July 10, 2019, *https://www.brennancenter.org/our-work/research-reports/automatic-voter-registration-bills-2015-present*.

⁴⁷ Nathaniel Rakich, "What Happened When 2.2 Million People Were Automatically Registered to Vote," FiveThirtyEight, October 10, 2019, *https://fivethirtyeight.com/features/what-happened-when-2-2-million-people-were-automatically-registered-to-vote*.

⁴⁸ Top ten turnout states: Minnesota, Colorado, Montana, Wisconsin, Oregon, Maine, Washington, North Dakota, Michigan, and Iowa. See George Pillsbury, "America Goes to the Polls 2018: Voter Turnout and Election Policy in the 50 States," Nonprofit VOTE and U.S. Elections Project, March 2019, p. 7, *https://www.voteathome.org/wp-content/uploads/2019/03/america-goes-polls-2018.pdf*.

Chapter 2

⁴⁹ This is a composite of several true stories from Americans. See Angela Caputo, Geoff Hing, and Johnny Kauffman, "'They Didn't Vote . . . Now They Can't," Reveal, October 22, 2018, *https://www.revealnews.org/article/they-didnt-vote-now-they-cant/*; Dale Ho, "The Ohio Purge and the Future of Voting," New York Times, June 12, 2018, *https://www.nytimes.com/2018/06/12/opinion/the-ohio-purge-and-the-future-of-voting.html*; and Andy Sullivan and Grant Smith, "Use It or Lose It: Occasional Ohio Voters May Be Shut Out in November," Reuters, June 2, 2016, *https://www.reuters.com/article/us-usa-votingrights-ohio-insight/use-it-or-lose-it-occasional-ohio-voters-may-be-shut-out-in-november-idUSKCN0YO19D*.

⁵⁰ This is a composite of several true stories from Americans. See Ari Berman, "A 90-Year-Old Woman Who's Voted Since 1948 Was Disenfranchised by Wisconsin's Voter ID Law," Nation, October 5, 2016, *https://www.thenation.com/article/a-90-year-old-woman-whos-voted-since-1948-was-disenfranchised-by-wisconsins-voter-id-law/*; Sari Horwitz, "Getting a Photo ID so You Can Vote Is Easy. Unless You're Poor, Black, Latino or Elderly," Washington Post, May 23, 2016, *https://www.washingtonpost.com/politics/courts_law/getting-a-photo-id-so-you-can-vote-is-easy-unless-youre-poor-black-latino-or-elderly/2016/05/23/8d5474ec-20f0-11e6-8690-f14ca9de2972_story.html*; Laurel White, "Conservative Advocacy Group Files Lawsuit against Wisconsin Elections Agency," Wisconsin Public Radio, November 13, 2019, *https://www.wpr.org/conservative-advocacy-group-files-lawsuit-against-wisconsin-elections-agency*; Philip Bump, "17,000 Wisconsinites in Two Counties Likely Didn't Vote in 2016 because of the State's Voter-ID Law," Washington Post, September 26, 2017, *https://www.washingtonpost.com/news/politics/wp/2017/09/26/17000-wisconsinites-in-two-counties-likely-didnt-vote-in-2016-due-to-the-states-voter-id-law/*; Heather Smith, "Are States Trying to Stop Students from Voting?" Sierra, September 4, 2018, *https://www.sierraclub.org/sierra/cool-schools-2018/are-states-trying-stop-students-voting-teens-disenfranchisement-elections*; and Ari Berman, "Rigged: How Voter Suppression Threw Wisconsin to Trump," Mother Jones, November 2017, *https://www.motherjones.com/politics/2017/10/voter-suppression-wisconsin-election-2016*.

⁵¹ People might be ineligible to vote because they are not citizens, have a felony conviction, are deceased, or no longer live in that jurisdiction.

⁵² Cameron Smith, "Voter ID Linked to Lower Turnout; Students, People of Color, Elderly Most Affected," Wisconsin Public Radio, October 2, 2018, *https://www.wpr.org/voter-id-linked-lower-turnout-students-people-color-elderly-most-affected*.

⁵³ Danny Hakim and Michael Wines, "'They Don't Really Want Us to Vote': How Republicans Made It Harder," New York Times, November 3, 2018, *https://www.nytimes.com/2018/11/03/us/politics/voting-suppression-elections.html*.

⁵⁴ "Debunking the Voter Fraud Myth," Brennan Center for Justice, January 31, 2017, *https://www.brennancenter.org/analysis/debunking-voter-fraud-myth*.

[55] Kevin Drum, "Voter Fraud Literally Less Likely Than Being Hit by Lightning," Mother Jones, August 6, 2014, *https://www.motherjones.com/kevin-drum/2014/08/voter-fraud-literally-less-likely-being-hit-lightning.*

[56] The fraud rate is around 0.00002 percent (see Id.), while the prison escape rate is around 0.5 percent. "How Often Do Prisoners Escape?" Slate, February 1, 2001, *https://slate.com/news-and-politics/2001/02/how-often-do-prisoners-escape.html.*

[57] Justin Levitt, "The Truth about Voter Fraud," Brennan Center for Justice, 2007, *http://www.brennancenter.org/sites/default/files/analysis/The%20Truth%20About%20Voter%20Fraud.pdf.*

[58] "Got Voter ID?" Kansas Secretary of State Elections Division, 2012, *http://www.gotvoterid.com.*

[59] Ed Espinoza, "Updated: Texas Voter ID Law Allows Gun Licenses, not Student IDs," Progress Texas, *https://progresstexas.org/blog/stricken-texas-voter-id-law-allowed-gun-licenses-not-student-id.*

[60] "Oppose Voter ID Legislation — Fact Sheet," American Civil Liberties Union, 2020, *https://www.aclu.org/other/oppose-voter-id-legislation-fact-sheet.*

[61] Kaveh Waddell and National Journal, "Here's How Much It Costs to Vote in States with Voter ID Laws," Atlantic, October 8, 2014, *https://www.theatlantic.com/politics/archive/2014/10/heres-how-much-it-costs-to-vote-in-states-with-voter-id-laws/458109.*

[62] Richard Sobel, "The High Cost of 'Free' Photo Voter Identification Cards," Charles Hamilton Houston Institute for Race & Justice, June 2014, *https://today.law.harvard.edu/wp-content/uploads/2014/06/FullReport-VoterIDJune20141.pdf.*

[63] See Federal Rules of Civil Procedure 45(c)(3). Texas v. Holder, p. 74.

[64] Keesha Gaskins and Sundeep Iyer, "The Challenge of Obtaining Voter Identification," Brennan Center for Justice, 2012, *https://www.brennancenter.org/sites/default/files/legacy/Democracy/VRE/Challenge_of_Obtaining_Voter_ID.pdf.*

[65] Maggie Astor, "North Dakota Voter ID Law Stands after Last-Ditch Lawsuit," New York Times, November 1, 2018, *https://www.nytimes.com/2018/11/01/us/politics/north-dakota-voter-id-tribe.html.*

[66] Keesha Gaskins and Sundeep Iyer, "The Challenge of Obtaining Voter Identification," Brennan Center for Justice, 2012, *https://www.brennancenter.org/sites/default/files/legacy/Democracy/VRE/Challenge_of_Obtaining_Voter_ID.pdf.*

[67] J. Mijin Cha and Liz Kennedy, "Millions to the Polls: Practical Policies to Fulfill the Freedom to Vote for All Americans," Demos, 2014, *https://www.demos.org/sites/default/files/publications/Millions%20to%20the%20Polls%20Restrictive%20Photo%20ID%20Law%20for%20Voting.pdf.*

[68] Richard Sobel, "The High Cost of 'Free' Photo Voter Identification Cards," Charles Hamilton Houston Institute for Race and Justice, June 2014, *http://today.law.harvard.edu/wp-content/uploads/2014/06/FullReport-VoterIDJune20141.pdf;* and "The Real Cost of Photo ID," Voting Rights Institute, accessed January 12, 2020, *http://media.cleveland.com/open_impact/other/Dems-report-real_cost_of_voting_ID.pdf.*

[69] Kelly Phillips Erb, "Taxpayers Spend Millions on New Voter ID Laws," Forbes, March 26, 2012, *https://www.forbes.com/sites/kellyphillipserb/2012/03/26/taxpayers-spend-millions-on-new-voter-id-laws/#1d3f31da43e4.*

[70] Michael Miller and Bernard Fraga, "Who Does Voter ID Legislation Keep from Voting?" MIT Election Data and Science Lab, 2017, *http://electionlab.mit.edu/sites/default/files/2019-01/fraga-miller_2017summary.pdf.*

[71] Phoebe Henninger, Marc Meredith, and Michael Morse, "Who Votes without Identification? Using Affidavits from Michigan to Learn about the Potential Impact of Strict Photo Voter Identification Laws," Social Science Research Network, July 13, 2018, *https://papers.ssrn.com/sol3/papers.cfm?abstract_id=3205769.*

[72] Mackenzie Weinger, "Pa. Pol: Voter ID Helps GOP Win State," Politico, June 25, 2012, *https://www.politico.com/story/2012/06/pa-pol-voter-id-helps-gop-win-state-077811.*

[73] Dan Hopkins, "What We Know about Voter ID Laws," FiveThirtyEight, August 21, 2018, *https://fivethirtyeight.com/features/what-we-know-about-voter-id-laws.*

[74] Scott Douglas, "The Alabama State Race May Already Have Been Decided (Opinion)," New York Times, December 11, 2017, *https://www.nytimes.com/2017/12/11/opinion/roy-moore-alabama-senate-voter-suppression.html.*

[75] Kevin Morris, "Voter Purge Rates Remain High, Analysis Finds," Brennan Center for Justice, August 1, 2019, *https://www.brennancenter.org/blog/voter-purge-rates-remain-high-analysis-finds.*

[76] Husted v. A. Philip Randolph Institute, 584 U.S. 16 (6th Cir. 2018), *https://www.scotusblog.com/wp-content/uploads/2017/02/16-980-cert-petition.pdf.*

[77] "National Voter Registration Act of 1993 (NVRA)," U.S. Department of Justice, last modified August 7, 2017, *https://www.justice.gov/crt/national-voter-registration-act-1993-nvra.*

[78] Husted v. A. Philip Randolph Institute, 584 U.S. 16-980 (6th Cir. 2018), dissent, p. 12, *https://www.supremecourt.gov/opinions/17pdf/16-980_f2q3.pdf.*

79 Sharad Goel, Marc Meredith, Michael Morse, David Rothschild, and Houshmand Shirani-Mehr, "One Person, One Vote: Estimating the Prevalence of Double Voting in U.S. Presidential Elections," Gregpalast.com, October 24, 2017, *https://gregpalast.com/wp-content/uploads/OnePersonOneVote.pdf*.

80 "Participation in the Interstate Crosscheck System," Center for American Progress Action Fund, accessed January 12, 2020, *https://healthofstatedemocracies.org/factors/intercross.html*; Lauren Harmon, Charles Posner, Michele Jawando, and Matt Dhaiti, "The Health of State Democracies," Center for American Progress Action Fund, July 2015, *https://cdn.americanprogressaction.org/wp-content/uploads/2015/07/HSD-report-FINAL.pdf*.

81 Mark Hedin, "Voter Crosscheck May Wrongly Purge Missouri Voters from Voting Rolls," St. Louis American, September 6, 2018, *http://www.stlamerican.com/news/local_news/voter-crosscheck-may-wrongly-purge-missouri-voters-from-voting-rolls/article_f0b5c3fc-b17a-11e8-b095-03c2e17fad71.html*.

82 Jessica Huseman and Derek Willis, "The Voter Fraud Commission Wants Your Data — But Experts Say They Can't Keep It Safe," ProPublica, October 23, 2017, *https://www.propublica.org/article/crosscheck-the-voter-fraud-commission-wants-your-data-keep-it-safe*.

83 Ibid.

84 "ACLU of Kansas Settlement Puts Crosscheck Out of Commission for Foreseeable Future; Program Suspended until Safeguards Added," ACLU Kansas, December 10, 2019, *https://www.aclukansas.org/en/press-releases/aclu-kansas-settlement-puts-crosscheck-out-commission-foreseeable-future-program*.

85 "Interstate Voter Registration Crosscheck Program," Wikipedia, last modified December 17, 2019, *https://en.wikipedia.org/wiki/Interstate_Voter_Registration_Crosscheck_Program*.

86 David Becker, "Electronic Registration Information Center Helps States Keep Pace with Mobile Electorate," Pew Charitable Trusts, August 2, 2016, *https://www.pewtrusts.org/en/research-and-analysis/articles/2016/08/02/electronic-registration-information-center-helps-states-keep-pace-with-mobile-electorate*.

87 "ERIC at Work," Electronic Registration Information Center, last modified November 22, 2019, *https://ericstates.org/statistics*.

88 "Who We Are," Electronic Registration Information Center, *https://ericstates.org/who-we-are*.

89 "ERIC at Work," Electronic Registration Information Center, last modified November 22, 2019, *https://ericstates.org/statistics*.

90 Ibid.

91 Justin Levitt, "The Truth about Voter Fraud," Brennan Center for Justice, 2007, p. 9, *http://www.brennancenter.org/sites/default/files/analysis/The%20Truth%20About%20Voter%20Fraud.pdf*.

92 "Electronic Registration Information Center," Common Cause Florida, accessed January 13, 2020, *https://www.commoncause.org/florida/our-work/expand-voting-rights-election-integrity/electronic-registration-information-center*.

93 "Protecting Voting Rights by Ending Crosscheck," Indivisible, accessed January 13, 2020, *https://indivisible.org/resource/protecting-voting-rights-ending-crosscheck*.

Chapter 2

94 This is a composite of several true stories from Americans. See Pema Levy, "Equipment Malfunctions and Voting Machine Shortages Bring Long Lines in Georgia," Mother Jones, November 6, 2018, *https://www.motherjones.com/politics/2018/11/equipment-malfunctions-and-voting-machine-shortages-bring-long-lines-in-georgia/*; Amy Gardner and Beth Reinhard, "Broken Machines, Rejected Ballots and Long Lines: Voting Problems Emerge as Americans Go to the Polls," Washington Post, November 6, 2018, *https://www.washingtonpost.com/politics/broken-machines-rejected-ballots-and-long-lines-voting-problems-emerge-as-americans-go-to-the-polls/2018/11/06/ffd11e52-dfa8-11e8-b3f0-62607289efee_story.html*; Adam Cohen, "No One Should Have to Stand in Line for 10 Hours to Vote," New York Times, August 25, 2008, *https://www.nytimes.com/2008/08/26/opinion/26tue4.html*; Barrett Holmes Pitner, "Early Voting Lines Are So Long, People Are Fainting. That Harms Democracy," Guardian, October 19, 2016, *https://www.theguardian.com/commentisfree/2016/oct/19/early-voting-lines-georgia*; Christina A. Cassidy, Colleen Long, and Michael Balsamo, "Machine Breakdowns, Long Lines Mar Vote on Election Day," Associated Press, November 6, 2018, *https://apnews.com/6fb6de6fdb034b889d301efd12602e21*; Ian MacDougall and Ariana Tobin, "Long Lines Test Voter Patience across the Nation," ProPublica Electionland, November 6, 2018, *https://www.propublica.org/article/long-lines-test-voter-patience-across-the-nation*; Nina Feldman and Miles Bryan, "Lines Were So Long at West Philly Polls That Some People Left without Voting," Billy Penn, November 6, 2019, *https://billypenn.com/2019/11/06/lines-were-so-long-at-west-philly-polls-that-some-people-left-without-voting/*; and Isaac Arnsdorf, "These Voters Had to Wait for Hours: 'It Felt like a Type of Disenfranchisement,'" ProPublica Electionland, November 6, 2018, *https://www.propublica.org/article/these-voters-had-to-wait-for-hours-it-felt-like-a-type-of-disenfranchisement*.

95 Combining the categories "Conflicting schedule," "Out of town," "Illness or disability," "Transportation problems," and "Inconvenient hours or polling locations." Gustavo Lopez and Antonio Flores, "Dislike of Candidates or Campaign Issues Was Most Common Reason for Not Voting in 2016," Pew Research Center, June 1, 2017, *https://www.pewresearch.org/fact-tank/2017/06/01/dislike-of-candidates-or-campaign-issues-was-most-common-reason-for-not-voting-in-2016*.

96   Anna North, "Why Long Lines at Polling Places Are a Voting Rights Issue," Vox, November 6, 2018, *https:// www.vox.com/2018/11/6/18068506/midterm-election-voting-lines-new-york-georgia*; Stef W. Kight, "Election Nightmares: Power Outages, Old Machines and Ballot Deficiencies," Axios, November 6, 2018, *https:// www.axios.com/midterms-2018-voters-failures-power-outage-broken-machines-1c8a038a-9c3c-4d81-8a23-5b71e692bbdd.html.*

97   Anna North, "Why Long Lines at Polling Places Are a Voting Rights Issue," Vox, November 6, 2018, *https:// www.vox.com/2018/11/6/18068506/midterm-election-voting-lines-new-york-georgia*; Tom Regan, Twitter post, November 16, 2018, 8:01 a.m., *https://twitter.com/tomreganWSB/status/1059838200699674624*; Ari Berman, "There Were 5-Hour Lines to Vote in Arizona because the Supreme Court Gutted the Voting Rights Act," Nation, March 23, 2016, *https://www.thenation.com/article/there-were-five-hour-lines-to-vote-in-arizona-because-the-supreme-court-gutted-the-voting-rights-act/*; Salisia's Kloset — Online Boutique official Twitter, Twitter post, November 6, 2018, 5:56 a.m., *https://twitter.com/salisiaskloset/status/1059806759311888384.*

98   Mark Nichols, "Closed Voting Sites Hit Minority Counties Harder for Busy Midterm Elections," USA Today, October 30, 2018, *https://www.usatoday.com/story/news/2018/10/30/midterm-elections-closed-voting-sites-impact-minority-voter-turnout/1774221002.*

99   Pema Levy, "Equipment Malfunctions and Voting Machine Shortages Bring Long Lines in Georgia," Mother Jones, November 6, 2018, *https://www.motherjones.com/politics/2018/11/equipment-malfunctions-and-voting-machine-shortages-bring-long-lines-in-georgia.*

100 Daniel Garisto, "Smartphone Data Show Voters in Black Neighborhoods Wait Longer," Scientific American, October 1, 2019, *https://www.scientificamerican.com/article/smartphone-data-show-voters-in-black-neighborhoods-wait-longer1.*

101 The states that require voters to have an "excuse" to request an absentee ballot are Alabama, Arkansas, Connecticut, Delaware, Indiana, Kentucky, Louisiana, Missouri, New Hampshire, New York, South Carolina, Tennessee, and West Virginia.

102 The 13 states allowing any voter to request an absentee ballot, with no "excuse" needed, are Georgia, Illinois, Iowa, Maine, Michigan, North Carolina, Ohio, Oklahoma, Pennsylvania, Rhode Island, South Dakota, Virginia, and Wisconsin.

103 The states mailing out all ballots in certain elections are Alaska, Arizona, Florida, Kansas, Maryland, Missouri, Montana, and Wyoming.

104 The states mailing out all ballots in certain jurisdictions are California, Idaho, Minnesota, Nebraska, Nevada, New Jersey, New Mexico, and North Dakota.

105 Arizona, California, DC, Montana, Nevada, and New Jersey allow voters to sign up for permanent absentee voting.

106 The five states that let all voters Vote At Home in all elections are Colorado, Hawaii, Oregon, Utah, and Washington.

107 The 9 states that waived or loosened their "excuse" requirements to absentee vote during the 2020 COVID-19 pandemic were Alabama, Connecticut, Delaware, Kentucky, Massachusetts, New Hampshire, New York, South Carolina, and West Virginia.

108 The following jurisdictions mailed ballots to all voters in the primary or general election in 2020: California (general), Idaho (primary), DC (general), Nevada (general), New Jersey (general), Vermont (general), Montana (primary and general).

109 Vote At Home counties in Utah saw a 5.5 percent participation increase in down-ballot races. This was lower than the 5 to 7 percent increase in turnout in up-ballot races, so Vote At Home brought in more voters, but those voters weren't necessarily more likely to make it down the ballot. Amelia Showalter, "Vote At Home: The Turnout Effects of All-Mail Election Systems in Upballot and Downballot Races in Utah 2016," National Vote at Home Institute, November 26, 2019, *https://www.voteathome.org/wp-content/uploads/2019/01/Utah-2016-Downballot-Analysis-FINAL-Pantheon-Analytics.pdf.*

110 "The Higher the Use of Mailed-Out Ballots, the Lower the Gap for Disabled Voter Participation," MIT Election Data and Science Lab, accessed January 14, 2020, *https://www.voteathome.org/wp-content/uploads/2019/09/VAH-lowers-disability-voting-gap.pdf.*

111 Danielle Root, "Increasing Voter Participation in America," Center for American Progress, July 11, 2018, *https://www.americanprogress.org/issues/democracy/reports/2018/07/11/453319/increasing-voter-participation-america.*

112 Devin Kelly, "Anchorage's Vote-by-Mail Election Was Supposed to Boost Turnout. It Shattered a Record," Anchorage Daily News, April 5, 2018, *https://www.adn.com/alaska-news/anchorage/2018/04/04/anchorages-vote-by-mail-election-was-supposed-to-boost-turnout-its-now-shattered-a-record.*

113 "Nebraska County Pilots Vote at Home, Sees 58% Turnout vs. 24% Statewide Average in 2018 Primary," National Vote at Home Coalition, May 17, 2018, *https://docs.wixstatic.com/ugd/ef45f5_13d9763efa1f4b6fb-3d4a8782f98c376.pdf.*

[114] Mori Kessler, "Voter Turnout Doubles for Washington City versus Previous Municipal Election," St. George News, November 14, 2019, *https://www.stgeorgeutah.com/news/archive/2019/11/14/mgk-voter-turnout-doubles-for-washington-city-versus-previous-municipal-election.*

[115] "City of Tucson General and Special Election Unofficial Results," City of Tucson, November 5, 2019, *https://www.tucsonaz.gov/files/clerks/COT_2019_UnofficialResults_General_11082019.pdf.*

[116] Elvyn Jones, "Clerk Estimates Mail-In Ballot Increased Turnout for Sales Tax Election by 20 Percent; State Law Limits How Such Ballots Can Be Used," Lawrence Journal-World, May 21, 2018, *http://www2.ljworld.com/news/2018/may/21/voter-turnout-proposition-1-illustrates-mail-ballo.*

[117] Blake Gumprecht, "Las Cruces Voters Approve All Four GO Bond Measures," Las Cruces Sun News, last modified August 22, 2018, *https://www.lcsun-news.com/story/news/2018/08/21/las-cruces-voters-approve-all-four-go-bond-measures-special-election/1059601002.*

[118] "Will Vote-by-Mail Elections Increase Turnout," U.S. Election Assistance Commission, February 23, 2017, *https://www.eac.gov/documents/2017/02/23/will-vote-by-mail-elections-increase-turnout.*

[119] Amelia Showalter, "Utah 2016: Evidence for the Positive Turnout Effects of 'Vote At Home' (also known as Vote By Mail) in Participating Counties," Pantheon Analytics, May 3, 2018, *https://kwtri4b8r0ep8ho61118ipob-wpengine.netdna-ssl.com/wp-content/uploads/2018/06/Utah-2016-Voter-File-Analysis-Pantheon-Analytics.pdf.*

[120] Alan S. Gerber, Gregory A. Huber, and Seth J. Hill, "Identifying the Effect of All-Mail Elections on Turnout: Staggered Reform in the Evergreen State," Political Science Research and Methods, June 12, 2013, *https://www.cambridge.org/core/journals/political-science-research-and-methods/article/identifying-the-effect-of-allmail-elections-on-turnout-staggered-reform-in-the-evergreen-state/3725E51B9B7F331D77DC9B49130D7F7D.*

[121] "Editorial: Absentee but Extremely Engaged," Traverse City Record Eagle, November 7, 2019, *https://www.record-eagle.com/opinion/editorials/editorial-absentee-but-extremely-engaged/article_1063d5bc-00d1-11ea-bbf6-97f1c567e66b.html.*

[122] "Colorado Voting Reforms: Early Results," Pew Charitable Trusts, March 2016, *https://www.pewtrusts.org/~/media/assets/2016/03/coloradovotingreformsearlyresults.pdf.*

[123] Randy Dotinga, "King of All He Tabulates," Voice of San Diego, January 3, 2014, *https://www.voiceofsandiego.org/topics/news/king-of-all-he-tabulates.*

[124] Provisional ballots are special ballots used to record a vote when there are questions about the voter's eligibility that must be resolved before the vote can count. "Colorado Voting Reforms: Early Results," Pew Charitable Trusts, March 2016, *https://www.pewtrusts.org/~/media/assets/2016/03/coloradovotingreformsearlyresults.pdf.*

[125] Anjali Enjeti, "Voting Rights Are Being Threatened More Than We Realize," Zora, August 2, 2019, *https://zora.medium.com/protecting-voting-rights-is-the-hot-topic-too-few-are-talking-about-a5c4769f0597.*

[126] "2016 General Election Survey," DHM Research, October 14, 2016, *https://www.voteathome.org/wp-content/uploads/2018/12/Oregon-Public-Brodcasting-Statewide-Survey-October-2016-2.pdf.*

[127] Charles Stewart III, "2016 Survey of the Performance of American Elections," MIT Election Data and Science Lab, 2017, *https://www.doi.org/10.7910/DVN/Y38VIQ/2NJDL9.*

[128] "Most Voters Have Positive Views of Their Midterm Voting Experiences," Pew Research Center, December 17, 2018, *https://www.people-press.org/2018/12/17/most-voters-have-positive-views-of-their-midterm-voting-experiences.*

[129] Allegra Chapman, Amber Mcreynolds, Tierra Bradford, Kiyana Asemanfar, Elena Nunez, and Gerry Langeler, "The Colorado Voting Experience: A Model That Encourages Full Participation," Common Cause and National Vote at Home Institute, 2019, p. 5, *https://www.commoncause.org/resource/the-colorado-voting-experience-a-model-that-encourages-full-participation.*

[130] Ibid., p. 4.

[131] "Colorado Voting Reforms: Early Results," Pew Charitable Trusts, March 22, 2016, *https://www.pewtrusts.org/en/research-and-analysis/issue-briefs/2016/03/colorado-voting-reforms-early-results.*

[132] Amelia Showalter, "Colorado 2014: Comparisons of Predicted and Actual Turnout," Pantheon Analytics, August 8, 2017, *https://www.voteathome.org/wp-content/uploads/2018/12/Colorado-2014-voter-turnout-study.pdf.*

[133] U.S. Government Accountability Office Report to Congressional Requesters, "Elections: Issues Related to Registering Voters and Administering Elections," June 2016, *https://www.gao.gov/assets/680/678131.pdf#page=35.*

[134] States that don't require election officials to notify voters and give them a chance to cure problems with their signature: Alabama, Alaska, Arkansas, Connecticut, Delaware, Idaho, Indiana, Kansas, Kentucky, Louisiana, Maine, Maryland, Michigan, Mississippi, Missouri, Nebraska, New Hampshire, New Mexico, New York, North Carolina, North Dakota, Oklahoma, Pennsylvania, South Carolina, South Dakota, Tennessee, Texas, Vermont, Virginia, West Virginia, Wisconsin and Wyoming.

[135] The 15 states that don't allow local officials to start processing absentee ballots early enough are Alabama, Kentucky, Maine, Maryland, Massachusetts, Michigan, Mississippi, New Hampshire, New York, Pennsylvania, South Carolina, South Dakota, West Virginia, Wisconsin, and Wyoming.

[136] "A Tool Kit of Resources for Scaling Up Vote by Mail," Center for Civic Design, last modified June 18, 2020, *https://civicdesign.org/tool-kit-for-scaling-up-vbm.*

[137] Sean Greene and Kyle Ueyama, "Vote-By-Mail Rates More Than Double Since 2000," Pew Charitable Trusts, April 29, 2015, *https://www.pewtrusts.org/en/research-and-analysis/blogs/stateline/2015/4/29/vote-by-mail-practices-more-than-double-since-2000.*

[138] Ibid.

[139] The 17 states that provide postage-prepaid return envelopes for ballots are Arizona, California, Delaware, Hawaii, Idaho, Iowa, Kansas, Maryland, Minnesota, Missouri, Nevada, New Mexico, Oregon, Rhode Island, Washington, West Virginia, and Wisconsin.

[140] Massoud Hayoun, "Could Washington State Be a Model for Native Voting Rights Reform?," Pacific Standard, March 20, 2019, *https://psmag.com/social-justice/could-washington-state-be-a-model-for-native-voting-rights-reform.* See Washington State's 2019 Native American Voting Rights Act, Engrossed Substitute S.B. 5079, 66th Leg., regular sess. (Washington 2019), *http://lawfilesext.leg.wa.gov/biennium/2019-20/Pdf/Bills/Senate%20Passed%20Legislature/5079-S.PL.pdf.*

[141] Vote At Home does not exclude voters experiencing homelessness or housing insecurity. These community members can have their ballots mailed to a shelter, park, or motor home, or they can pick up their ballots in person at the county elections office. "Homeless Voters and Those Wishing Confidentiality," Oregon Secretary of State, *https://sos.oregon.gov/voting/Pages/homeless-confidential.aspx.* Oregon Revised Statutes 247.038. Individuals who are homeless or reside in shelters, vehicles, marinas, or other identifiable locations cannot be denied the opportunity to register to vote. Residence addresses can be descriptions of the person's physical location or the office of the county clerk.

[142] The National Conference of State Legislatures supplies the most current information on states implementing Vote At Home. "All-Mail Elections (aka Vote-By-Mail)," National Conference of State Legislatures, November 7, 2019, *https://www.ncsl.org/research/elections-and-campaigns/all-mail-elections.aspx.*

Chapter 4

[143] This is a composite of several true stories from Americans. See "SPLC Sues Florida Officials to Keep Citizens from Losing Right to Vote Again," Southern Poverty Law Center, July 2, 2019, *https://www.splcenter.org/news/2019/07/02/splc-sues-florida-officials-keep-citizens-losing-right-to-vote-again;* Greg Allen, "Felons in Florida Want Their Voting Rights Back without a Hassle," National Public Radio, July 5, 2018, *https://www.npr.org/2018/07/05/625671186/felons-in-florida-want-their-voting-rights-back-without-a-hassle;* Joseph Williams, "Want to Vote? Pay Up," New Republic, October 24, 2019, *https://newrepublic.com/article/155483/florida-felon-voting-rights-court-debts-disenfranchisement;* Shirin Jaafari, "'I Lost My Right to Vote Before I Ever Had the Right to Vote,'" Public Radio International, October 9, 2018, *https://www.pri.org/stories/2018-10-09/i-lost-my-right-vote-i-ever-had-right-vote;* and Ben Botkin, "After Prison, Many Oklahomans Are Banned from Voting for Years," Oklahoma Watch, June 18, 2018, *https://oklahomawatch.org/2018/06/18/after-prison-many-oklahomans-are-prohibited-from-voting-for-years.*

[144] Christopher Uggen, Ryan Larson, and Sarah Shannon, "6 Million Lost Voters: State-Level Estimates of Felony Disenfranchisement, 2016," Sentencing Project, 2016, *http://www.sentencingproject.org/publications/6-million-lost-voters-state-level-estimates-felony-disenfranchisement-2016.*

[145] "Voting and Registration in the Election of November 2016," U.S. Census Bureau, May 2017, *https://www.census.gov/data/tables/time-series/demo/voting-and-registration/p20-580.html.*

[146] "Democracy Restoration Act," Brennan Center for Justice, August 8, 2019, *https://www.brennancenter.org/legislation/democracy-restoration-act.*

[147] Probation is part of a criminal sentencing to be served in the community under supervision, rather than in prison. Parole is granted by a parole board when someone has served some or most of their prison sentence and has exhibited signs of rehabilitation — they reenter the community under supervision.

[148] Wendy R. Weiser, "Testimony before House Committee on Administration in Support of the For the People Act," Brennan Center for Justice, February 13, 2019, *https://www.brennancenter.org/analysis/testimony-house-committee-administration-support-people-act.*

[149] Jean Chung, "Felony Disenfranchisement: A Primer," Sentencing Project, June 27, 2019, *https://www.sentencingproject.org/publications/felony-disenfranchisement-a-primer.*

[150] Martin Austermuhle, "DC Clears the Way for Incarcerated Felons to Vote, Joining Only Two States That Allow It," DCist, July 9, 2020, *https://dcist.com/story/20/07/09/dc-incarcerated-felons-vote-voting-rights.*

[151] Jean Chung, "Felony Disenfranchisement: A Primer," Sentencing Project, June 27, 2019, *https://www.sentencingproject.org/publications/felony-disenfranchisement-a-primer.*

152 Morgan McLeod, "Expanding the Vote: Two Decades of Felony Disenfranchisement Reforms," Sentencing Project, October 17, 2018, *https://www.sentencingproject.org/publications/expanding-vote-two-decades-felony-disenfranchisement-reforms.*

153 For example, Louisiana authorized voting rights for residents who have not been incarcerated for five years, including those on probation or parole. Ibid.

154 For example, Nevada passed a law to automatically restore voting rights upon release from prison, with no waiting period. "Voting Rights Restoration Efforts in Nevada," Brennan Center for Justice, May 30, 2019, *https://www.brennancenter.org/analysis/voting-rights-restoration-efforts-nevada.*

155 On August 5, 2020, Governor Kim Reynolds issued an executive order restoring voting rights to those who have completed prison, parole, probation, and special sentences. The order will benefit tens of thousands of people. "Voting Rights Restoration Efforts in Iowa," Brennan Center for Justice, last modified August 5, 2020, *https://www.brennancenter.org/our-work/research-reports/voting-rights-restoration-efforts-iowa.*

156 "Want to Help Restore the Vote? Take Action Today!" Restore the Vote — Minnesota, May 9, 2019, *https://restorethevotemn.org.*

157 Unfortunately, activists in Washington faced a setback when a bill to automatically restore rights once released from prison died in the state senate in February 2020. The change would have benefited about 10,000 people. David Hawkings, "Voting Bill in Washington Killed by Impasse on Which Felons Should Benefit," Fulcrum, February 2020, *https://thefulcrum.us/felons-voting-rights.*

158 "Want to Help Restore the Vote? Take Action Today!" Restore the Vote — Minnesota, May 9, 2019, *https://restorethevotemn.org.*

159 "Voting Rights Restoration Efforts in Virginia," Brennan Center for Justice, April 20, 2018, *https://www.brennancenter.org/analysis/voting-rights-restoration-efforts-virginia;* "State Felon Voting Laws," ProCon.org, last modified January 16, 2020, *https://felonvoting.procon.org/view.resource.php?resourceID=000286#virginia.*

160 "Voting Rights Restoration Efforts in Virginia," Brennan Center for Justice, April 20, 2018, *https://www.brennancenter.org/our-work/research-reports/voting-rights-restoration-efforts-virginia.*

161 Laura Vozzella, "Va. Gov. McAuliffe Says He Has Broken U.S. Record for Restoring Voting Rights," Washington Post, April 27, 2017, *https://www.washingtonpost.com/local/virginia-politics/va-gov-mcauliffe-says-he-has-broken-us-record-for-restoring-voting-rights/2017/04/27/55b5591a-2b8b-11e7-be51-b3fc6ff7faee_story.html?utm_term=.d7c0c68d0a6a.*

162 This is why Virginia remains in the right-most column — serving time in prison, parole, and probation are not enough for someone to get their voting rights back; they must still wait for further action by the governor.

163 Exec. Order No. 2015-0871, Ken. Gov. (November 24, 2015), *http://apps.sos.ky.gov/Executive/Journal/execjournalimages/2015-MISC-2015-0871-242277.pdf.*

164 "Kentucky Governor Creates New Process to Help Restore Voting Rights to 170,000 Citizens," Brennan Center for Justice, November 24, 2015, *https://www.brennancenter.org/our-work/analysis-opinion/kentucky-governor-creates-new-process-help-restore-voting-rights-170000.*

165 Samantha Lachman, "A GOP Governor Just Undid a Major Voting Rights Victory in His State," HuffPost, last modified January 4, 2017, *https://www.huffpost.com/entry/matt-bevin-voting-rights_n_567ac72ee4b014efe0d-7aaec.*

166 Exec. Order No. 2019-003, Ken. Gov. (December 12, 2019), *https://www.brennancenter.org/sites/default/files/2019-12/Executive%20Order%202019-003.pdf.*

167 "Florida Attorney General Election, 2018," Ballotpedia, accessed January 25, 2020, *https://ballotpedia.org/Florida_Amendment_4,_Voting_Rights_Restoration_for_Felons_Initiative_(2018).*

168 "Voting Rights Restoration Efforts in Florida," Brennan Center for Justice, May 31, 2019, *https://www.brennancenter.org/analysis/voting-rights-restoration-efforts-florida.*

169 "Voter Registration — by Party Affiliation," Florida Department of State Division of Elections, last modified September 30, 2019, *https://dos.myflorida.com/elections/data-statistics/voter-registration-statistics/voter-registration-monthly-reports/voter-registration-by-party-affiliation.*

170 Ex-felons could appeal to restore their rights, but the Florida process was arbitrary. As Governor Rick Scott said, "We can make any decisions we want." Kevin Morris, "A Transformative Step for Democracy in Florida," Brennan Center for Justice, November 7, 2018, *https://www.brennancenter.org/blog/transformative-step-democracy-florida.*

171 German Lopez, "Florida votes to restore ex-felon voting rights with Amendment 4," Vox, last modified November 7, 2018, *https://www.vox.com/policy-and-politics/2018/11/6/18052374/florida-amendment-4-felon-voting-rights-results.*

172 Rebekah Diller, "The Hidden Costs of Florida's Criminal Justice Fees," Brennan Center for Justice, 2010, *https://www.brennancenter.org/sites/default/files/legacy/Justice/FloridaF&F.pdf.*

[173] Lawrence Mower and David Ovalle, "How Much Will Regaining the Right to Vote Cost Florida Felons? It Could Be a Lot." Miami Herald, March 21, 2019, https://www.miamiherald.com/news/politics-government/state-politics/article228192699.html.

[174] "2018 Annual Assessments and Collections Report," Florida Court Clerks & Comptrollers, 2018, https://cdn.ymaws.com/www.flclerks.com/resource/resmgr/public_documents_/1_final_front_matter_cover_s.pdf.

[175] "Poll Taxes," National Museum of American History, accessed January 10, 2020, https://americanhistory.si.edu/democracy-exhibition/vote-voice/keeping-vote/state-rules-federal-rules/poll-taxes.

[176] Congress proposed the 24th Amendment in 1962, and it passed the House and Senate with the required two-thirds vote. By 1964, 38 states had ratified it, enough for it to take effect. At that time, 5 states still retained a poll tax: Alabama, Arkansas, Mississippi, Texas, and Virginia.

[177] P. R. Lockhart, "A Controversial Florida Law Stops Some Former Felons from Voting. A Judge Just Blocked Part of It." Vox, last modified October 19, 2019, https://www.vox.com/policy-and-politics/2019/7/2/20677955/amendment-4-florida-felon-voting-rights-lawsuits-fines-fees.

[178] Myrna Pérez, "Federal Appeals Court Rules Florida Voting Restrictions Unconstitutional," Brennan Center for Justice, February 19, 2020, https://www.brennancenter.org/our-work/analysis-opinion/federal-appeals-court-rules-florida-voting-restrictions-unconstitutional.

[179] Lawrence Mower, "Florida Felons Lose Voting Rights Case in Federal Appeals Court," Tampa Bay Times, September 11, 2020, https://www.tampabay.com/florida-politics/buzz/2020/09/11/florida-felons-lose-voting-rights-case-in-federal-appeals-court.

[180] "Criminal Justice Fact Sheet," NAACP, accessed January 10, 2020, https://www.naacp.org/criminal-justice-fact-sheet.

[181] "QuickFacts Population Estimates," U.S. Census Bureau, accessed January 16, 2020, https://www.census.gov/quickfacts/fact/table/US/PST045218.

[182] Bernadette Rabuy and Daniel Kopf, "Prisons of Poverty: Uncovering the Pre-incarceration Incomes of the Imprisoned," Prison Policy Initiative, July 9, 2015, https://www.prisonpolicy.org/reports/income.html.

[183] P. R. Lockhart, "A Controversial Florida Law Stops Some Former Felons from Voting. A Judge Just Blocked Part of It," Vox, last modified October 19, 2019, https://www.vox.com/policy-and-politics/2019/7/2/20677955/amendment-4-florida-felon-voting-rights-lawsuits-fines-fees.

[184] "Voting Rights Restoration," Brennan Center for Justice, accessed February 29, 2020, https://www.brennancenter.org/issues/ensure-every-american-can-vote/voting-rights-restoration.

[185] "Zero Disenfranchisement: The Movement to Restore Voting Rights," Common Cause Education Fund, accessed January 10, 2020, https://www.commoncause.org/page/zero-disenfranchisement.

Section II

[186] In Germany, big parties routinely spend between 20 and 30 million euros to win around 200 seats and the chancellor (head of government) position. That's an average of around $100,000 per race. Olga Khazan, "Why Germany's Politics Are Much Saner, Cheaper, and Nicer Than Ours," Atlantic, September 30, 2013, https://www.theatlantic.com/international/archive/2013/09/why-germany-s-politics-are-much-saner-cheaper-and-nicer-than-ours/280081. In Canada in 2015, the Liberal Party spent CAN $43 million total to win 184 seats, including the prime minister (head of government) position. That's an average of around $20,000 per race. Joan Bryden, "Liberals Outspent Conservatives by $1.2 million in 2015 Election," Globe and Mail, June 20, 2016, https://www.theglobeandmail.com/news/politics/liberals-outspent-conservatives-by-12-million-in-2015-election/article30524115.

[187] Sarah Holder, "City Elections Take Aim at the Spiraling Costs of Local Elections," CityLab, September 4, 2018, https://www.citylab.com/equity/2018/09/cities-take-aim-at-the-spiraling-costs-of-local-elections/567727.

[188] Citizens United v. Federal Election Commission, 558 U.S. 310, 396, and 450 (2010).

[189] "Citizens United v. Federal Election Commission," SCOTUS blog, January 21, 2010, https://www.scotusblog.com/case-files/cases/citizens-united-v-federal-election-commission.

[190] Dan Eggen, "Poll: Large Majority Opposes Supreme Court's Decision on Campaign Financing," Washington Post, February 17, 2010, http://www.washingtonpost.com/wp-dyn/content/article/2010/02/17/AR2010021701151.html; and Megan Thee-Brenan, "Polls Show Broad Support for Campaign Spending Caps," New York Times, April 2, 2014, https://www.nytimes.com/2014/04/03/us/politics/polls-show-broad-support-for-campaign-spending-caps.html.

[191] "McCutcheon v. Federal Election Commission," SCOTUS blog, April 2, 2014, https://www.scotusblog.com/case-files/cases/mccutcheon-v-federal-election-commission/.

[192] The opinion was signed by only a plurality, not a majority, of the nine justices. Only four justices joined the opinion: Roberts, Scalia, Kennedy, and Alito. Justice Thomas filed a separate opinion but concurred in the judgment.

[193] McCutcheon v. Federal Election Commission, 572 U.S. 185 (2014), *https://www.supremecourt.gov/opinions/13pdf/12-536_e1pf.pdf*.

[194] Lawrence Lessig, Republic, Lost: How Money Corrupts Congress — and a Plan to Stop It (New York: Twelve Books, 2011), 270.

Chapter 5

[195] This is a composite of true stories from Americans. Sarah Kliff, "Seattle's Radical Plan to Fight Big Money in Politics," Vox, November 5, 2018, *https://www.vox.com/2018/11/5/17058970/seattle-democracy-vouchers*; Susan Russell, "Democracy Vouchers Gave This Seattle Resident a Voice," Washington Community Action Network, March 12, 2018, *https://www.washingtoncan.org/civic-engagement-stories/2018/3/12/democracy-vouchers-gave-this-seattle-resident-a-voice*; "Seattle Tries Voucher System to Reform Campaign Finance," Marketplace, February 21, 2017, *https://www.marketplace.org/2017/02/21/seattle-tries-voucher-system-reform-campaign-finance/*; Sarah Kliff and Kenny Malone, "#873: The Seattle Experiment," Planet Money, podcast audio, November 2, 2018, *https://www.npr.org/transcripts/663541365*; Mark Joseph Stern, "Janus Unleashed," Slate, December 26, 2018, *https://slate.com/news-and-politics/2018/12/seattle-democracy-vouchers-elster-janus.html*; Gene Balk, "Do Seattle's Democracy Vouchers Work? New Analysis Says Yes," Seattle Times, last modified October 15, 2017, *https://www.seattletimes.com/seattle-news/data/do-seattles-democracy-vouchers-work-new-analysis-says-yes/*; and Adam Eichen, "The Case for Giving Every American $25 'Democracy Vouchers' for Every Election," Salon, October 26, 2018, *https://www.salon.com/2018/10/26/the-case-for-giving-every-american-25-democracy-vouchers-for-every-election_partner*.

[196] Kristin Eberhard, "Big Donors Dominated Portland's 2016 Mayoral Race," Sightline Institute, June 7, 2016, *https://www.sightline.org/2016/06/07/big-donors-dominated-portlands-2016-mayoral-race*; and Kristin Eberhard, "In Portland Elections, 600 Big Donors Tip the Campaign Scales," Sightline Institute, May 27, 2016, *https://www.sightline.org/2016/05/27/in-portland-elections-600-big-donors-tip-the-campaign-scales*.

[197] Serena Cruz, "Portland City Council Election Reform Would Make Each Voice Count," Street Roots, October 20, 2016, *https://news.streetroots.org/2016/10/20/portland-city-council-election-reform-would-make-each-voice-count*.

[198] Maggie Koerth, "Everyone Knows Money Influences Politics . . . except Scientists," FiveThirtyEight, June 4, 2019, *https://fivethirtyeight.com/features/everyone-knows-money-influences-politics-except-scientists*.

[199] Washington Post Staff, "Annotated Transcript: The Aug. 6 GOP Debate," Washington Post, August 6, 2015, *https://www.washingtonpost.com/news/post-politics/wp/2015/08/06/annotated-transcript-the-aug-6-gop-debate*.

[200] Adam Smith, "Joe Biden on Money in Politics: 'A Hell of a Way to Run a Democracy,'" Every Voice, July 17, 2015, *https://everyvoice.org/featured/joe-biden-money-politics-hell-way-run-democracy*.

[201] Maggie Koerth, "Everyone Knows Money Influences Politics . . . except Scientists," FiveThirtyEight, June 4, 2019, *https://fivethirtyeight.com/features/everyone-knows-money-influences-politics-except-scientists*.

[202] Ryan Grim and Sabrina Siddiqui, "Call Time for Congress Shows How Fundraising Dominates Bleak Work Life," HuffPost, last modified December 6, 2017, *https://www.huffpost.com/entry/call-time-congressional-fundraising_n_2427291*.

[203] Alan Durning, "Charts: Honest Elections Seattle Is an Incredible Bargain," Sightline Institute, May 4, 2015, *https://www.sightline.org/2015/05/04/charts-honest-elections-seattle-is-an-incredible-bargain*.

[204] Alan Durning, "Democracy Vouchers Are Fraud-Repellent," Sightline Institute, April 30, 2015, *https://www.sightline.org/2015/04/30/democracy-vouchers-are-fraud-repellent*.

[205] The program was designed for voters to be able to support only candidates for city council in its first year, and mayoral candidates and city attorney thereafter. City elections happen every two years in Seattle, so the first opportunity voters had to support mayoral candidates was in 2019.

[206] Teresa Mosqueda, "Seattle's Democracy Vouchers Helped Me Get Elected & Here's What I Want You to Know," Bustle, August 14, 2018, *https://www.bustle.com/p/seattles-democracy-vouchers-helped-me-get-elected-heres-what-i-want-you-to-know-10052772*.

[207] Margaret Morales, "Seattle's Democracy Vouchers Are Changing the Campaign Trail for Candidates and City Residents," Sightline Institute, November 28, 2017, *https://www.sightline.org/2017/11/28/seattles-democracy-vouchers-are-changing-the-campaign-trail-for-candidates-and-city-residents*.

[208] Jennifer Heerwig and Brian J. McCabe, "Expanding Participation in Municipal Elections: Assessing the Impact of Seattle's Democracy Voucher Program," University of Washington Center for Studies in Demography and Ecology, *https://www.jenheerwig.com/uploads/1/3/2/1/13210230/mccabe_heerwig_seattle_voucher_4.03.pdf*.

[209] The 2017 total includes Seattleites who donated a voucher even when a candidate's campaign wasn't able to use it because they had already used the maximum amount of voucher dollars under the Democracy Voucher rules. Ibid.

[210] "Seattle Democracy Voucher Program Evaluation," City of Seattle Ethics and Elections Commission, April 25, 2018, p. 26, *https://www.seattle.gov/Documents/Departments/EthicsElections/DemocracyVoucher/DVP%20Evaluation%20Final%20Report%20April%2025%202018.pdf#page=26*.

[211] "First Look: Seattle's Democracy Voucher Program," Win/Win Network and Every Voice Center, November 15, 2017, *https://everyvoice.org/wp-content/uploads/2018/08/2017-11-15-Seattle-Post-Election-Report-FINAL. pdf.*

[212] Dale Eisman, "Democracy Vouchers Leveling the Political Playing Field in Seattle," Common Cause, August 2, 2017, *https://www.commoncause.org/democracy-wire/democracy-vouchers-leveling-political-field.*

[213] "How States Can Fight Money in Politics," Indivisible, *https://indivisible.org/resource/how-states-can-fight-money-politics.*

Section III

[214] The first constitution was the Articles of Confederation, an agreement among the 13 original states written in 1777, ratified in 1781, and clearly not working by 1786, when James Madison called a convention in Annapolis to revise it. Not enough states sent delegates that year, but in 1787 states sent delegates to the Philadelphia Convention, which produced the second constitution that is still in place today.

[215] Maurice Duverger, Political Parties: Their Organization and Activity in the Modern State (London: Metheun, 1954); William H. Riker, "The Two-Party System and Duverger's Law: An Essay on the History of Political Science," American Political Science Review 76(4):753–66 (1982), *https://www.jstor.org/stable/1962968;* Arend Lijphart, "The Political Consequences of Electoral Law, 1945–85," American Political Science Review 84(2):481–96 (1990).

[216] V. O. Key, Politics, Parties, and Pressure Groups, 3rd ed. (New York: Thomas Y. Crowell Co., 1952), 224–25.

[217] "Gerrymandering," Wikipedia, last modified January 24, 2020, *https://en.wikipedia.org/wiki/Gerrymandering#Etymology.*

[218] Editorial Board, "When Politicians Pick Their Voters," New York Times, May 30, 2017, *https://www.nytimes.com/2017/05/30/opinion/gerrymandering-supreme-court.html?_r=0.*

[219] John Oliver, "Gerrymandering," Last Week Tonight with John Oliver, April 9, 2017, YouTube video, *https://www.youtube.com/watch?v=A-4dIImaodQ.*

[220] Alexander Burns and Jonathan Martin, "Eric Holder to Lead Democrats' Attack on Republican Gerrymandering," New York Times, January 11, 2017, *https://www.nytimes.com/2017/01/11/us/eric-holder-to-lead-democrats-attack-on-republican-gerrymandering.html.*

[221] "Governor Arnold Schwarzenegger Took His Mission to Terminate Gerrymandering to DC," USC Schwarzenegger Institute, March 29, 2019, *http://schwarzenegger.usc.edu/institute-in-action/article/governor-arnold-schwarzenegger-took-his-mission-to-terminate-gerrymandering.*

[222] "Washington's Farewell Address 1796," Avalon Project (Yale University), *https://avalon.law.yale.edu/18th_century/washing.asp.*

[223] "From John Adams to Jonathan Jackson" (letter, dated October 2, 1780), Founders Online (National Archives), *https://founders.archives.gov/documents/Adams/06-10-02-0113.*

[224] "James Madison to Robert Walsh" (letter, dated November 27, 1819), in The Writings of James Madison, vol. 3, ed. Gaillard Hunt (New York: G. P. Putnam's Sons, 1900–1910), 298, *http://press-pubs.uchicago.edu/founders/print_documents/a1_9_1s20.html.*

[225] "III. Thoughts on Government" (dated April 1776), Papers of John Adams, vol. 4, ed. Robert J. Taylor (Cambridge: Harvard University, 1979), *http://www.masshist.org/publications/adams-papers/view?&id=PJA04d040.*

[226] Kristin Eberhard, "This Is How New Zealand Fixed Its Voting System," Sightline Institute, June 19, 2017, *https://www.sightline.org/2017/06/19/this-is-how-new-zealand-fixed-its-voting-system.*

[227] Jack Denvir, "Single-Winner Districts: Not What the Founding Fathers Intended," FairVote, August 17, 2015, *https://www.fairvote.org/single-winner-districts-not-what-the-founding-fathers-intended.*

[228] As an example, in 1840, Whigs garnered 43 percent of the Alabama statewide vote yet did not receive a single seat. But Whigs won control of both Congress and the presidency and passed a bill requiring single-winner districts with the aim of preventing an Alabama-like result for themselves in the future. Erik J. Engstrom, "The United States: The Past — Moving from Diversity to Uniform Single-Member Districts," in The Handbook of Electoral System Choice, ed. Josep M. Colomer (London: Palgrave Macmillan, 2004).

[229] "VRA Remedy Database," FairVote, 2020, *https://www.fairvote.org/vra_remedy_database.*

[230] Lee Drutman, Breaking the Two-Party Doom Loop (Oxford: Oxford University Press, 2019).

[231] Ezra Klein, Why We're Polarized (New York: Simon & Schuster, 2020).

[232] "Marriage," Gallup Polls, accessed September 20, 2020, *https://news.gallup.com/poll/117328/marriage.aspx.*

[233] Kevin Enochs, "In US, 'Interpolitical' Marriage Increasingly Frowned Upon," Voice of America, February 3, 2017, *https://www.voanews.com/usa/us-interpolitical-marriage-increasingly-frowned-upon.*

[234] By the turn of the twentieth century, more Americans could vote than had been allowed in the eighteenth century. Most land-owning and religious requirements had been removed, the post–Civil War amendments technically allowed men of color to vote, and in 1920 women gained the right to vote too.

[235] In Federalist Paper No. 68, the founding fathers argued that the Electoral College would prevent an unqualified man with "talents for low intrigue, and the little arts of popularity" from becoming president, because the electors would be more likely to select men with "characters preeminent for ability and virtue." Avalon Project (Yale University), https://avalon.law.yale.edu/18th_century/fed68.asp.

[236] George C. Edwards III, Why the Electoral College Is Bad for America, 3rd ed. (New Haven, CT: Yale University Press, 2019); John P. Roche, "The Founding Fathers: A Reform Caucus in Action," American Political Science Review 55(4):799–816 (1961), https://www.cambridge.org/core/journals/american-political-science-review/article/founding-fathers-a-reform-caucus-in-action/CE50156024A1189BFA965DBBE1094B3A.

[237] Dave Roos, "Why Was the Electoral College Created?," History.com, January 7, 2020, https://www.history.com/news/electoral-college-founding-fathers-constitutional-convention.

[238] Garrett Epps, "The Electoral College Wasn't Meant to Overturn Elections," Atlantic, November 27, 2016, https://www.theatlantic.com/politics/archive/2016/11/the-electoral-college-shouldnt-save-us-from-trump/508817.

[239] In 1824, Andrew Jackson won only 99 Electoral College votes, 32 fewer than he needed for a majority of the total votes cast. John Quincy Adams won 84 electoral votes followed by 41 for William H. Crawford, and 37 for Henry Clay. All four candidates in the election identified with the Democratic-Republican Party. "Democratic-Republican Party," Wikipedia, accessed January 20, 2020, https://en.wikipedia.org/wiki/Democratic-Republican_Party. In 1876, Tilden won 184 electoral votes to Hayes's 165, with 20 votes unresolved. "United States Electoral College," Wikipedia, accessed January 20, 2020, https://en.wikipedia.org/wiki/United_States_Electoral_College.

[240] The original U.S. Constitution gave state legislatures great power in the federal government: in addition to choosing presidential electors, state legislatures also chose their respective U.S. senators. This did not change until 1913, when the 17th Amendment changed to instead elect U.S. senators by a popular vote of the people. U.S. Constitution, amend. 17, art. 1, sec. 3, http://constitutionus.com/#x17.

[241] U.S. Constitution, art. 2, sec. 1, cl. 2, http://constitutionus.com/#a2s1c2.

[242] McPherson v. Blacker, 146 U.S. 1 (1892), https://scholar.google.com/scholar_case?case=12718508074854824379.

[243] Erik J. Engstrom, "The United States: The Past — Moving from Diversity to Uniform Single-Member Districts," in The Handbook of Electoral System Choice, ed. Josep M. Colomer (London: Palgrave Macmillan, 2004).

[244] Ibid.

[245] The exceptions are Maine and Nebraska, where one electoral vote is awarded to the presidential candidate who wins the popular vote in each congressional district, while the remaining two electoral votes are awarded to the candidates receiving the most votes statewide. "The Electoral College," National Conference of State Legislatures, January 6, 2020, http://www.ncsl.org/research/elections-and-campaigns/the-electoral-college.aspx#distribution.

[246] "The Federalist Papers: No. 68," Avalon Project (Yale University), accessed September 20, 2020, https://avalon.law.yale.edu/18th_century/fed68.asp.

[247] By today's standards, the number of voters a presidential candidate had to win over was shockingly small — there were fewer than 44,000 voters total in the first presidential election. Compare that to around 200,000 voters in each of the United States' 435 congressional districts in 2018. Michael J. Dubin, United States Presidential Elections, 1788–1860: The Official Results by County and State (Jefferson, NC: McFarland, 2002).

[248] In 2020 the Supreme Court agreed to decide whether electors must be rubber stamps, or if they may choose to cast their vote for a candidate of their own choice. Adam Liptak, "Supreme Court to Hear Timely Case on Electoral College," New York Times, January 17, 2020, https://www.nytimes.com/2020/01/17/us/supreme-court-electoral-college.html.

[249] George C. Edwards III, Why the Electoral College Is Bad for America, 3rd ed. (New Haven, CT: Yale University Press, 2019).

[250] "The Federalist Papers: No. 22," Avalon Project (Yale University), accessed September 20, 2020, https://avalon.law.yale.edu/18th_century/fed22.asp.

[251] "Madison Debates — June 30," Avalon Project (Yale University), accessed September 20, 2020, https://avalon.law.yale.edu/18th_century/debates_630.asp.

252 Noah Feldman, "Revamping the Senate Is a Fantasy," Bloomberg Opinion, October 10, 2018, *https://www.bloomberg.com/opinion/articles/2018-10-10/u-s-senate-is-undemocratic-but-there-s-no-way-to-change-it.*

253 "The Federalist Papers: No. 22," Avalon Project (Yale University), accessed September 20, 2020, *https://avalon.law.yale.edu/18th_century/fed22.asp.*

254 Michael Lind, "75 Stars," Mother Jones, January/February 1998, *https://www.motherjones.com/politics/1998/01/75-stars.*

255 No other democratic nation fills its top job quite the way the United States does, and only a handful are even similar. The only other democracies that indirectly elect a leader who combines the roles of head of state and head of government (as the U.S. president does) are Botswana, the Federated States of Micronesia, the Marshall Islands, Nauru, South Africa, and Suriname. Even those countries give the task of choosing the president to their national legislature, not a onetime body with no other duties like the U.S. Electoral College. In more than half (65) of the world's 125 democracies, voters directly elect the head of state — nearly always called a president. Thirty other democracies are classified as constitutional monarchies, and in the remaining 30, including the United States, the head of state is indirectly elected. Drew DeSilver, "Among Democracies, U.S. Stands Out in How It Chooses Its Head of State," Pew Research Center, November 22, 2016, *https://www.pewresearch.org/fact-tank/2016/11/22/among-democracies-u-s-stands-out-in-how-it-chooses-its-head-of-state.*

Chapter 6

256 This is a composite of several true stories from Americans. See Jonathan Martin, "Many Democrats Love Elizabeth Warren. They Also Worry about Her," New York Times, August 15, 2019, *www.nytimes.com/2019/08/15/us/politics/elizabeth-warren-2020-campaign.amp.html*; Marco della Cava, Sarah Elbeshbishi, and Ledyard King, "Elizabeth Warren's Latest Hurdle to the Presidency: Democrats' Belief Women Face Tougher Fight against Trump," USA Today, September 10, 2019, *https://www.usatoday.com/amp/2055209001*; and Molly Hensley-Clancy, "Democrats Like the Idea of a Gay President. But They Are Quietly Worried about Mayor Pete," BuzzFeed News, May 23, 2019, *www.buzzfeednews.com/amphtml/mollyhensleyclancy/mayor-pete-buttigieg-gay-2020-win.*

257 Steven Levitsky, How Democracies Die (Crown Publishing Group, 2018).

258 Ray La Raja and Jonathan Rauch, "Too Much Democracy Is Bad for Democracy," Atlantic, December 2019, *https://www.theatlantic.com/magazine/archive/2019/12/too-much-democracy-is-bad-for-democracy/600766.*

259 Donald Trump in 2016, George Bush in 2000, and Bill Clinton in 1996. The Electoral College of course complicates the presidential election, but even without it, the presence of additional candidates outside the two major parties, combined with plurality voting, enables candidates to win without majority support.

260 "Partisanship and Political Animosity in 2016," Pew Research Center, June 22, 2016, *https://www.pewresearch.org/politics/2016/06/22/partisanship-and-political-animosity-in-2016.*

261 "Political Polarization in the American Public," Pew Research Center, June 12, 2014, *https://www.pewresearch.org/politics/2014/06/12/political-polarization-in-the-american-public.*

262 "Maine Voters Handle Ranked Choice Voting Well," FairVote, November 15, 2018, *https://www.fairvote.org/congressman_elected_with_instant_runoff.*

263 Brian Naylor, "Ranked Choice Voting Could Play a Deciding Role in Maine's Senate Race," NPR, October 8 2020, *https://www.npr.org/2020/10/08/920830640/ranked-choice-voting-could-play-a-deciding-role-in-maines-senate-race.*

264 Some researchers have found that voters can think about and distinguish up to six candidates, but a ballot with more starts to seem overwhelming.

265 Chapter 8 gives more detail about how to select multiple top candidates from a ranked choice ballot.

266 Washington and California use open top-two, also known as nonpartisan blanket primaries.

267 Grace Ramsey and Sarah John, "Ranked Choice Voting: Lessons about Political Polarization from Civility Studies of Local Elections," National Democracy Slam 2015, April 22, 2015, *https://eventmobi.com/api/events/8461/documents/download/f0d0c6d5-8f6c-4c34-ae52-f93dc4a1203d.pdf/as/Sarah%20John%20and%20Grace%20Ramsey_RCV%20Lessons%20from%20Civility%20Study_Reform#14.pdf.*

268 Dean E. Murphy, "New Runoff System in San Francisco Has the Rival Candidates Cooperating," New York Times, September 30, 2004, *https://www.nytimes.com/2004/09/30/us/new-runoff-system-in-san-francisco-has-the-rival-candidates-cooperating.html.*

269 Catherine Rauch, "Group Hugs on the Oakland Campaign Trail," Oakland Magazine, September 3, 2014, *http://www.oaklandmagazine.com/Oakland-Magazine/September-2014/Group-Hugs-on-the-Oakland-Campaign-Trail.*

270 "Andrew Douglas, "Ranked Choice Voting and Civility: New Evidence from American Cities," Ranked Choice Voting Civility Project, April 2014, *https://fairvote.app.box.com/v/rcv-civility-study-april-2014.*

271 "Campaign Civility," FairVote, accessed January 20, 2020, *https://www.fairvote.org/research_rcvcampaigncivility.*

272 David Daley, "Ranked Choice Voting Is on a Roll: 6 States Have Opted In for the 2020 Democratic Primary," In These Times, July 9, 2019, *http://inthesetimes.com/article/21959/ranked-choice-voting-2020-democratic-primary-maine-kansas.*

273 "Alaska RCV 2020," FairVote, 2020, *https://www.fairvote.org/alaskarcv2020.*

274 David Daley, "Ranked-Choice Voting = Super Saturday in Alaska, Hawaii," RealClearPolitics, April 13, 2019, *https://www.realclearpolitics.com/articles/2019/04/13/ranked-choice_voting__super_saturday_in_alaska_hawaii.html.*

275 John Hanna, "Kansas Democrats Are Planning Ranked-Choice Voting for Presidential Primary," PBS NewsHour, June 11, 2019, *https://www.pbs.org/newshour/politics/kansas-democrats-are-planning-ranked-choice-voting-for-presidential-primary.*

276 "Wyoming RCV 2020," FairVote, 2020, *https://www.fairvote.org/wyomingrcv2020.*

277 David P. Redlawsk, "Iowa Democrats' Innovative Changes May Have Saved the Caucuses," Des Moines Register, February 12, 2019, *https://www.desmoinesregister.com/story/opinion/columnists/caucus/2019/02/12/iowa-democrats-innovative-changes-may-have-saved-caucuses-2020-presidential-new-hampshire-primary/2846267002.*

278 Dan Merica, "Here Is How Early Voting Works in the Nevada Caucuses," CNN, February 18, 2020, *https://www.cnn.com/2020/02/17/politics/how-does-early-voting-work-nevada-caucuses/index.html.*

279 "Alaska RCV 2020," FairVote, 2020, *https://www.fairvote.org/alaskarcv2020.*

280 "Utah Voters Rank Their Choices: The 2019 Municipal Elections in Payson and Vineyard," FairVote, accessed February 16, 2020, *https://infogram.com/utah-voters-use-rcv-1hzj4o9kmrv74pw?live.*

281 "The Primaries Are Just Dumb," New York Times, February 26, 2020, *https://www.nytimes.com/2020/02/26/opinion/democrats-primary-south-carolina.html.*

282 "Large Majority of Maine Voters Want to Keep Ranked Choice Voting and Find it Easy," FairVote, November 15, 2018, *https://www.fairvote.org/maine_voters_want_to_keep_rcv.*

283 Maggie Astor, "Maine Voters Will Rank Their Top Presidential Candidates in 2020," New York Times, September 6, 2019, *https://www.nytimes.com/2019/09/06/us/politics/maine-elections.html*; Adam Crepeau, "Here's What RCV for Presidential Elections Means for Maine," Maine Heritage Policy Center, September 9, 2019, *https://mainepolicy.org/heres-what-rcv-for-presidential-elections-means-for-maine.*

284 "Ranked Choice Voting — Where It's Used," Ranked Choice Voting Resource Center, accessed January 20, 2020, *https://www.rankedchoicevoting.org/where_used.*

285 Li Zhou, "Live Results for New York City Ranked-Choice Voting Ballot Initiative," Vox, November 5, 2019, *https://www.vox.com/policy-and-politics/2019/11/5/20948132/live-results-new-york-city-ranked-choice-voting.*

286 "Ranked Choice Voting — Where It's Used," Ranked Choice Voting Resource Center, accessed January 20, 2020, *https://www.rankedchoicevoting.org/where_used.*

287 "About Ranked Choice Voting," Voter Choice for Massachusetts, accessed January 2020, *https://voterchoice2020.org/about.*

288 James Brooks, "On Election-Reform Ballot Measure 2, Backers and Opponents Don't Follow Party Lines," Anchorage Daily News, last modified September 12, 2020, *https://www.adn.com/politics/2020/09/09/on-election-reform-ballot-measure-2-backers-and-opponents-dont-follow-party-lines.*

289 "Making Votes Count: Ranked Choice Voting Ballots and the Contest for the Democratic Presidential Nomination in 2020," FairVote, October 2019, *https://fairvote.app.box.com/s/lr5uioq4km12zskrfic8157hp214gnk6.*

290 "Where Ranked Choice Voting Is Used," FairVote, accessed January 20, 2020, *https://www.fairvote.org/where_is_ranked_choice_voting_used.*

291 "RCV in Campus Elections," FairVote, accessed January 20, 2020, *https://www.fairvote.org/rcv_in_campus_elections.*

292 "Ranked Choice Voting Will Be Question 1 on the Ballot This November!" Common Cause New York, accessed January 20, 2020, *https://www.commoncause.org/new-york/wp-content/uploads/sites/20/2018/08/RCV-Education-One-Pager.pdf.*

Chapter 7

[293] This is a composite of several true stories from Americans. See Justin Mattingly, "Senate Panel Punts on Virginia Joining States Pushing Popular Vote over Electoral College," Roanoke Times, February 25, 2020, https://roanoke.com/z-no-digital/senate-panel-punts-on-virginia-joining-states-pushing-popular-vote/article_bb34c0d8-6142-5acb-94ea-a394d519e6e4.html; "Janine Reid: Our Republic Is Strengthened by the National Popular Vote," Greeley Tribune, July 11, 2020, https://www.greeleytribune.com/2020/07/01/janine-reid-our-republic-is-strengthened-by-the-national-popular-vote/; and Saul Anuzis, "The Popular Vote Should Prevail in Presidential Elections: Here's How to Do It," Miami Herald, August 19, 2020, https://www.miamiherald.com/opinion/op-ed/article245093180.html.

[294] In Maine and Nebraska, the winner in each congressional district receives one electoral vote, and the statewide winner receives two more.

[295] John R. Koza, Barry F. Fadem, Mark Grueskin, Michael S. Mandell, Robert Richie, and Joseph F. Zimmerman, "Every Vote Equal: A State-Based Plan for Electing the President by National Popular Vote," 4th ed., National Popular Vote, 2013, http://www.every-vote-equal.com/sites/default/files/everyvoteequal-4th-ed-2013-02-21.pdf.

[296] Ibid.

[297] CGP Grey, The Trouble with the Electoral College, November 7, 2011, YouTube video, https://www.youtube.com/watch?v=7wC42HgLA4k&feature=youtu.be&t=259.

[298] "List of United States Presidential Elections by Popular Vote Margin," Wikipedia, accessed February 4, 2020, https://en.wikipedia.org/wiki/List_of_United_States_presidential_elections_by_popular_vote_margin.

[299] John R. Koza, Barry F. Fadem, Mark Grueskin, Michael S. Mandell, Robert Richie, and Joseph F. Zimmerman, "Every Vote Equal: A State-Based Plan for Electing the President by National Popular Vote," 4th ed., National Popular Vote, 2013, http://www.every-vote-equal.com/sites/default/files/everyvoteequal-4th-ed-2013-02-21.pdf.

[300] "Presidential Elections," FairVote, accessed February 4, 2020, https://www.fairvote.org/presidential_elections#.UJBM-8XA-6U.

[301] Aaron Blake, "Donald Trump Says He Would Have Won a Popular-Vote Election. And He Could Be Right." Washington Post, November 5, 2016, https://www.washingtonpost.com/news/the-fix/wp/2016/11/14/trump-lost-the-popular-vote-that-doesnt-mean-he-would-have-lost-a-popular-vote-election.

[302] Ann-Derrick Gaillot, "11 Must-Read Quotes from Donald Trump's '60 Minutes' Interview," Bustle, November 14, 2016, https://www.bustle.com/articles/195039-11-must-read-quotes-from-donald-trumps-60-minutes-interview.

[303] "Presidential Elections," FairVote, accessed February 4, 2020, https://www.fairvote.org/presidential_elections#.UJBM-8XA-6U.

[304] "America Goes to the Polls 2012," NonProfit Vote, 2012, http://www.elon.edu/docs/e-web/org/nccc/AmericaGoesToThe%20Polls2012.pdf#page=9.

[305] "Presidential Elections," FairVote, accessed February 4, 2020, https://www.fairvote.org/presidential_elections#.UJBM-8XA-6U.

[306] "Two-Thirds of Presidential Campaign Is in Just 6 States," National Popular Vote, accessed February 4, 2020, https://www.nationalpopularvote.com/campaign-events-2016.

[307] Tim Meko, Denise Lu, and Lazaro Gamio, "How Trump Won the Presidency with Razor-Thin Margins in Swing States," Washington Post, November 11, 2016, https://www.washingtonpost.com/graphics/politics/2016-election/swing-state-margins.

[308] "2016 Presidential Candidate General Election Events Tracker (maintained by FairVote)," FairVote, accessed February 29, 2020, https://docs.google.com/spreadsheets/d/14Lxw0vc4YBUwQ8cZouyewZvOGg6PyzS2mAr-WNe3iJcY.

[309] "Agreement Among the States to Elect the President by National Popular Vote," National Popular Vote, accessed February 4, 2020, http://www.nationalpopularvote.com/pages/explanation.php.

[310] John Hudak, Presidential Pork: White House Influence over the Distribution of Federal Grants (Washington, DC: Brookings Institution Press, 2014).

[311] Douglas Kriner and Andrew Reeves, "Presidents Create Political Inequality by Allocating Federal Dollars to Electorally Useful Constituencies across the Country," LSE US Centre, April 6, 2015, https://blogs.lse.ac.uk/usappblog/2015/04/06/presidents-create-political-inequality-by-allocating-federal-dollars-to-electorally-useful-constituencies-across-the-country.

[312] "President Obama's 'No Swing State Left Behind' Policy," Wall Street Journal, June 5, 2012, https://www.wsj.com/articles/SB10001424052702303640104577440803786176064.

[313] Douglas L. Kriner, The Particularistic President: Executive Branch Politics and Political Inequality (Cambridge, UK: Cambridge University Press, 2015).

[314] See analysis by National Popular Vote for 2016: *https://drive.google.com/file/d/0B716mDiwCPFhaVZRb-k9MN0ZfMXFIZVQxQTZkOENPX1BJVlBN/view* and 2012: *https://drive.google.com/file/d/0B716mDi-wCPFhTm0tX20wSERZMVNBODhpZE4xdWtsTjMyajBB/view.*

[315] Chris Kirk, "How Powerful Is Your Vote?," Slate, November 2, 2012, *http://www.slate.com/articles/news_and_politics/map_of_the_week/2012/11/presidential_election_a_map_showing_the_vote_power_of_all_50_states.html.*

[316] Donald Applestein, "The Three-Fifths Compromise: Rationalizing the Irrational," Constitution Daily, February 12, 2013, *https://constitutioncenter.org/blog/the-three-fifths-compromise-rationalizing-the-irrational.*

[317] Wilfred Codrington III, "The Electoral College's Racist Origins," Atlantic, November 17, 2019, *https://www.theatlantic.com/ideas/archive/2019/11/electoral-college-racist-origins/601918.*

[318] Rick Perlstein, "Exclusive: Lee Atwater's Infamous 1981 Interview on the Southern Strategy," Nation, November 13, 2012, *https://www.thenation.com/article/exclusive-lee-atwaters-infamous-1981-interview-southern-strategy.*

[319] The five are Alabama, Georgia, Louisiana, Mississippi, and South Carolina. The sixth state is Maryland.

[320] Alabama, Mississippi, and South Carolina.

[321] "List of United States Presidential Election Results by State," Wikipedia, last modified December 30, 2019, *https://en.wikipedia.org/wiki/List_of_United_States_presidential_election_results_by_state.*

[322] John R. Koza, Barry F. Fadem, Mark Grueskin, Michael S. Mandell, Robert Richie, and Joseph F. Zimmerman, "Every Vote Equal: A State-Based Plan for Electing the President by National Popular Vote," 4th ed., National Popular Vote, 2013, *http://www.every-vote-equal.com/sites/default/files/everyvoteequal-4th-ed-2013-02-21.pdf.*

[323] Claire Davis, "Oklahoma Voter Turnout Suffers without National Popular Vote Plan," FairVote, March 13, 2015, *https://www.fairvote.org/oklahoma-voter-turnout-suffers-without-national-popular-vote-plan.*

[324] Kristin Eberhard, "Oregon Legislature Passes New Motor Voter Law," Sightline Institute, March 9, 2015, *https://www.sightline.org/2015/03/09/oregon-legislature-passes-new-motor-voter-law.*

[325] "The Federalist Papers: No. 68," Avalon Project (Yale University), *https://avalon.law.yale.edu/18th_century/fed68.asp.*

[326] "Home," National Popular Vote, accessed February 8, 2020, *http://www.nationalpopularvote.com/index.php.*

[327] "Text of the National Popular Vote Compact Bill," National Popular Vote, *https://www.nationalpopularvote.com/bill-text.*

[328] Kristin Eberhard, "Oregon Just Joined the National Popular Vote Interstate Compact," Sightline Institute, June 5, 2019, *https://www.sightline.org/2019/06/05/oregon-just-joined-the-national-popular-vote-interstate-compact;* "Status of National Popular Vote Bill in Each State," National Popular Vote, accessed February 29, 2020, *https://www.nationalpopularvote.com/state-status.*

[329] "Election 2016: Restrictive Voting Laws by the Numbers," Brennan Center for Justice, September 28, 2016, *https://www.brennancenter.org/our-work/research-reports/election-2016-restrictive-voting-laws-numbers.*

[330] "Two-Thirds of Presidential Campaign Is in Just 6 States," National Popular Vote, accessed February 8, 2020, *https://www.nationalpopularvote.com/campaign-events-2016.*

[331] Alaska, DC, Delaware, Hawaii, Idaho, Maine, Montana, North Dakota, Rhode Island, South Dakota, Vermont, and Wyoming.

[332] "Myths That Candidates Reach Out to All the States under the Current System," National Popular Vote, *https://www.nationalpopularvote.com/section_9.2.*

[333] Kristin Eberhard, "The Electoral College Trumped the People. Again," Sightline Institute, November 28, 2016, *https://www.sightline.org/2016/11/28/the-electoral-college-trumped-the-people-again.*

[334] Alaska, Idaho, Montana, North Dakota, South Dakota, and Wyoming.

[335] DC, Delaware, Hawaii, Maine, Rhode Island, and Vermont.

[336] Anna Fahey, "We the People Say: The Electoral College Is Not for Us," Sightline Institute, November 18, 2016, *https://www.sightline.org/2016/11/18/we-the-people-say-the-electoral-college-is-not-for-us.*

[337] National Popluar Vote Inc., "Myths about Small States," *https://www.nationalpopularvote.com/section_9.4#myth_9.4.4.*

[338] DC, Hawaii, Rhode Island, and Vermont.

[339] Delaware and Maine.

[340] Alaska, Idaho, Montana, and North Dakota.

Chapter 8

[341] Sabrina Tavernise, "'These Americans Are Done with Politics,'" New York Times, November 17, 2018, https://www.nytimes.com/2018/11/17/sunday-review/elections-partisanship-exhausted-majority.html; Christina Zdanowicz, "Neither Republican or Democrat: Why I'm an Independent," CNN, November 2, 2012, https://www.cnn.com/2012/11/02/politics/irpt-independent-voters/index.html; Bente Birkeland, "With Voters Sour on Major Parties, Group Recruits 'None of the Above' Candidates," National Public Radio, October 14, 2018, https://www.npr.org/2018/10/14/656576055/with-voters-sour-on-major-parties-group-recruits-none-of-the-above-candidates; Krosbie Carter, "Why Many Americans Are Registering as Independents, Instead of GOP or Democrat," Mic, January 13, 2012, https://www.mic.com/articles/3301/why-many-americans-are-registering-as-independents-instead-of-gop-or-democrat; and Susan Page, "Divided We Fall? Americans See Our Angry Political Debate as 'a Big Problem,'" USA Today, last modified December 9, 2019, https://www.usatoday.com/story/news/politics/elections/hiddencommonground/2019/12/05/hidden-common-ground-americans-divided-politics-seek-civility/4282301002.

[342] See videos by Washington Post, Vox, and John Oliver, and commitments from Eric Holder and Arnold Schwarzenegger. Christopher Ingraham, "This Is Actually What America Would Look Like without Gerrymandering," Washington Post, January 13, 2016, video, https://www.washingtonpost.com/news/wonk/wp/2016/01/13/this-is-actually-what-america-would-look-like-without-gerrymandering; "The Algorithm That Could Help End Partisan Gerrymandering," Vox, April 10, 2017, YouTube video, https://www.youtube.com/watch?v=gRCZR_BbjTo; John Oliver, "Gerrymandering," Last Week Tonight with John Oliver, April 9, 2017, YouTube video, https://www.youtube.com/watch?v=A-4dIImaodQ; Alexander Burns and Jonathan Martin, "Eric Holder to Lead Democrats' Attack on Republican Gerrymandering," New York Times, January 11, 2017, https://www.nytimes.com/2017/01/11/us/eric-holder-to-lead-democrats-attack-on-republican-gerrymandering.html?_r=1; and Judy Kurtz, "Schwarzenegger Rips Gerrymandering: Congress 'Couldn't Beat Herpes in the Polls,'" Hill, February 15, 2017, https://thehill.com/blogs/in-the-know/in-the-know/319678-schwarzenegger-rips-gerrymandering-congress-couldnt-beat-herpes.

[343] Michael C. Li and Thomas P. Wolf, "Supreme Court Has Historic Chance to End Extreme Gerrymandering," American Prospect, June 21, 2017, http://prospect.org/article/supreme-court-has-historic-chance-end-extreme-gerrymandering.

[344] Erica Klarreich, "Gerrymandering Is Illegal, but Only Mathematicians Can Prove It," Wired, April 16, 2017, https://www.wired.com/2017/04/gerrymandering-illegal-mathematicians-can-prove.

[345] Ibid.; Elizabeth Kolbert, "Drawing the Line," New Yorker, June 27, 2016, https://www.newyorker.com/magazine/2016/06/27/ratfcked-the-influence-of-redistricting; and Christopher Ingraham, "This Is the Best Explanation of Gerrymandering You Will Ever See," Washington Post, March 1, 2015, https://www.washingtonpost.com/news/wonk/wp/2015/03/01/this-is-the-best-explanation-of-gerrymandering-you-will-ever-see.

[346] "Monopoly Politics 2018," FairVote, February 2017, https://docs.google.com/spreadsheets/d/1P3WA35-_XNs1Tm1KfJdxlhQ90dzrK9mWTmFnPlHSNr4/edit#gid=1867046879.

[347] In 35 states, the state legislatures are responsible for drawing district lines. In practice, this often means that the party in control of the state legislature at the time of redistricting is able to draw lines that lock that party into power for a decade, no matter what the voters say.

[348] Heather Gerken, "A Wisconsin Court Case May Be the Last Best Hope to Fix Gerrymandering by 2020," Vox, December 1, 2016, https://www.vox.com/the-big-idea/2016/12/1/13800348/wisconsin-gerrymander-supreme-court-parties.

[349] Michael Li and Thomas Wolf, "5 Things to Know about the Wisconsin Partisan Gerrymandering Case," Brennan Center for Justice, June 19, 2017, https://www.brennancenter.org/blog/5-things-know-about-wisconsin-partisan-gerrymandering-case.

[350] Aaron Blake, "Why You Should Stop Blaming Gerrymandering So Much. Really," Washington Post, April 8, 2017, https://www.washingtonpost.com/news/the-fix/wp/2017/04/08/why-you-should-stop-blaming-gerrymandering-so-much-really/?utm_term=.1b78f5f77fb4; Ben Anderstone, "Puget Sound Really Is a Political Bubble, and It's Getting Worse," Crosscut, December 28, 2016, http://crosscut.com/2016/12/puget-sound-really-is-a-political-bubble-and-its-getting-worse/; and "2014 Political Polarization Survey: Table 3.2 Ideal Community Type," Pew Research Center, June 12, 2014, http://www.people-press.org/2014/06/12/ideal-community-type.

[351] Jowei Chen and Jonathan Rodden, "Don't Blame the Maps," New York Times, January 24, 2014, https://www.nytimes.com/2014/01/26/opinion/sunday/its-the-geography-stupid.html?_r=0.

[352] Bill Bishop, The Big Sort: Why the Clustering of Like-Minded America Is Tearing Us Apart (Boston, MA: Mariner Books, 2009); and David Wasserman and Ally Flinn, "Introducing the 2017 Cook Political Report Partisan Voter Index," Cook Political Report, April 7, 2017, https://cookpolitical.com/introducing-2017-cook-political-report-partisan-voter-index.

[353] Tim Wallace, "The Two Americas of 2016," New York Times, November 16, 2016, https://www.nytimes.com/interactive/2016/11/16/us/politics/the-two-americas-of-2016.html.

[354] Vieth v. Jubelirer, 541 U.S. 267 (2004), https://supreme.justia.com/cases/federal/us/541/267/opinion.html.

[355] Nicholas Goedert, "Gerrymandering or Geography? How Democrats Won the Popular Vote but Lost the Congress in 2012," Research & Politics, April 1, 2014, *http://journals.sagepub.com/doi/abs/10.1177/2053168014528683.*

[356] Ibid.

[357] Gill v. Whitford, 585 U.S. ___ (2018), *http://www.scotusblog.com/wp-content/uploads/2017/04/16-1161-cert-amicus-rnc.pdf.*

[358] Jowei Chen and Jonathan Rodden, "Unintentional Gerrymandering: Political Geography and Electoral Bias in Legislatures," Quarterly Journal of Political Science 8:239–69 (2013), *http://web.stanford.edu/~jrodden/wp/florida.pdf.*

[359] "California Citizens Redistricting Commission," Wikipedia, last modified September 27, 2019, *https://en.wikipedia.org/wiki/California_Citizens_Redistricting_Commission.*

[360] Brian Olson, "Engineering Elections without Bias | Brian Olson | TEDxCambridge," TEDx Talks, June 22, 2016, YouTube video, *https://www.youtube.com/watch?v=EC3L2lSSONQ.*

[361] Molly E. Reynolds, "Republicans in Congress Got a 'Seats Bonus' This Election (Again)," Brookings, November 22, 2016, *https://www.brookings.edu/blog/fixgov/2016/11/22/gop-seats-bonus-in-congress.*

[362] "America's Electoral System Gives the Republicans Advantages over Democrats," Economist, July 12, 2018, *https://www.economist.com/briefing/2018/07/12/americas-electoral-system-gives-the-republicans-advantages-over-democrats.*

[363] Christopher Ingraham, "This Computer Programmer Solved Gerrymandering in His Spare Time," Washington Post, June 3, 2014, *https://www.washingtonpost.com/news/wonk/wp/2014/06/03/this-computer-programmer-solved-gerrymandering-in-his-spare-time/?utm_term=.9fa9e83d72c6.*

[364] Jowei Chen and Jonathan Rodden, "Unintentional Gerrymandering: Political Geography and Electoral Bias in Legislatures," Quarterly Journal of Political Science 8:253 (2013), *https://sites.tufts.edu/vrdi/files/2018/06/Chen-Rodden-unintentional.pdf.*

[365] John A. Henderson, Brian Hamel, and Aaron Goldzimer, "Gerrymandering Incumbency: Does Non-Partisan Redistricting Increase Electoral Competition?," May 1, 2017, *https://papers.ssrn.com/sol3/papers.cfm?abstract_id=2961564.*

[366] Nearly 70 million eligible American voters — that's nearly one-third of all eligible voters — live in districts that are safe for the political party they oppose. Drew Penrose, "Uncompetitive and Unrepresented: Voters Locked Out of Representation," FairVote, April 17, 2020, *https://www.fairvote.org/uncompetitive_and_unrepresented_voters_locked_out_of_representation.*

[367] "Washington House of Representatives Elections, 2016," Ballotpedia, accessed February 20, 2020, *https://ballotpedia.org/Washington_House_of_Representatives_elections,_2016.*

[368] Amanda Skuldt, "Could a Third-Party Candidate Win the U.S. Presidency? That's Very Unlikely," Washington Post, August 2, 2016, *https://www.washingtonpost.com/news/monkey-cage/wp/2016/08/02/could-a-third-party-candidate-win-the-u-s-presidency-very-unlikely/?utm_term=.99431b70f280.*

[369] "Results for National, Statewide Races," Seattle Times, last modified November 22, 2016, *http://projects.seattletimes.com/2016/election-results/#Congressional.*

[370] "Do America's Elected Officials Reflect Our Population?," Who Leads Us?, accessed February 23, 2020, *https://wholeads.us/electedofficials.*

[371] "Women in National Parliaments," Inter-Parliamentary Union archive, last modified February 1, 2019, *http://www.ipu.org/wmn-e/classif.htm.*

[372] Karl Evers-Hillstrom, "Majority of Lawmakers in 116th Congress Are Millionaires," OpenSecrets, April 23, 2020, https://www.opensecrets.org/news/2020/04/majority-of-lawmakers-millionaires.

[373] Juliana Menasche Horowitz, Ruth Igielnik, and Rakesh Kochnar, "Trends in Income and Wealth Inequality," Pew Research Center, January 9, 2020, https://www.pewsocialtrends.org/2020/01/09/trends-in-income-and-wealth-inequality.

[374] John Hart Ely, "Gerrymanders: The Good, the Bad, and the Ugly," Stanford Law Review, February 1998, *https://www.jstor.org/stable/1229319.*

[375] Angela Helm, "Crooked Lines: Ahead of the Midterms, 3 Women of Color Highlight Racial Gerrymandering in North Carolina," Root, November 2, 2018, *https://www.theroot.com/crooked-lines-ahead-of-the-midterms-3-women-of-color-1830176927.*

[376] Arend Lijphart, Patterns of Democracy (New Haven, CT: Yale University Press, 2012).

[377] Joseph Zeballos-Roig and Angela Wang, "Americans Really Want the US to Adopt Renewable Energy like Wind and Solar Power, while Rejecting Fossil Fuels like Coal," Business Insider, October 1, 2019, https://www.businessinsider.com/americans-really-want-the-us-adopt-renewable-energy-sources-2019-10.

[378] Kristin Eberhard, "The United States Needs More Than Two Political Parties," Sightline Institute, April 28, 2016, https://www.sightline.org/2016/04/28/the-united-states-needs-more-than-two-political-parties.

[379] "Political Party Affiliation," Pew Research Center, http://www.pewresearch.org/data-trend/political-attitudes/party-identification.

[380] "A Deep Dive into Party Affiliation," Pew Research Center, April 7, 2015, http://www.people-press.org/2015/04/07/a-deep-dive-into-party-affiliation.

[381] Kristin Eberhard, "5 Pictures to Explain the Voter Referendum in British Columbia," Sightline Institute, October 1, 2018, https://www.sightline.org/2018/10/01/proportional-representation-vs-first-past-the-post-british-columbia-2018.

[382] Kristin Eberhard, "Glossary of Methods for Electing Legislative Bodies," Sightline Institute, May 18, 2017, https://www.sightline.org/2017/05/18/glossary-of-methods-for-electing-legislative-bodies/#multi-winner-ranked-choice-voting-aka-single-transferable-vote.

[383] Ibid.

[384] Andrew Douglas, "Cambridge, Massachusetts, Elections a Model for America," FairVote, November 1, 2013, https://www.fairvote.org/cambridge-massachusetts-elections-a-model-for-america.

[385] "Preference Voting and Voter Turnout: The Case of Cambridge, MA," FairVote, January 1, 2009, https://www.fairvote.org/preference_voting_and_voter_turnout_the_case_of_cambridge_ma.

[386] "QuickFacts: Cambridge Massachusetts," U.S. Census Bureau, https://www.census.gov/quickfacts/table/PST045215/2511000.

[387] Kristin Eberhard, "Glossary of Methods for Electing Legislative Bodies," Sightline Institute, May 18, 2017, https://www.sightline.org/2017/05/18/glossary-of-methods-for-electing-legislative-bodies/#multi-winner-ranked-choice-voting-aka-single-transferable-vote.

[388] Matthew Yglesias, "Proportional Representation Could Save America," Vox, October 15, 2018, https://www.vox.com/policy-and-politics/2018/10/15/17979210/proportional-representation-could-save-america.

[389] Robert Richie and Steven Hill, "The Case for Proportional Representation," Boston Review, March 1, 1998, https://bostonreview.net/politics/robert-richie-steven-hill-case-proportional-representation.

[390] To calculate each typology's left–right placement, I used seven Pew survey questions that seemed to address the changing values versus traditional values divide, including whether being open to immigrants is a good thing, whether abortion should be legal, and whether the country's success depends on its ability to change.

[391] To calculate each typology's up–down placement, I used five Pew survey questions about business and government, including whether corporations make too much profit, whether regulation of business is a good thing, and whether government should do more to help needy Americans.

[392] Voters don't form their views in a vacuum; they respond to party cues. American voters in 2017 were pulled into alignment with the two major parties: Democrats in the lower left, and Republicans in the upper right. Once multiple parties emerged and took hold in the popular imagination, the groupings of voters might diverge from the two-party pattern and we might see more voters migrating to the upper left or lower right.

[393] For a similar take on a potential five-party system in the U.S., but using a different methodology, see "What If the U.S. Were a Multi-Party Democracy?" Echelon Insights, October 25, 2019, http://echeloninsights.com/wp-content/uploads/Omnibus-October-2019_Party.pdf.

[394] Per G. Fredriksson and Daniel L. Millimet, "Electoral Rules and Environmental Policy," Economics Letters, August 2004, https://www.sciencedirect.com/science/article/pii/S0165176504000886.

[395] Salomon Orellana, Electoral Systems and Governance: How Diversity Can Improve Policy-Making (Abingdon, Oxfordshire: Routledge, 2014).

[396] Darcie Roschen Cohen, "Do Political Preconditions Affect Environmental Outcomes? Exploring the Linkages between Proportional Representation, Green Parties and the Kyoto Protocol" (thesis, Simon Fraser University, 2010), http://summit.sfu.ca/item/10084.

[397] Kristin Eberhard, "Proportional Representation Gives More Voting Power to Low-Income People," Sightline Institute, October 30, 2018, https://www.sightline.org/2018/10/30/proportional-representation-more-voting-power-low-income-workers.

[398] Julian Bernauer, Nathalie Giger, and Jan Rosset, "Mind the Gap: Do Proportional Electoral Systems Foster a More Equal Representation of Women and Men, Poor and Rich?," International Political Science Review, August 28, 2013, http://journals.sagepub.com/doi/abs/10.1177/0192512113498830.

[399] Kristin Eberhard, "How to End Gerrymandering for Good," Sightline Institute, September 25, 2017, https://www.sightline.org/2017/09/25/how-to-end-gerrymandering-for-good.

[400] Anna Fahey, "This Voting Reform May Get More Women into Elected Office," Sightline Institute, October 25, 2018, https://www.sightline.org/2018/10/25/getting-more-women-elected-us-canada-proportional-representation.

[401] Pippa Norris, "The Impact of Electoral Reform on Women's Representation," Acta Politica, 2006, https://link.springer.com/content/pdf/10.1057%2Fpalgrave.ap.5500151.pdf.

[402] Arend Lijphart, Patterns of Democracy (New Haven, CT: Yale University Press, 2012).

[403] "Differential Impact of Electoral Systems on Female Political Representation," European Parliament Directorate-General for Research Women's Rights' Series, March 1997, *https://www.europarl.europa.eu/workingpapers/femm/w10/2_en.htm*.

[404] Margaret Morales, "How to Improve Underrepresentation of Elected Officials of Color in the US," Sightline Institute, June 6, 2018, *https://www.sightline.org/2018/06/06/how-to-improve-underrepresentation-of-elected-officials-of-color-in-the-us*.

[405] Robert Richie and Steven Hill, "The Case for Proportional Representation," Boston Review, March 1, 1998, *https://bostonreview.net/politics/robert-richie-steven-hill-case-proportional-representation*.

[406] Here is a database of Voting Rights Act cases that resulted in a switch to cumulative voting, limited voting, or multi-winner ranked choice voting: "VRA Remedy Database," FairVote, *https://www.fairvote.org/vra_remedy_database*.

[407] David Brockington, Todd Donovan, Shaud Bowler, and Robert Brischetto, "Minority Representation under Cumulative and Limited Voting," Journal of Politics 60(4):1108–25 (November 1998), *https://www.researchgate.net/publication/231782598_Minority_Representation_under_Cumulative_and_Limited_Voting*.

[408] Margaret Morales, "How to Improve Underrepresentation of Elected Officials of Color in the US," Sightline Institute, June 6, 2018, *https://www.sightline.org/2018/06/06/how-to-improve-underrepresentation-of-elected-officials-of-color-in-the-us*.

[409] Kristin Eberhard, "Old Voting Systems Run the Risk of Electing a Hitler," Sightline Institute, June 11, 2018, *https://www.sightline.org/2018/06/11/old-voting-systems-run-the-risk-of-electing-a-hitler*.

[410] Jennifer McCoy and Murat Somer, "Toward a Theory of Pernicious Polarization and How It Harms Democracies: Comparative Evidence and Possible Remedies," Annals of the American Academy of Political and Social Science, December 6, 2018, *https://journals.sagepub.com/doi/10.1177/0002716218818782*.

[411] Norm Ornstein, "I've Witnessed the Decline of the Republican Party," Atlantic, August 6, 2020, *https://www.theatlantic.com/ideas/archive/2020/08/decline-gop/614983*.

[412] Well, except Russia. In 2013 President Vladimir Putin ordered a reversal from full proportional representation to using some single-winner districts, a change that helped his party consolidate power. David M. Herszenhorn, "Putin Orders Change in Election Rules," New York Times, January 2, 2013, *https://www.nytimes.com/2013/01/03/world/europe/putin-orders-new-system-for-russian-parliamentary-elections.html*.

[413] Kristin Eberhard, "This Is How New Zealand Fixed Its Voting System," Sightline Institute, June 19, 2017, *https://www.sightline.org/2017/06/19/this-is-how-new-zealand-fixed-its-voting-system*.

[414] Kristin Eberhard, "Sightline's Guide to Methods for Electing Legislative Bodies," Sightline Institute, May 18, 2017, *https://www.sightline.org/2017/05/18/sightlines-guide-to-methods-for-electing-legislative-bodies/#proportional-solution-legislative-bodies-that-more-fairly-represent-we-the-people*.

[415] Margaret Morales, "Over 300 Places in the United States Have Used Fair Voting Methods," Sightline Institute, November 8, 2017, *https://www.sightline.org/2017/11/08/over-300-places-in-the-united-states-have-used-fair-voting-methods*.

[416] Eastpointe, Michigan, and Palm Desert, California, both settled Voting Rights Act lawsuits by adopting multi-winner ranked choice voting, to provide greater opportunities for minority voters to elect candidates. In 2019, Eastpointe ran its first multi-winner ranked choice election: voters saw a broader slate of options, and more than 80 percent of voters ranked two or more candidates. What's more, Eastpointe enjoyed higher voter turnout. Twenty percent of the city's voters participated in the 2019 election, compared to 14 percent in 2017 and 12 percent in 2015. Though 20 percent is still low, the upward trend of the turnout over the aughts is encouraging. Drew Penrose, "2019 RCV Election Day Roundup," FairVote, November 21, 2017, *https://www.fairvote.org/2019_rcv_election_day_roundup*.

[417] Don Beyer, "Let's Change How We Elect the House of Representatives," Washington Post, June 27, 2017, *https://www.washingtonpost.com/opinions/lets-change-how-we-elect-the-house-of-representatives/2017/06/27/92f28570-5ab9-11e7-a9f6-7c3296387341_story.html?utm_term=.10c671148180#comments*.

[418] "Fair Representation in Kansas," FairVote, September 2017, *https://fairvote.app.box.com/v/FairRepKansas*.

[419] "Fair Representation in Ohio," FairVote, September 2017, *https://fairvote.app.box.com/v/FairRepOhio*.

[420] "Fair Representation in California," FairVote, September 2017, *https://fairvote.app.box.com/v/FairRepCalifornia*.

Chapter 9

[421] Kirsten Scharnberg, "Where the U.S. Military Is the Family Business," Chicago Tribune, March 11, 2007, https://www.chicagotribune.com/news/ct-xpm-2007-03-11-0703110486-story.html; Blaine Harden, "Guam's Young, Steeped in History, Line Up to Enlist," Washington Post, January 27, 2008, https://www.washingtonpost.com/wp-dyn/content/article/2008/01/26/AR2008012602050.html; Josh Hicks, "Guam: A High Concentration of Veterans, but Rock-Bottom VA Funding," Washington Post, October 29, 2014, https://www.washingtonpost.com/news/federal-eye/wp/2014/10/29/guam-a-high-concentration-of-veterans-with-little-va-funding/; and Janela Carrera, "Twin Sisters Sue Feds over Denial of SSI Benefits All because 1 Sister Lives in Guam," Pacific News Center, December 7, 2018, https://www.pncguam.com/twin-sisters-sue-feds-over-denial-of-ssi-benefits-all-because-1-sister-lives-in-guam.

[422] Reynolds v. Sims, 1964.

[423] Matthew Yglesias, "American Democracy's Senate Problem, Explained," Vox, December 17, 2019, https://www.vox.com/policy-and-politics/2019/12/17/21011079/senate-bias-2020-data-for-progress.

[424] David Leonhardt, "The Senate: Affirmative Action for White People," New York Times, October 14, 2018, https://www.nytimes.com/2018/10/14/opinion/dc-puerto-rico-statehood-senate.html.

[425] Ibid.

[426] Maine, Montana, New Hampshire, North Dakota, South Dakota, Vermont, and Wyoming are all among both the ten smallest and the ten whitest states.

[427] Frances E. Lee and Bruce I. Oppenheimer, Sizing Up the Senate (Chicago: University of Chicago Press, 1999).

[428] Adam Liptak, "Smaller States Find Outsize Clout Growing in Senate," New York Times, March 11, 2013, https://www.nytimes.com/2013/03/11/us/politics/senate-gives-small-states-power-beyond-their-size.html.

[429] "The Senate Is an Irredeemable Institution," Data for Progress, https://filesforprogress.org/memos/the-senate-is-an-irredeemable-institution.pdf.

[430] A majority of Americans live in nine states (in order from largest to smallest population): California, Texas, Florida, New York, Illinois, Pennsylvania, Ohio, Georgia, and North Carolina. See Ian Millhiser, "America's Democracy Is Failing. Here's Why," Vox, July 31, 2020.

[431] "Fixing the Senate: Equitable and Full Representation for the 21st Century," Roosevelt Institute, 2019, https://rooseveltinstitute.org/wp-content/uploads/2020/07/RI_Fixing-The-Senate_report-201903.pdf.

[432] Demographics Research Group, "National Population Projections," University of Virginia, Weldon Cooper Center for Public Service, 2018, https://demographics.coopercenter.org/national-population-projections.

[433] J. J. McCullough, "Why States Still Matter," National Review, September 11, 2018, https://www.nationalreview.com/2018/09/states-key-to-senate-legitimacy.

[434] Jonathan Chait, "The Senate Is America's Most Structurally Racist Institution," New York Magazine Intelligencer, August 10, 2020, https://nymag.com/intelligencer/2020/08/senate-washington-dc-puerto-rico-statehood-filibuster-obama-biden-racist.html.

[435] Demographics Research Group, "National Population Projections," University of Virginia, Weldon Cooper Center for Public Service, 2018, https://demographics.coopercenter.org/national-population-projections.

[436] Juan J. Linz and Alfred Stepan, "Comparative Perspectives on Inequality and the Quality of Democracy in the United States," Perspectives on Politics 9(4):845 (2011), www.jstor.org/stable/41623697.

[437] Robert A. Dahl, How Democratic Is the American Constitution? (New Haven, CT: Yale University Press, 2001).

[438] Lowell Barrington, Comparative Politics: Structures and Choices (Boston: Wadsworth Cengage Learning, 2009), 174.

[439] Juan J. Linz and Alfred Stepan, "Comparative Perspectives on Inequality and the Quality of Democracy in the United States," www.jstor.org/stable/41623697.

[440] Frances E. Lee and Bruce I. Oppenheimer, Sizing Up the Senate: The Unequal Consequences of Equal Representation (Chicago: University of Chicago Press, 1999).

[441] Ian Millhiser, "America's Democracy Is Failing. Here's Why," Vox, July 31, 2020, https://www.vox.com/policy-and-politics/2020/1/30/20997046/constitution-electoral-college-senate-popular-vote-trump.

[442] Ian Millhiser, "Britain's Brilliant Method of Picking Supreme Court Justices, Explained," Vox, September 25, 2019, https://www.vox.com/2019/9/25/20881843/supreme-court-britian-judicial-selection-brexit.

[443] "The Federalist Papers: No. 22," Avalon Project (Yale University), https://avalon.law.yale.edu/18th_century/fed22.asp.

[444] Robert A. Dahl, How Democratic Is the American Constitution? (New Haven, CT: Yale University Press, 2001), https://catalyst.library.jhu.edu/catalog/bib_6374470.

[445] Ibid.

446 Ibid., 847.

447 "Fixing the Senate: Equitable and Full Representation for the 21st Century," Roosevelt Institute, *https://roos-eveltinstitute.org/wp-content/uploads/2020/07/RI_Fixing-The-Senate_report-201903.pdf.*

448 "The Senate Is an Irredeemable Institution," Data for Progress, p. 8, *https://filesforprogress.org/memos/the-sen-ate-is-an-irredeemable-institution.pdf.*

449 Shelby County v. Holder, 570 U.S. 529 (2013), *https://www.supremecourt.gov/opinions/12pdf/12-96_6k47.pdf.*

450 Daniel J. Hopkins, The Increasingly United States: How and Why American Political Behavior Nationalized (Chicago: University of Chicago Press, 2018).

451 Lee Drutman, "The Senate Has Always Favored Smaller States. It Just Didn't Help Republicans Until Now," FiveThirtyEight, July 29, 2020, *https://fivethirtyeight.com/features/the-senate-has-always-favored-smaller-states-it-just-didnt-help-republicans-until-now.*

452 Ezra Klein, "The Rigging of American Politics," Vox, October 16, 2018, *https://www.vox.com/policy-and-poli-tics/2018/10/16/17951596/kavanaugh-trump-senate-impeachment-avenatti-democrats-2020-supreme-court.*

453 "New State Ice Co. v. Liebmann," Cornell Law School, Legal Information Institute, *https://www.law.cornell.edu/supremecourt/text/285/262.*

454 Mark Pulliam, "Red State, Blue Cities," City Journal, 2016, *https://www.city-journal.org/html/red-state-blue-cit-ies-14731.html.*

455 David A. Graham, "Red State, Blue City," Atlantic, March 2017, *https://www.theatlantic.com/magazine/ar-chive/2017/03/red-state-blue-city/513857.*

456 "POP Culture: 1790," U.S. Census Bureau, December 17, 2019, *https://www.census.gov/history/www/through_the_decades/fast_facts/1790_fast_facts.html.*

457 Cindy Dampier, "Meet the People Working to Kick Chicago out of Illinois," Chicago Tribune, August 1, 2019, *https://www.chicagotribune.com/lifestyles/ct-life-illinois-state-secession-movement-0801-20190801-iesnu74ogvfjx-fk35sn72lq7ya-story.html.*

458 John D. Dingell, "I Served in Congress Longer Than Anyone. Here's How to Fix It," Atlantic, December 4, 2018, *https://www.theatlantic.com/ideas/archive/2018/12/john-dingell-how-restore-faith-government/577222.*

459 Noah Feldman, "Revamping the Senate Is a Fantasy," Bloomberg Opinion, October 10, 2018, *https://www.bloomberg.com/opinion/articles/2018-10-10/u-s-senate-is-undemocratic-but-there-s-no-way-to-change-it.*

460 Sanford V. Levinson, Our Undemocratic Constitution: Where the Constitution Goes Wrong (And How We the People Can Correct It) (Oxford: Oxford University Press, 2006).

461 Article V: "no State, without its Consent, shall be deprived of its equal Suffrage in the Senate."

462 Ezra Klein, "The Definitive Case for Ending the Filibuster," Vox, October 1, 2020, *https://www.vox.com/21424582/filibuster-joe-biden-2020-senate-democrats-abolish-trump.*

463 Sam Berger and Alex Tausanovitch, "The Impact of the Filibuster on Federal Policymaking," Cen-ter for American Progress, December 5, 2019, *https://www.americanprogress.org/issues/democracy/re-ports/2019/12/05/478199/impact-filibuster-federal-policymaking.*

464 "Read the Full Transcript of Obama's Eulogy for John Lewis," New York Times, July 30, 2020, *https://www.nytimes.com/2020/07/30/us/obama-eulogy-john-lewis-full-transcript.html.*

465 "New States may be admitted by the Congress into this Union; but no new State shall be formed or erected within the Jurisdiction of any other State; nor any State be formed by the Junction of two or more States, or Parts of States, without the Consent of the Legislatures of the States concerned as well as of the Congress," U.S. Constitution, art. 4, sec. 3, and "Article IV," Cornell Law School, Legal Information Institute, *https://www.law.cornell.edu/constitution/articleiv#section3.*

466 The last time a state divided was in 1863, when West Virginia calved off from Virginia to stay in the Union. "Election of Virginia's First Civil War Senators," U.S. Senate, *https://www.senate.gov/artandhistory/history/common/generic/Civil_War_VAFirstCivilWarSen.htm.*

467 American Samoa is also a U.S. territory, but its residents are not U.S. citizens. They are called U.S. nation-als. Heather Brady, "Why Are American Samoans Not U.S. Citizens," National Geographic, March 30, 2018, *https://www.nationalgeographic.com/news/2018/03/american-samoa-citizenship-lawsuit-history.*

468 "Quotes Supporting Full Democracy for the District of Columbia," DC Vote, 2003–2020, *https://www.dcvote.org/support-dc-equality/quotes-supporting-full-democracy-district-columbia.*

469 Once such a bill gets signed into law, there is a constitutional wrinkle. The 23rd Amendment gives DC three electors in the Electoral College. It would need to be repealed because it would be irrelevant once DC is a state, so until Congress and the states got their act together to repeal the 23rd Amendment, there could be some legal ambiguity about the number of electors DC had.

470 Frances Robles, "23% of Puerto Ricans Vote in Referendum, 97% of Them for Statehood," New York Times, June 11, 2017, *https://www.nytimes.com/2017/06/11/us/puerto-ricans-vote-on-the-question-of-statehood.html.*

[471] Heather Cox Richardson, "When Adding New States Helped the Republicans," Atlantic, September 19, 2019, *https://www.theatlantic.com/ideas/archive/2019/09/when-adding-new-states-helped-republicans/598243.*

[472] Simon Barnicle, "The 53-State Solution," Atlantic, February 11, 2020, *https://www.theatlantic.com/ideas/archive/2020/02/case-new-states/606148.*

[473] Alan Greenblatt, "The US Almost Tore Itself Apart to Get to 50 States. Can DC Make It 51?" Vox, last modified September 25, 2019, *https://www.vox.com/the-highlight/2019/9/18/20863026/50-states-dc-puerto-rico-statehood.*

[474] "List of U.S. States by Date of Admission to the Union," Wikipedia, last modified December 13, 2019, *https://en.wikipedia.org/wiki/List_of_U.S._states_by_date_of_admission_to_the_Union.*

[475] "The Senate Is an Irredeemable Institution," Data for Progress, pp. 11–12, *https://filesforprogress.org/memos/the-senate-is-an-irredeemable-institution.pdf.*

[476] For a slightly different version of this proposal, see Burt Neuborne, "Divide States to Democratize the Senate," Wall Street Journal Opinion, November 19, 2018, *https://www.wsj.com/articles/divide-states-to-democratize-the-senate-1542672828.*

[477] Texas already has permission from Congress to break up into as many as five states. Erick Trickey, "For More Than 150 Years, Texas Has Had the Power to Secede . . . from Itself," Smithsonian Magazine, March 2, 2017, *https://www.smithsonianmag.com/history/more-150-years-texas-has-had-power-secede-itself-180962354.*

[478] There have been at least 220 efforts to divide California into smaller states, including at least five just since 2000. The most recent was a 2016 ballot initiative to break the Golden State into six states, and a 2018 proposal to break it into three. Alice Walton and KPCC staff, "Splitting up California: 7 Times They've Tried to Break Up the Golden State," KPCC, *https://www.scpr.org/news/2018/04/13/45392/six-californias-from-jefferson-to-colorado-the-cal.*

[479] The 13 largest states, in order from biggest to smallest, are California, Texas, Florida, New York, Pennsylvania, Illinois, Ohio, Georgia, North Carolina, Michigan, New Jersey, Virginia, and Washington.

[480] The states with fewer than 3.3 million people, in order from smallest to largest, are Wyoming, Vermont, Alaska, North Dakota, South Dakota, Delaware, Rhode Island, Montana, Maine, New Hampshire, Hawaii, Idaho, West Virginia, Nebraska, New Mexico, Kansas, Mississippi, Arkansas, Nevada, Iowa, and Utah.

[481] Douglas Perry, "Another Eastern Oregon County Is Ready to Gather Signatures to Switch State Allegiance; Idaho Governor: 'It Doesn't Surprise Me One Bit,'" Oregonian, February 26, 2020, *https://www.oregonlive.com/pacific-northwest-news/2020/02/another-eastern-oregon-county-ready-to-gather-signatures-to-switch-state-allegiance-idaho-governor-it-doesnt-surprise-me-one-bit.html.*

[482] Theodore Wyckoff, "The Navajo Nation Tomorrow: 51st State, Commonwealth, Or . . . ?" American Indian Law Review 5(2):267–97 (1977).

[483] A majority of senators could employ the so-called nuclear option to establish a new precedent that debate can be ended by a majority vote. Molly E. Reynolds, "What Is the Senate Filibuster, and What Would It Take to Eliminate It?" Brookings, last modified September 9, 2020, *https://www.brookings.edu/policy2020/votervital/what-is-the-senate-filibuster-and-what-would-it-take-to-eliminate-it.*

Section IV

Chapter 10

[484] Evy Beekers, "Are Citizens' Assemblies the Future of Participation?" Citizen Lab, October 15, 2019, *https://www.citizenlab.co/blog/civic-engagement/are-citizens-assemblies-the-future-of-participation*; Louise Caldwell, "I Took Part in a Citizens' Assembly — It Could Help Break the Brexit Deadlock," Guardian, January 16, 2019, *https://www.theguardian.com/commentisfree/2019/jan/16/citizens-assembly-ireland-abortion-referendum*; and James Fishkin and Larry Diamond, "This Experiment Has Some Great News for Our Democracy," New York Times, October 2, 2019, *https://www.nytimes.com/2019/10/02/opinion/america-one-room-experiment.html.*

[485] "Federalist No. 10 (1787)," Bill of Rights Institute, *https://billofrightsinstitute.org/founding-documents/primary-source-documents/the-federalist-papers/federalist-papers-no-10.*

[486] Tanza Loudenback, "The Net Worth It Takes at Every Age to Be Richer Than Most People You Know," Business Insider, August 21, 2019, *https://www.businessinsider.com/net-worth-to-be-wealthy-at-every-age-2019-8.*

[487] Randy Leonard and Paul V. Fontelo, "Every Member of Congress' Wealth in One Chart," Roll Call, March 2, 2018, *https://www.rollcall.com/news/politics/every-member-congress-wealth-one-chart.*

[488] "Comparison of State Legislative Salaries," Ballotpedia, last modified March 5, 2020, *https://ballotpedia.org/Comparison_of_state_legislative_salaries.*

[489] Gloria Guzman, "New Data Show Income Increased in 14 States and 10 of the Largest Metros," U.S. Census Bureau, September 26, 2019, *https://www.census.gov/library/stories/2019/09/us-median-household-income-up-in-2018-from-2017.html.*

[490] "Members Literally Don't Have Enough Time to Read Some Bills Before a Vote Is Held. This Change Would Require They Do," GovTrack Insider, March 29, 2018, *https://govtrackinsider.com/members-literally-dont-have-enough-time-to-read-some-bills-before-a-vote-is-held-e8691c86c91d.*

[491] Nathan Grasse and Brianne Heidbreder, "The Influence of Lobbying Activity in State Legislatures: Evidence from Wisconsin," Legislative Studies Quarterly 36(4):567–89 (2011), *https://www.jstor.org/stable/23053277.*

[492] Antony P. Mueller, "Forget Electoral Democracy — Give 'Demarchy' a Chance," Mises Institute, April 6, 2018, *https://mises.org/wire/forget-electoral-democracy-%E2%80%94-give-demarchy-chance.*

[493] Tim Dunlop, "Voting Undermines the Will of the People — It's Time to Replace It with Sortition," Guardian, October 13, 2018, *https://www.theguardian.com/australia-news/2018/oct/14/voting-undermines-the-will-of-the-people-its-time-to-replace-it-with-sortition.*

[494] Michael Schulson and Samuel Bagg, "Give Political Power to Ordinary People," Dissent, July 19, 2019, *https://www.dissentmagazine.org/online_articles/give-political-power-to-ordinary-people-sortition.*

[495] "Citizens' Initiative Review," Healthy Democracy, 2017, *https://healthydemocracy.org/cir.*

[496] John Gastil, Katherine Knobloch, and Robert Richards, "Vicarious Deliberation: How the Oregon Citizens' Initiative Review Influenced Deliberation in Mass Elections," International Journal of Communication 8:62–89 (2014), *https://ijoc.org/index.php/ijoc/article/view/2235.*

[497] John Gastil, Genevieve Fuji Johnson, Soo-Hye Han, and John Rountree, "Assessment of the 2016 Oregon Citizens' Initiative Review on Measure 97," State College, PA: Pennsylvania State University, 2016, *https://sites.psu.edu/citizensinitiativereview/files/2015/01/Assessment-of-the-2016-Oregon-CIR-zmzb9i.pdf.*

[498] John Gastil, Katherine R. Knobloch, Justin Reedy, Mark Henkels, and Katherine Cramer, "Assessing the Electoral Impact of the 2010 Oregon Citizens' Review," American Politics Research, 2017, *https://sites.psu.edu/citizensinitiativereview/files/2015/01/APR2017-1vsxasz.pdf.*

[499] Terrill Bouricius, "Why Hybrid Bicameralism Is Not Right for Sortition," Politics and Society, August 13, 2018, *https://journals.sagepub.com/doi/abs/10.1177/0032329218789893.*

[500] James S. Fishkin, "Random Assemblies for Lawmaking? Prospects and Limits," Politics and Society, August 13, 2018, *https://journals.sagepub.com/doi/10.1177/0032329218789889.*

[501] A "charter city" is a city that writes its own charter, which is sort of like a constitution for a city, rather than taking a generic blueprint of laws about governance from the state.

[502] This could be an extension of the 2011 deliberative poll "What's Next California." See James S. Fishkin, "Random Assemblies for Lawmaking? Prospects and Limits," Stanford University, Center for Deliberative Democracy, August 13, 2018, https://cdd.stanford.edu/mm/2018/08/fishkin-ps-random-assemblies.pdf.

[503] Climate Assembly UK, "The Path to Net Zero," last modified September 11, 2020, *https://www.climateassembly.uk/report.*

[504] "Milwaukie Citizens Jury Pilot Project," Healthy Democracy, 2017, *https://healthydemocracy.org/cj/milwaukie.*

[505] David Farrell, Clodagh Harris, and Jane Suiter, "The Irish Vote for Marriage Equality Started at a Constitutional Convention," Washington Post, June 5, 2015, *https://www.washingtonpost.com/news/monkey-cage/wp/2015/06/05/the-irish-vote-for-marriage-equality-started-at-a-constitutional-convention.*

[506] Michela Palese, "The Irish Abortion Referendum: How a Citizens' Assembly Helped Break Years of Political Deadlock," Electoral Reform Society, May 29, 2018, *https://www.electoral-reform.org.uk/the-irish-abortion-referendum-how-a-citizens-assembly-helped-to-break-years-of-political-deadlock.*

[507] "Citizen Assembly Votes on Eighth Amendment — A Majority of Members Recommend that the Termination of Pregnancy without Restriction Should Be Lawful," Citizens' Assembly, April 23, 2017, *https://2016-2018.citizensassembly.ie/en/News/Citizens-Assembly-Votes-on-Eighth-Amendment-A-Majority-of-Members-Recommend-That-The-Termination-of-Pregnancy-Without-Restriction-Should-Be-Lawful.html.*

[508] "Citizen Assemblies Are Increasingly Popular," Economist, September 19, 2020, *https://www.economist.com/international/2020/09/19/citizens-assemblies-are-increasingly-popular.*

[509] Caroline Bannock and Guardian readers, "'Transparency and Fairness': Irish Readers on Why the Citizens' Assembly Worked," Guardian, January 22, 2019, *https://www.theguardian.com/commentisfree/2019/jan/22/irish-readers-citizens-assembly-worked-brexit.*

[510] Larry Diamond and James Fishkin, "This Experiment Has Some Great News for Our Democracy," New York Times, October 2, 2019, *https://www.nytimes.com/2019/10/02/opinion/america-one-room-experiment.html.*

[511] "America in One Room Results," Stanford University, Center for Deliberative Democracy, October 2, 2019, *https://cdd.stanford.edu/2019/america-in-one-room-results.*

[512] Sean Kates, Jonathan M. Ladd, and Joshua A. Tucker, "New Poll Shows Dissatisfaction with American Democracy, Especially Among the Young," Vox, October 31, 2018, *https://www.vox.com/mischiefs-of-faction/2018/10/31/18042060/poll-dissatisfaction-american-democracy-young.*

[513] "Healthy Democracy," 2017, *https://healthydemocracy.org.*

514 "How We Work | Citizens Juries," Jefferson Center, 2020, *https://jefferson-center.org/about-us/how-we-work.*

515 "Demands," Extinction Rebellion PDX, *https://www.xrpdx.org/truth*; "Citizens' Assembly," Extinction Rebellion PDX, 2020, *https://rebellion.earth/act-now/resources/citizens-assembly.*